GOD LIVES

...From Religious Fear
To Spiritual Freedom

GOD LIVES

...From Religious Fear
To Spiritual Freedom

by

James Kavanaugh

Steven J. Nash Publishing

God Lives...
From Religious Fear To Spiritual Freedom

Library of Congress Catalog # 93-086218

    Kavanaugh, James J.
    God Lives...

    ISBN #1-878995-21-9   First Edition, Steven J. Nash Publishing

To my beloved brothers who struggled to escape the myths that limited our love and joy as boys, and crippled us as men until we stood up and walked in spiritual freedom, each to our Personal God!

Frank, John, Bob, Phil, Tom, Dan

All My Love—
Jamie

BOOKS BY JAMES KAVANAUGH

NON-FICTION
There's Two Of You
Man In Search of God
Journal of Renewal
A Modern Priest Looks At His Outdated Church
The Struggle of the Unbeliever (Limited Edition)
The Birth of God
Between Man And Woman(co-authored)
Search: A Guide For Those Who Dare
God Lives...From Religious Fear To Spiritual Freedom
POETRY
There Are Men Too Gentle To Live Among Wolves
Will You Be My Friend?
America, I Love You But Not Like I Used To (A Ballad)
The Crooked Angel (a children's book)
Sunshine Days And Foggy Nights
Maybe If I Loved You More
Winter Has Lasted Too Long
Walk Easy On The Earth
Laughing Down Lonely Canyons
Today I Wondered About Love
(Adapted from: Faces In The City)
From Loneliness To Love
Tears and Laughter Of A Man's Soul
Mystic Fire: The Love Poetry Of James Kavanaugh
Quiet Water: The Inspirational Poetry of James Kavanaugh
And On The Sixth Day God Made Man... Honest!
(Humorous Reflections of James Kavanaugh)
FICTION
A Coward For Them All
The Celibates
ALLEGORY
Celebrate The Sun: A Love Story
A Village Called Harmony—A Fable

"With willingness and trust, you set out to rejoin the river of life. There is no charted course, no signposts other than those that appear in your own heart. Yet in time, the river will gather you up and sweep you along, without your knowing how, into the sea of bliss that makes all life possible."

—Deepak Chopra M.D.

"On our planet itself all dividing horizons have been shattered. We can no longer hold our loves at home and project our aggressions elsewhere; for on this spaceship Earth there is no 'elsewhere' any more. And no mythology that continues to speak or teach of 'elsewheres' and 'outsiders' meets the requirements of this hour."

—Joseph Campbell

CONTENTS

You Are Your Own Answer

You are your own answer
   Beyond books and seers,
      psychic or doctors
   Beyond the strength that comes
      from what you have accomplished.
Your weakness is as valuable as your strength,
Your helplessness as loveable as your charm.
You are God's child and each step of the way,
   He gives you bread and not a stone,
      food and not a serpent.
All is part of the plan, as you look within
   And listen to the quiet, persistent voice
      that tells you who you are.
There is no strength greater than yours.
   No wisdom not available to you.
And love and light will flood your being
When you believe deeply enough to know
   that you are your own answer
In the beauty and creativity that make us all one.
No one beyond our love, no one not connected.
Abandon anger and fear to the wind,
   sadness and pseudo-strength to the earth.
Be who you are, in whatever state,
   and you will discover
That you are your own answer
   in the silence of your own heart.
Where all light and power dwell forever.

From Quiet Water

Note: All poetry written by James Kavanaugh unless otherwise stated.

INTRODUCTION

A generation ago the cover of *Time* Magazine proclaimed the "Death of God". There ensued a massive uproar among religious leaders and the people alike. No uproar was any louder than my own! And yet, *Time* was right! An, ancient historic God was dying, the God Whom I'd known from childhood, and His gradual demise has continued until this day. The "Dying God" was the angry God of Christian myth and theology, the God we heard about in parochial schools and Sunday sermons, the angry God Who punished and got even, the God who catalogued sins and wrote them in stone, but most of all the God Who could send a struggling human to an eternal, fiery hell. That was the God I was expected to love and never could. Although He existed to a degree in other cultures, none was as universally vicious, vengeful, and terrifying as the Christian God I have finally escaped. He is the focus of my personal odyssey from terror and imprisonment to truth, but it took more than a simple dismissal of Him and walking away. My mind and heart did not work that way. It took a minute investigation of the origin and evolution of how He came to be. Only then could I exorcize and release Him, and attempt to help others do the same because as a priest I felt responsible for the damage I had done.

And while the death of this God is more obvious in ever widening circles in and outside the churches, He continues to contaminate the air waves and some fundamentalist sects. But most of all, the new and living God Who resides in each of us, the universal God beyond hostile pettiness and bullying vengeance, an unconditionally loving and caring God is being newly reborn. He is the God of Jesus stripped of biblical bias and personal prejudices that tarnished even the gospels with the distortions and wrath of early Christian communities and made of them not "good news" but a legal brief not unlike the ancient Jewish laws Jesus was trying to purify. Now I finally begin to know a God beyond the archaic and terrifying myths manufactured by man in a reflection of personal guilt and fear: the one GOD WHO LIVES and communicates within each of us whether Jew or Gentile, male or female, slave or free, Hindu or Bhuddist, or even the avowed atheist! My own struggle has not been an easy one, and I hope that sharing it with you may help to free you as it has me.

I now know there is but one God and one people, an unconditionally loving God Who did not create the dogmas and laws that made me a slave, even as I knew it all had to be wrong. I knew it at five more clearly than I knew it at thirty. What helped me in my own release was to see the origin of the myths, especially the myth of the bible itself which was not dictated by God, but borrowed from a variety of traditions and various sources. John's gospel, for example was written three or four entire generations after that of Mark, and presents a whole new vision. Even as we speak, new myths are emerging from New Age religions which can be as guilt producing and destructive as the old: e.g. that we are somehow the source of our cancer, our clinical depression, our poverty and even a murdered child. The fact is, that beyond all New Age or Old Age religions we already know the truth, but the power of personal decision and spiritual intuition has been stripped from many of us through artificial authority, unwarranted fear, needless guilt, and history's twisted distortions turned to infallible truth. We look to some human authority for validation when there is none, and within our very being, GOD LIVES.

In this small book I attempt to make known without theological jargon and double talk, the origin of long-standing religious myths which prevented men and women from being themselves. I reflect upon modern man and woman, the ones Marshall McLuhan once fittingly called "the man of the global village," those who wear "all mankind on their skin," and I try to delineate our need to escape slavery fashioned by cruel superstition and sterile tradition. I believe modern women and men will gradually free themselves from religious sects which enslave or intimidate, for this is not of God and I want to help in their liberating struggle which can lead them to God.

I recognize that such an undertaking is an ambitious one, but I owe a debt to those I unwittingly led astray. I have rewritten and rethought this book many times over. It's been a more difficult book to write than **A Modern Priest Looks At His Outdated Church** because it did not flow as much from the intensity of my personal anguish as from quiet research, long reflection, several revisions, and a new way of life. I consider it an even more important book because it attempts to examine in reasonable detail the historical roots of the religious experience of the ordinary man without drowning him in detail. I don't write to scholars since that has been done for decades. I write to men and women attempting to find love, raise families, live responsibly, to believe honestly, and to attain personal freedom and maturity.

I am aware this book will be offensive to many because religious myths, meant to enlighten, grew to enslave the naive and uninformed as containing "divine significance and "infallible truth." I choose never to argue with Fundamentalists who see the bible as a textbook dictated by God, and presume that religious truth does not expand and evolve as do men and women themselves. But I welcome and can accept viewpoints other than mine, because I no longer attempt to defend the Church that I inherited, but to discover the God Within Who gives meaning to my own and every life. I learn from sincere critics who do not transform what was into what is and what must be! And I respect the path, even that of the Fundamentalist, on which they are led by their own Inner Spirit of God, "the comforter", that Jesus promised to each of us. I have no ability or need to say the "last word," only to say an honest one to the extent I can.

And regardless of critics, I know that millions are ready for what is written here or perhaps have moved beyond me. We want to be free from any archaic religious legends that hold us captive. We want to escape any religious institution that attempts to decide human value by decaying traditions, and in the process detract from our personal strength and limit our own responsibility. We will find our brother and sister everywhere and will not be impeded by historic prejudice. I write for countless millions like me who choose to be free of man-made laws and folklore. We will be responsible for our own behavior without obsolete and self appointed religious authorities.

Free persons pay a heavy price for freedom. No longer can they blame society for shortcomings, nor expect "divine" deliverance from inhumanity. They do not hide behind a hero nor cower behind elaborate rationalizations of a religious tradition. They must bear the burden of human pain themselves, look not to Adam and Eve but to their own hearts to understand evil. They must rely on contact with their Inner Guide to pursue peace and meaning in their own lives. It is to the person who wants to be free that I write, that one who is prepared to be responsible for his own actions and the condition of his world. And in the free and responsible behavior of such a one is the genuine proof, beyond incarcerating myths, that GOD LIVES.

For many, I know that freedom may still be too difficult, even as it was for me when I wrote these words some twenty years ago:

> *Man does not want freedom, he only talks of it,*
> *Satisfied to choose his slavery and to pay it homage.*
> *Freedom asks too much: Silence and strength.*
> *The death of empty alliances, an end to ego baths.*
> *Freedom confronts loneliness and lives with it,*
> *Makes more of larks than lust, builds no monuments to itself.*
> *Freedom, content to live without goals,*
> *Satisfied that living is enough, scoffs at titles,*
> *Laughs at greed, too free to propose reforms.*
>
> *Man does not want freedom, he fears its demands,*
> *And only needs to talk of it—*
> *The Free Man has no such need.*

But man can live without freedom,
Content to laugh at slavery,
And to know today that yesterday's pain is gone.

From **There Are Men Too Gentle To Live Among Wolves**

It is hard for me to believe the changes that have taken place in my life. Actually I have gradually changed my whole way of life. I expected to live and die as a Catholic priest, and had no idea that I would one day reject the very laws and dogmas I preached so sincerely. I'm not even sure how it happened, but I think it came from the people I worked with as a priest. Their beauty and sincerity was so obvious that it became impossible to hear confessions or to preach of sin and hell, salvation, no divorce and easy excommunication, and the inhuman sexual code of a celibate Church. Yet, I did not anticipate a personal conversion to a new vision of God. I think it began long before I was a priest, and crystallized finally by the traitorous inaction of the bishops after the promise of a Second Vatican Council in the Sixties.

After ten years as a priest, I was completing my doctoral studies at Catholic University in Washington, D.C. and in Europe. Like most of my priest classmates from all over the world, I was filled with indignation and heartbreak at the refusal of my Church even to honor decisions made at the Council. When I later toured the country in open dialogue, I was increasingly aware of the great religious unrest. I painfully learned that I no longer accepted what I had been taught. An Inner Guide was speaking after three years of graduate study exploring the roots of my faith.

I realized I was not an Orthodox Catholic. I could not honestly be, but the Catholic Church held me in a strangling childhood bond, but God was leading me beyond that position. This book tells of my own odyssey in personal, spiritual growth and where life has taken me. I anticipate rejection and condemnation even from dear friends, as happened when I wrote **A Modern Priest....** My mother was not able to speak to me for several years. I would not be honest if I were to say that this made no difference. Harsh words and rejection hurt me, but they will not prevent me from writing what I know to be my truth. Nor do I expect others to believe as I do. I believe GOD LIVES in all of us, and we take the path along which we are led.

I wrote and rewrote this book to be honest, because I did not want to appear as something I am not. I wrote it because I am convinced that millions of men are at the same stage of religious development as I am, and that they will profit from what I have to say. I wrote it in the hope that they will not have to suffer the guilt and anguish that I have suffered in attempting to escape the fierce hold of the religious institution that chained me as a helpless child. I wrote it in the hope that parents who have lived honestly and successfully within the religious institution, who have raised their families by its codes and doctrines, will better understand that their children are not rejecting them when they reject their churches. I wrote it to offer leadership for the young whose faith will never be satisfied by the narrow goals of the churches. I wrote it because I felt qualified to write it, because only a man who has taken the Church as seriously as I have in the past and has explored its roots as minutely can know the power of its grasp on men and women.

Millions have turned away from the churches; millions more will follow as they discover how exhilarating it is to be free. But they will often suffer when they leave the Church, not merely because their families and friends may judge them harshly, not merely because they will feel cut off from childhood, but most of all because they will feel responsible to be a part of the whole world, a brother to every man and woman, a part of every injustice that makes us prisoners.

Once as a priest I could demand people's obedience and force their compliance by mythical threats of punishment. Now I can but offer my friendship and open my heart, recognizing by myself I am as feeble as anyone, and in this common feebleness, I sense our concerted strength. In our personal struggle, I experience the gradual death of an archaic God and the birth of the One God Within. I know that whoever we are and whatever we now believe, despite brutal wars and ancient hatreds, drugs, murders, and human abuse, religious discord and racial hatred, in each and every one of us, no matter how it may seem, GOD LIVES!

My Easy God Is Gone

I have lost my easy God —the one whose name
   I knew since childhood.
I knew his temper, his sullen outrage, his ritual forgiveness.
I knew the strength of his arm, the sound of his insistent voice.
His beard bristling, his lips full and red
   With moisture at the moustache,
His eyes clear and piercing, too blue to understand all,
His face too unwrinkled to feel my child's pain...

I never told him how he frightened me,
   How he followed me as a child
When I played with friends or begged for candy on Halloween.
He was a predictable God, I was the unpredictable one...

He, the mysterious, took all mystery away, corroded my imagination,
Controlled the stars and would not let them speak for themselves.
Now he haunts me seldom: some fierce umbilical cord is broken,
I live with my own fragile hopes and sudden rising despair.
Now I do not weep for my sins; I have learned to love them
And to know that they are the wounds that make love real.
His maxims memorized in boyhood do not
   Make fruitless and pointless my experience.
I walk alone, but not so terrified as when he held my hand.
I do not splash in the blood of his son
   Nor hear the crunch of nails and thorns piercing protesting flesh.
I am a boy again—I whose boyhood was turned to manhood
   in a brutal myth.
Now wine is only wine with drops that do not taste of blood...

Now my easy God is gone—he knew too much to be real,
He talked to much to listen, he knew my words before I spoke.
But I knew his answers as well—computerized

And turned to dogma...
Now the world is mine with all its pain and
    Warmth, with its every color and sound;
The setting sun is my priest with the ocean for its altar.
I lie on the grass and boy-like, search the sky.
The clouds do not turn to angels, the winds
        do not whisper of heaven or hell.
    Perhaps I have no God—what does it matter?
I have beauty and joy and transcending loneliness,
I have the beginning of love—as beautiful as it
    is feeble—as free as it is human.
I have the mountains that whisper secrets held before man could speak,
I have the ocean that belches life on
    the beach and caresses it in the sand,
I have a friend who smiles when he sees me,
    who weeps when he hears my pain,
I have a future full of suprises, a present full of wonder.
I have no past—the steps have disappeared
    the wind has blown them away.

I stand in the Heavens and on earth, I feel the breeze in my hair.
I sense the call of creation, I feel its swelling in my hands.
    I can lust and love, eat and drink, sleep and rise,
But my easy God is gone—and in his stead
    the mystery of loneliness and love!

From There Are Men To Gentle To Live Among Wolves

Time To Start Anew

Life has its beginnings
Coming at intervals,
Time to start anew.
None is first or last,
Save birth and death,
Nor can we decide
Which is most significant,
Transforming, or long enduring.
It only matters that
Each beginning, like spring,
Be given its due,
 To nourish the earth
  for flowers,
 To respect sun and rain
  for fertility
 Not to trample feeble life,
  our own or another's,
Before it is strong enough
 To bend in the wind!

From Quiet Water

Chapter 1

A Man Alone

$\mathcal{J}$t was June 5, in the late sixties the very anniversary of my ordination to the priesthood. I backed out of the driveway of my parents' home in Michigan; I had said "good-bye" to them even though they did not understand the reason for my journey. My mother stood in the doorway and cried openly. My dad was flushed and upset. I wanted to get out of the car and tell them I loved them, but I knew I had to go. I left in a little blue Volkswagen filled with everything I owned. My destination was my brother's home in California. I had five hundred dollars to my name.

The day before, I had talked to my bishop and had tried to tell him why I wanted to take a leave of absence from the priesthood. He did not understand. He asked me to remain and be a pastor in a parish in Southwestern Michigan. But I couldn't. So he reluctantly gave me a leave of absence and I left to go to California. There, I was to write a book about why I found it difficult to be a priest. My bishop would read it and not understand and plead with me not to print it.

I arrived in San Diego after stopping briefly in Mexico. I had planned to stay in Mexico to brush up on my Spanish. I took up residence with a family in Morelia. They offered me room and board for sixty dollars a month. But the book gnawed at me so I only stayed a few weeks. I tried to tell the family in faltering Spanish that I had not been disappointed with my accommodations. I just had to leave to write, but they did not understand and were deeply hurt.

In San Diego, I took an apartment. It was a strange sensation since, already in my 30's, I never had an apartment of my own. I bought some food and dishes, a cookbook, a few sheets and towels, and dug in to write a book without any idea I would write it in six weeks and that it would turn my world upside down. I met some of my neighbors but only gradually dared to tell them that I was a priest. Later, when I told people, it didn't seem to matter. No one seemed concerned or even especially interested.

When I finished the book, I took a job in a counseling institute. I was more fortunate than most priests who leave. My brother was a director of the institute and offered me a job. Looking back, perhaps it was immature of me to lean on him, but I was afraid, unprepared for the world and did not know what else to do. Shortly after I came to the institute, we stopped receiving referrals from Catholic parishes. My brother was not considered a good enough Catholic. He did not go to church and he now harbored an "ex-priest." My presence in the institute undoubtedly cost him a lot of money, but in his characteristic way he said, "The hell with it." Now I know I might have stood on my own feet, but I had never learned such independence in the priesthood.

Several months after I came to the institute I met the young woman who would later become my wife. I liked her the instant I met her while at a friend's apartment. We only talked a few minutes that night. When she asked me what kind of work I did, I was afraid to tell her that I was a priest on leave. I told her on our first real date, and it didn't seem to trouble her. She was not a Catholic and had never really known a priest, but she seemed to remain interested in me. She said I always made her laugh.

Working at the institute was difficult. I was self-conscious and worried about what people might think of me. My clients didn't seem to care about my past; they were in search of understanding and help. Through those early months at the institute, I still thought frequently about remaining in the priesthood. But I did not know what I wanted. I was lonely and confused and my mind was in constant turmoil. I had known nothing but the Church since I was a little boy.

I had gone to the seminary when I was fifteen and had worked hard. I received praise for my efforts and was told I would make a good priest. Ten years later I was ordained and sent to the Cathedral parish in Lansing, Michigan. It was the first of three assignments. For a time, I worked among the Mexican migrants and I enjoyed it. Later, I would have a chance to work among the Blacks. This turned out to be my favorite assignment. It was work that had interested me, since I had served as a director of a Black playground a few years before I became a priest. But most of the time I worked among the middle class, people whose attitudes and background were similar to my own. I worked with college students and taught in high school. I was often lonely, but I seemed to have no doubts about the teaching of the Church that I dared admit—I kept too busy to reflect.

In the summer of 1963, I was sent to the Catholic University of America in Washington D.C., to earn a doctoral degree in religious philosophy. I was still narrow and unswerving in my loyalty to the Pope and to the Church. When the birth control problem was discussed, I was violent in my defense of the Church's position. I could not think for myself; the consequences were too great. I could not endanger my faith. While I was at the University Vatican II was taking place. The discussions about the council began to open my eyes. I began to ask questions that had always been vaguely at the back of my mind. In the confessional and in private discussions with my friends, I began to admit the doubts that came to me and gradually I became associated with the more liberal of the graduate students. I read everything I could get my hands on which explored the doctrine and moral teachings of my church, books which once had been forbidden reading. My doubts increased and Kennedy's death that fall made me wonder not only about myself but the whole world.

I was among ten selected to study in Europe in the summer of 1964 and attend the lectures of the great theological minds of England, Germany and France. This was a high honor and an important period in my life. I met personally the men whose great books I had read, and I asked them the questions that had gone unanswered in their treatises, even quarreling with the future Cardinal Ratzinger, the present pope's guardian of the faith, who told me we were not "in America". I was unhappy with their professional answers; they did not seem to understand the real problems of our time. They were serious and sincere scholars who seemed to know little about real people. They were not able to help me, and at times treated me with arrogance and contempt.

One of my associates that summer, Dr.Ernst Borinski, was a professor of sociology at a small black college in Alabama. He was Jewish, brilliant, and twice my age, but more important, he was human and of considerable help to me. He helped me to understand that I could not look to other men for answers that I must provide myself. He said that scholarship could not help me now, only courage. We often talked far into the night, and up to that point in my life, I had never met such an open and honest man. He helped me believe in myself and find my own answers. He helped me dare to overcome the handicap of my priestly education that had forced me to base any personal opinion on some ancient authority. One night he said to me over a cold stein of German Beer:

"Jim, you are as bright as any of these great men, and you have one advantage. You know and love people. They love research and footnotes and the past! You are of the future. When you begin to answer your own questions, you will become some kind of man!" Something changed deep inside of me that night. I knew my summer with Dr. Ernst was of God.

I returned to the university in the fall and my confusion grew but so did my confidence. I found it difficult to hear confessions and to say Mass. Yet I went through the motions and tried desperately to be a priest. I said Mass at Trinity girls' college near the university, and the students seemed to sense my struggle. I gave their retreat and refused to cater to the theological traditions of the Catholic Church especially about sexual pettiness. Rumors spread, questions were asked, several priests attacked my "liberalism". When I heard confessions, I refused to listen to "sins". Any sins! I only wanted to know their spiritual hopes and dreams for a meaningful life. The confessional line of young women was a block long till two in the morning and they shared feelings forever hidden before—often sitting face to face and smoking a cigarette. Their dreams were beautiful, and I really felt like a priest, a "father" for the first time in my life.

Somehow, when I reached San Diego, all this was past. I had taken off my collar and had begun wearing a tie. Then the book, *Modern Priest*, which I had written several months before was featured in *Look Magazine*, and my life was no longer quiet. I was asked to appear on major television, to be interviewed by the press. For weeks, I did not have a minute to myself. My religious struggle was shared with millions of people. I was still battling with my own problems of faith, and I was asked to pass judgment on the feelings of thousands of other men and women.

I had been trying to learn to be a good counselor. I had been trying to understand my own feelings about the priesthood and the Church. I had been trying to get to know the woman who would share my life. I had been trying to learn to live as a layman. Suddenly I was in the midst of a giant struggle I never anticipated. Mail poured in and phone calls came from all over America and Canada. Walter Cronkite and Johnny Carson were on the phone. I had not been fully aware of the kind of book I had written. I had only wanted to tell my bishop and the friends who had trusted me, indeed to tell myself, why I found it difficult to be a priest. I had thought that some others would be interested, but I did not know the extent of the religious confusion in the world.

My friends realized that I was under tremendous pressure. It was not television that bothered me, though at times I was very nervous. I did not usually mind the reporters or the endless antagonists who felt compelled to "take me on." I was struggling with my own conscience. I did not know the future of the Church. I did not know the future of my own life. I only knew that I was struggling to find meaning and peace for myself, and the questions asked by thousands of people obliged me to examine and reexamine my own convictions. The struggle was not with my interrogators, but with my own heart and mind.

The Catholic press began to scream at me. They simplified my struggle and said that I was in "search of sex" or that I had "lost my faith." They called me "traitor," "Judas," "theological imbecile," "money hungry," or "publicity hound." Their words hurt me deeply. I did not feel like any of the things they called me. I had pondered for months over the contents of my book. I had weighed the words, felt each feeling at the core of my being, and longed to find my God. I was restless in my job, unsure in my romance, and fearful of the new responsibility that was mine. I wanted to run, but something inside of me would not let me. No one seemed to understand what I was about. Some called me "courageous" when I was only trying to find meaning in my life. Others called me "insane" when I asked questions that no one seemed to answer.

In August of 1967, I had started on the last leg of a television tour. I had broken up with my future wife and had told her that I was confused about my life. I loved her, I needed her, but I could not have her amid the struggle in which I was engaged. I made the appearances that were expected of me. I appeared on the *Today* show in August, and shortly after my interview I returned home. I was determined to make no more public appearances until I had taken stock of myself. I remember walking the beaches of San Diego and wrote:

The Quiet Mornings
I like the quiet mornings
When the waves have washed the footprints from the shore,
When even the gulls are just beginning to stir
And the heat of the day has not yet aroused the flies
   to search the seaweed for breakfast,
When the beach still has the sand of sleep in its eyes
And the driftwood looks like tired swimmers resting on the shore
When the waves laugh at the rocks
And playfully wash the night from their eyes.
Soon enough the hungry gulls will dive for fish
And the waves will beat shape into the rocks.

Feet will pound on the beach
And ladies will snatch the driftwood for lamps,
And I will face the day's demands,
Tramples like the sand, Wounded like the rocks,
Torn up like the wood,
Living for another quiet morning!

From Quiet Water

I spent hours in solitude, rethought my position, and asked myself a thousand more profound questions than any interviewer had posed. I watched the waves for hours, read a bit, occasionally went to Mass.

Suddenly I realized that I had already given up on the institutional church. It was then that a huge weight was lifted from my shoulders. I resolved never to wear the collar again. I could no longer be a priest. I started dating my future wife again, although by this time she was ready to give me up for lost. I was still struggling, I still did not have the answers I needed about life's meaning, but I was asking nothing from the institutional church. I was on my own with God and Jesus, and I began to feel like a human being after what seemed like a hundred years of trying.

I thought of my summers at home during the seminary days. I remembered walking by the shore of the lake where we lived. I remembered how I prayed, how I begged God to make me feel worthwhile, how I pleaded with Him to give me the strength to go on and be a priest. Though I had six great brothers, no one really knew me then. I hid from everyone, although I appeared friendly and at peace and usually kept the family laughing with outrageous stories. I was in the midst of a lifelong turmoil, struggling to be free from sin, struggling to be dedicated to the service of men, struggling to find God, not yet knowing He would find me.

I now realized that I had never found Him in all the years of trying, I only found an historic church filled with ritual, dogmas, moral laws, and unyielding legalism that deep inside I knew were wrong, even though the priests and nuns were by

27

and large tender, loving people. I found a church that could not change, a church that had no structure or organization for change. It was a monarchy that was laden with rigid structures that had lost their meaning. I found mighty schools, a strong hierarchy, loyal people, endless traditions, and frightened members. But this was not enough. I wanted God, I wanted peace and joy.

In October 1967, I was invited to speak at Notre Dame University. It was then that I formally announced my resignation from the priesthood, though I had not in any way intended to at the time. It happened as I talked to the students about the Church, I described its narrowness, its injustice, its superficial changes, and its lack of genuine contact with people. I saw the honest openness of the young faces about me. I had already told myself deep inside that I could no longer be a priest, and as I talked, I knew I had to tell the students. So I told them—in sudden and unexpected tears. I told them with the fury of unanticipated emotions that had been buried for a lifetime, ripping off my collar publicly and stepping on it with all the fury of repressed rage and hurt and profound self pity. Without shame, I told the Catholic Church with its abuse and distrust of people and its cruel laws, as I knew them, to "go to hell". The auditorium was deathly silent for several seconds until students, nuns, and even priests were on their feet shouting their long repressed approval. My priesthood was over.

A month later, I felt I was ready for marriage. I loved Pat very much, although the on-again, off-again status of our romance had nearly driven her mad. I wrote to the bishop and asked for permission to be married in the Church. It was not an honest thing to do. When I had resigned from the priesthood at Notre Dame, I had also left the institutional church. I really did not care to be married in the Church, but I thought it would make it easier for my parents to accept my marriage. But I was wrong. It was next to impossible for them to understand. There was too much confusion and hurt. But I corresponded with my bishop several times. When he told me to delay my marriage, I refused, and Pat and I were married by an Episcopal priest some months later. The local Catholic clergy were incensed, the local bishop was angry and almost rude, but I was content to take what seemed my next step.

I had no idea of the many more steps I would have to take to gain some semblance of balance, maturity, and true peace. I was no longer openly committed to any system of thought. I was no longer the slave of any traditional philosophy. My life was not a preplanned program, not a dedication to an ideal that men had forced upon me, but the excitement and pain of an honest search. I was not then looking for the ultimate truth, I just wanted enough meaning to get me through the day. This was not always easy. Sometimes I woke up early in the morning in terror, or lay awake at night and wondered what it all meant. I slowly realized that even marriage could not renew me. I had first to find the way back to a real and honest self.

One evening my wife and I gave a party for a few friends. Some of the people had never met. It was a quiet party—more realistically, it was a disappointment. Afterward we were both depressed. The next day we were alone. We talked quietly about our deepest feelings and admitted the depths of our loneliness, the feebleness of our human love. We hid nothing, we were a trifle sad, we accepted the uncertainty of our lives. It was a sacred moment that we shared. We did not demand answers, we did not demand ecstatic joy. We reached out our hands in trust and beginning love. We did not know certainty, only a quiet kind of peace. We did not know God, only a gentle kind of meaning. We did not know an overpowering strength, only a fragile kind of hope. I also knew in my deepest heart that I had a long journey before I was ready for marriage and was soon divorced. Emotionally I was still the adolescent that had entered the seminary—protected from reality and denied any real understanding of women.

Since leaving the Church, like most other men, I was lonely. But I could begin to be honest, genuine, legitimate, real. I wanted to be loved, to feel the power of love, to be able to reach out and ask for another's hand, to admit my fear, my loneliness, my anger, my confusion, my joy, my peace. I did not feel stronger than another man, nor weaker, but I had always been set apart as "special." I compared myself with everyone in some inane, fearful competition. I could not share the experience of another man and liken it to my own. I could not yet reveal my weakness to another and know that it was similar to his. I could not be myself and know that I really could be loved, since I had not yet learned to love myself. Only to be set apart and "special."

I could better understand why many men and women at that time were not able to leave the Church. It was not an easy way even for me with a broad theological background to draw from. The Church gave many of us something to lean on other than ourselves. It permitted us to escape the deep questions that tore at our hearts when we faced life as it is. The person in the institution usually does not have to know the anguish of those who wonder: "Does life mean anything?" They do not know the pain of a person who says; "Why live at all?" But neither do they often know the faith of such a one, a blind and feeble faith , not in a system but in the opaqueness of life and God. They do not usually know the hope of such a one, not in a cultural myth with all of its bold certainty but in the quiet uncertainty of every day, in the tiny spark of a real, unmythical, honest love.

I will always remember the past with a kind of nostalgia. Sometimes I used to lie on the beach and hum the Gregorian chants that I once sang in the seminary, the Kyrie with its solemn dignity, the psalms with their melancholic strain. I thought of a little boy who recited his catechism and gave up candy during Lent. I thought of a seminarian who served a quiet Mass in a crypt chapel and spent countless hours in a dark church on his knees, far into the night, pleading with God to help me hang on and become the priest I thought He wanted me to be against my deepest will. I thought of Christmas and Easter and the old church where I believed as a schoolboy, or thought I did.

But such thoughts were somehow little different from the ones I had of the woods I walked in, searching for rabbits and frogs. Nor were they different from the memories I had of football games on Sunday afternoons with the boys in my neighborhood, or of Halloween parties when we got sick on cider or laughed till our sides ached. I felt nostalgia about my six brothers when we were boys, about my parents when they watched us gulp down mashed potatoes and the Sunday roast, about my friends when we had no wrinkles or cares.

But I couldn't go back. Neither the Church nor the family life of my childhood could be restored. Neither was anything more than a memory. Now, I had to live with the realities beyond memory. Now, I had to live with the facts of today as painful and frightening as they often seemed.

I had not given up religion, I had only matured. Once I knelt before a statue of the Virgin Mary and poured out my heart. Now I could tell a woman that I loved her and knew that love was not the poetic affection I had imagined. Once I paid homage to the mystery of God by honoring Him in the Trinity. Now I began to feel the mystery of God's presence in men and know the pain of uncertainty, of blind and doubtful faith. Once I needed hell to tell me of man's suffering, of his inhumanity to other men. Now I felt the terror of human suffering, the horror of a life without love, the anguish of human loneliness including my own. Once I needed heaven to encourage me, to give me strength. Now I could try to face death with the little bit of meaning that I drew from every day. I knew that each dogma I accepted from the Church was a partial truth which, when stripped of its caustic mythology and historic bias could have contemporary meaning. I knew that each moral teaching, when purged and purified, and made human and universal, contained a beautiful idea for everyone, not the select few. I do not mock these truths; I treasure them as the door to freedom which lies far beyond them. Mythology has been the comfortable avenue to the more painful or powerful truth, a palatable symbol of what is far more profound and beyond our total vision. But in my Church, as most others, it had become a cruel and unfeeling nightmare. And I had to travel beyond myth to spiritual freedom.

To some, it may seem that I changed quickly. In a way, they are right. Once the door of my mind was opened, once I saw how completely I had leaned on the Church and its well-meaning myths, and saw how I had been tied to my family and my fears, I was able to abandon my childhood and try to begin to become a mature man. Then it was easier to see beyond sin and hell, sacrament and salvation. But that very first step toward openness, the first effort to pry open my mind and to face my fears seemed to take a thousand years. I feel that I have fought beside every pilgrim who said his rosary on the way to a roadside shrine, that I have struggled beside every bishop whose mitre I respected, whose ring I kissed. I have battled beside every priest who forgave my sins in kindness, beside every nun who told me of caressing angels and the devil's wrath. I have relived every memory of a mother who taught me to pray and who let me put the infant in the Christmas crib.

And even now, I cannot easily forget. I can only continue to search in the joyful agony of a new freedom, in the pain and joy of standing before God on my own. To be thus is not to "lose one's faith." It was for the first time in my life really to have faith. It was to be stripped of props and religious fantasies. It was to face the ultimate fear, the fear that life means nothing, and to live with it. It was to be a part of all the unrest that currently questions every traditional value in our society. It was to live with oneself, to learn one's own value, to abandon the religious myths of childhood, to grow mature enough to have faith beyond all symbol or myth. Pure, raw surrender to what is! And find God with myself and another.

Some years ago I had an important counseling experience with a father and his nineteen-year-old son. The father explained to me that his son was a failure at almost everything he tried to do. He had flunked out of college his second year. He had dated a girl who did not meet with the approval of the family. He had passed up a career in baseball because he got tired of practicing. He had very few friends, was unable to converse with people in the neighborhood, and spent far too much of his time protesting the draft and marching for civil rights. The father admitted that his son had a right to different attitudes about society than his parents, but he insisted that the young man was not realistic about making a living. He was learning to be a mechanic when he had the talent and abilities to be a professional man.

The son spoke quietly and seemed hurt that he had disappointed his father. He said that he had never wanted to go to college, but had agreed to try it when his parents applied pressure. He said that the girl he had dated was quiet and shy and his parents only seemed to approve the college cheerleader type. He admitted that the "all-American girl" made him uncomfortable and self-conscious. His girl friend, on the other hand, had a quiet kind of honesty that he loved. He also talked about his work and spoke of it with pride. He said that he was becoming a good mechanic and that the job fascinated him. He admitted that he might get tired of it, but he wanted to find out for himself.

As the discussion continued, the feelings of the father and the son grew more intense. The father felt that the son was purposely disappointing him in some kind of adolescent rebellion. He spoke of his own life, how hard he had worked, how many sacrifices he had made for his son's happiness and education. The young man tried to explain, but the father did not seem to be able to listen. Finally the son's eyes filled with tears, his face was flushed and frightened, and he looked right at his father and said, *"Dad, I'm trying to tell you who I am. I know you're disappointed. But can't you love me for what I am?"*

That night, in the tension of their struggle, I saw the struggle of the world, the struggle of my own life. I saw a son asking his father: If I am really myself, will you love me? If I throw away my masks, if I stop hiding what I feel, if I am weak and unsure, will you not reject me and demand that I be strong and successful and confident? If I am honest, can I not be your son? I saw a man begging his fellowman: "Please love me for what I am."

That's what the whole world asks! This is what I once

asked the Church and it refused. So I left the Church. And I have discovered that I do not need its certainties. I can live with uncertainty. I can take any position that seems honest. And I can change that position when new evidence or experience demands it. I live with wonder, with mystery, and in the midst of doubts which are the very condition of life. This is not to say that I do not know anything; it is merely to say that I do not know everything. And in my uncertainty I had to leave the certainty of the Church, and in doing this I have slowly begun to rediscover my fraternity with men and women. I have stopped asking my Church or any church or guru to accept me, to approve my behavior or my faith. I have begun tenuously to accept myself, to try to look beyond my myths, and, in this often painful acceptance and freedom, to discover the birth of God in my own way.

Several years ago a priest visited me in my office. He was kind and concerned. He told me that I was doing a great deal of harm to simple and unsuspecting men. He said that I should not take the Church away from people until I had something to put in its place. This priest was willing to admit that much of religion is mere custom and even superstition, that much of faith is myth. He did not believe in the Trinity, or in purgatory, or in hell. He had doubts about the sacraments and the Mass. But he did not want to betray people and leave them helpless in the face of life.

I told him that I had more confidence in men and women. I said that I did not believe that something untrue would ultimately help anyone. He said that the Church needed more time, that the Pope and bishops did not know where to turn. He pleaded with me to be patient. I liked him. He was a sincere man. But I did not like what he was saying. Systems of thought do not replace systems of thought like new buildings replace old ones. Change comes gradually, almost imperceptibly, but when most of us recognize it, it is already upon us. Often the institution is the last to know.

He asked me what I had to put in the place of the Church. I told him that I had bits and pieces, only a beginning, only the courage to search, the faith to face uncertainty as a man and not as a child. I said I believed that man will find his own system, his own religion, if we tear down the mythological idols that have kept him in slavery. The priest looked very sad when he told me that if the institution disappears, we will lose the values that we knew as children, there will be fear and confusion, authority will be undermined, sexual freedom will tear apart marriages and destroy young lives. He insisted that man will have no clear picture of the after life and will lose his reverence for God. He felt that religious traditions would pass away, that religious truths would be watered down or abandoned. He foresaw terror and savagery in the streets, misery and hostility in the homes, tears and hopelessness in human hearts. He asked finally, *"What will be left?"*

He will be left and so will I, so will the simple and hardworking, so will human love, and so will God. There will not be an end to authority, but a new authority based on honesty and not on superstition. There will be a genuine and fulfilling sexuality, not a preoccupation and prudishness nourished in the immaturity of the past. There will be an honest confrontation with death, not the morbidity and terror that have made of man a coward and a slave. There will be man and woman ever yearning, ever searching, ever changing, ever growing, even if we must pass through a period of death and darkness when rebirth takes place.

Life Stretches Ahead

Life stretches ahead
Like some uncharted, winding gravel road
   Passing through hills and valleys
With unfamiliar scenery and disappearing landmarks.
Even loyal friends who have seen me through
   madness and mounting fears
   Cannot tell me which way to turn
   Or when to turn back at the threat of sudden storms.
Even my lover struggles to survive and cannot

whisper comforting directions
When dawn burst on my consciousness,
*   confusing me with its exaggerated splendor,*
Or darkness calms my torrent of fright,
*   permitting me a momentary peace.*
So I walk, step by step,
*   Guided by sometimes friendly stars*
*   Washed by the wind and rain*
*   Chilled by the snow of mountain peaks*
*   Warmed by the desert's monotonous heat,*
Trusting blindly that the gravel road will take
*   me where I must go,*
Hoping quietly that the unfamiliar scenery is
*   only a friend dressed differently,*
Loving gently all I meet along the way
*   Where none who walks alone is ever a stranger,*
As life stretches ahead.

From Laughing Down Lonely Canyons

As I write I watch the sun slowly push away the fog. I watch the water wash against the rocks. I watch the birds in the wind. And I know that I am of the world of fog and rocks and flying birds. I am man and woman, the prince of the world, its pride and majestic monument. And in my being I feel the water and the sun, the joy of the sea gull and the quiet calm of the fog. I feel the ages gone and the ages ahead. I feel the victory of battles won and the challenge of battles yet to be fought. I feel in my bones the struggle of the animal to rise up and walk. In my blood I feel the heat of a thousand dead rebels and the passion of a thousand loves. In my heart I feel the joy and sadness of a thousand hearts who helped in the creation of mine. But most of all I feel a glowing thread of confidence and hope in the pain of the search. I do not need certainty. I do not need absolutes. I do not need unyielding structures or infallible teachers, because I am man and can live with questions.

I need to be loved; I am loved, and in this experience, I can search for a greater share of truth and a greater understanding of myself. But I need to be loved as I am, not as I could be, or might be, or will be. I need love now, first and foremost from myself, and without tasting it, I can only live in meaningless agony and vain competition, in empty ambition and pointless pain in utter loneliness and coldness, in childish devotion to the well meant, but restrictive religious myths of my past. And to live thus is for me to be dead. I cannot speak for others. Once I was a priest and I was unknowingly dead. Now I am a man and I am slowly coming alive. I know that I count to someone, that it really makes a difference if I live or die. I know that my words, my touch, my pain are important. I know that I am priceless to another as weak and human as I am. And in this knowledge I have ceased the more massive struggling and have begun more calmly and patiently to search and find. I do not regret my years in the priesthood. Perhaps they made me better able to appreciate what I have, a part of God's plan for my own work. Now I do not live in fantasy, or as often blame myself for what God has built within my heart: the longing to be loved as I am. Now I do not "save" anyone, or try to "save" myself. I search for life and meaning and do the best I can.

I have no system, only a few ideas. I have no church, only a few friends. I have no ritual, only an embrace, a handshake, a quiet conversation. I have no vestments, only hand and heart and mind, a smile, a laugh, a tear. I have no master plan for the religious reconstruction of the world, only a boundless confidence that the man who is led to abandon his religious myths and move beyond them to universal truth, who is free from his idols will discover God in the growing honesty of his own life, in the communities with others that he or she requires, whether in or outside of the institutional church—as long as we are free and open to be who we really are. I am searching now, not always struggling, and in this search and in the search of millions of other men in churches or temples, forests or laughter or by themselves, I sense the rebirth of God beyond restricting and punishing myths.

I Am But A Part Of It All

I am but a part of it all,
No more or less important
Than the cab driver in Manila
Who weeps with joy over the grandchild
    That makes his life newly worthwhile
With such radiance I have rarely known,
Such pure joy that usually eludes me
    With my options and optical illusions.
He is a beautiful man, still naive enough
To love MacArthur and name an eldest son Arturo,
Still grateful enough to remember Bataan
    Beyond any politics or government compromise,
Trusting enough to love God and have heroes.
I am heroless save for the peasants in rice paddies
    And the wrinkled grandmother squinting rapturously
        her smile into the sun,
    With a baby's brown face pressed against
        her complexion of a fragrant, decaying apple.
Heroless save for anyone who can still laugh easily
    Or stare silently in awe at a disappearing sun.
I am a man bursting with a strange love
    That finds ought but a child's memories to worship.
My own land has become an exploding real estate market,
    My own friends with no time to pluck blades of grass
        And whistle their wonder for the day,
Seeking instead victories that time has proved
    A thousand times are not victorious,
Seeking them with such passion and enthusiasm
    That I am ashamed to tell them
        About a cab driver in Manila
And that I am but a part of it all.

From Walk Easy On The Earth

38

Chapter 2

The Arrogance Of Authority

I was stunned one night some years ago while listening to the news. The commentator announced that a priest friend of mine had been excommunicated for marrying without the permission of the Church. I found it hard to believe that in the age of space technology a religious body could be so out of touch as to believe that such a mythological penalty could have any meaning left for man. (To excommunicate means to cut off a person from union with the Church.) This particular priest had served well as a pastor and as an educator within the system. He decided for his own reasons of conscience that he must live within the framework of marriage. He asked permission to leave honorably and was told that a petition would be sent to Rome. He waited for more that a year and then decided to ignore the Roman authority. He took a worthwhile job to support his wife and her children. The marriage took place and he settled down to the responsibilities of his new life. Then after a few months came the startling and public news that he was excommunicated.

Actually, even within the framework of the Church's own law, such an excommunication was totally invalid. There can be no excommunication unless it involves serious "sin" or "mortal sin" on the part of the subject who is punished in this way. The most any Church authority could say is that this man incurred excommunication by marrying, if in so doing he had acted contrary to his own conscience. In this case the religious authority made no such qualification. A man had peered into the soul of another man and found him guilty, in direct defiance of the verdict of the II Vatican Council. This is authoritarian arrogance of the most unpardonable kind. It was also an act of heroism on the priest's part that has currently led to a much more benign departure from the priesthood with some dignity, if not respect. As so often happens, the "lawless" and brave create new attitudes.

Excommunication had for centuries been authority's way of playing God. It was the inhuman and unchristian denial of man's freedom of conscience. But most of all it had been a deeply frightened authority's frantic effort to dominate and control men and woman rather than to direct them toward a free and mature love. Excommunication attempted to turn the religious experience into a boot camp where the officer in charge aspires to build loyal robots by smothering them with confinement and indignity. Perhaps such methods might have had meaning in preparing a man for combat. They are only childish and dishonest in dealing with a man or woman's relationship with God, but incredulously they still exist.

Excommunication had its origin in another culture, when people saw portents in thunderstorms and evil omens in the flow of a chicken's blood. It was the product of an age when subjects could think of investing a king with divine prerogatives and dividing persons into rigid social classes. These were days when the rights of individuals were few, when the wealthy could live off the poor without any effective social protest, when Popes and bishops had the outlook and accouterment of privileged lords. But although these days are long gone, their decayed remains are still present enough to invade the television news even today and speak of an official, public excommunication by a Bishop Rene Gracida of Corpus Christi, Texas in a Southwestern American diocese of a Catholic woman who ran an abortion clinic.

Such exaggerated authority could flourish in a divided and fragmented world where man is isolated from his fellowman. It was a world in which an individual could consider his own culture unique and special. The Frenchman could judge the German obese and stupid and could call him an esthetic illiterate. The German could despise the Jew who was as much a German as he was and vow to exterminate him because his blood was not "Aryan." And the Jew could hate the Arab and refuse him a homeland with some political distortion of a "biblical" title to another's land. It was a world in which the American could mock the passion of the Italian and think that his children were all budding members of the Mafia. It was a world in which the Black was a white man's valet and housemaid, as once my Irish forbears were to the English, and his mental capacity was said to be limited by his inferior protoplasm. It was a world in which the American thought the Japanese were cowardly and deceitful, that the Chinese were cruel and diabolically cunning. It was a world in which each was taught to see his own family as deserving of lifelong loyalty no matter how fiercely it held him a prisoner and fostered bigotry and guilt. It was a world in which a religious sect could call itself infallible and absolute, the mythological image of the one, true God, and hate as well as any fascist or Nazi.

In such a world extermination or censorship—just like excommunication—was the accepted principle of survival, and isolation was the very condition of flourishing life. It was not merely the censorship and isolation demanded by the elaborate Catholic Index of Forbidden Books or the banning of Ulysses or Henry Miller, but that created by man's inability to read any language but his own. Or that created by an educational administration which selected its own books and tailored its own courses. Or that created in a culture where the world of the East was a mystery to the man of the West and thus contraband and forbidden. The very philosophy of education, limited as it was by its devotion to the printed word and to the "logical" development of ideas, by its programs of degrees and its required courses, by its teaching methods and the nature of its standardized exams, locked man in the narrowness of his own culture. Even Huckleberry Finn was dangerous, and Nietzsche or Lenin were abominations.

The Book Burners

Well, the book burners are out in force these days,
Not worried so much about Darwin and Freud—who
must be chagrined to be old hat so soon,

But worrying instead about Steinbeck, The Merchant
    of Venice, and wily old Huckleberry Finn,
Attacking indecent language and racial slurs,
Unmindful that most healthy people speak indecent
    language on important occasions like love and
    hate and varying shades of exuberance or surprise,
Unaware that racial and sexual slurs are still a
    significant part of every culture and aren't
    eradicated by banning the books that reflect the way things are.
But I suppose Dante must go with his biased
    assignments to heaven and hell
Only to be certainly followed by Mencken, Shaw,
    Nietzsche, Voltaire, and, of course, a
    revivification of Ulysses and Henry Miller.
Assuredly the bible must not be overlooked with
    Josue's sadism and David's adultery, not to mention
        Paul's attitude towards Jews,
        Corinthians, homosexuals, and women.
And Christ's own blatant anarchy and attacks on the moral majority.
I presume Little Women is safe, though it does portray
    feminine stereotypes, while even Tom Sawyer
    supports laziness and lies and noxious attitudes towards Indians.
The Little Engine That Could is a direct attack on railroads,
And Dickens' Christmas Carol makes the rich seem heartless and greedy.
    Mother Goose is probably pornographic, Br'er Rabbit
    is racist, and Aesop is unquestionably a Communist.
I presume Dr. Seuss is not yet seen as subversive and
    Chaucer will survive because the censors can't understand him.
    Nixon's memoirs are safe and the Harlequin Romances sell like cereal.
But meanwhile I'm rewriting Little Black Sambo so
    that a white kid discovers a psychotic tiger, takes
    him to the zoo, and shares his pancakes made
    from all natural ingredients, thus rendering him a harmless pussycat.
So far the censors have not attacked me—nor the nutritionists
    —nor even the animal lovers—not to mention the book burners.
The problem is: I just can't get the damn boring thing published!

From Laughing Down Lonely Canyons

It was a world of walls, not merely the dramatic ones in Berlin and in Eastern Europe, not merely the tense one of the Mandelbaum Gate dividing the Arab from the Jew, but the wall in South America that divided the rich from the poor, the wall in Canada that separated the French and the English, the wall in America that held back the Polish immigrant and accepted the Irish, the wall that kept the Jew from country clubs and Blacks from almost anywhere. It was the wall that kept the African loyal to his colonial landlords, that kept the Communist pouring out his propaganda, that kept the United States supervising the various revolutions of the world, truly believing that it was a kind of Messianic Savior in a universe of Darth Vader's.

But now a new man is here, the product of an electronic age. He is a man to whom boundaries mean nothing, who has begun to conquer time and space. Marshall McLuhan wrote well of him years ago, describing the "imperceptible alteration" whereby he has been suddenly transformed in the "global village" in which he now lives. No longer can man be remote, no longer can he be out of touch; each man wears "all mankind as [his] skin." The new "medium" of contact in the world, the electronic medium, has a new "message": instantaneous communication. A revolt in Peru or Bolivia is heard and understood in Munich, Liverpool and Niles, Michigan. An American war in Vietnam is protested in London and Berlin, in Paris and San Francisco. A student riot at Berkeley or Columbia is reenacted in Budapest or at the Sorbonne, and an American military force lands in the desert to guard its interests in Kuwait.

The new citizen does not have to run to the giant cities to be a part of the world. The cities come to him in the remoteness of his own village, in the quiet privacy of his country estate. Men and women are, perhaps often unconsciously, being made "emotionally aware of their total interdependence with the rest of society." Once we relied on the wheel to take us to distant cities, or we depended on books to reveal foreign cultures. Now we can fly to lands which were once a

43

mystery, or we can remain at home and have these lands and their people brought to us. Even now we can hear instant translations of foreign tongues and talk of the day when there will be a universal language on the face of the earth. We can watch Olympic Games in Barcelona, golf matches in Georgia, prizefights in Germany, murders in Memphis and Dallas. Once we read about men and women who wore strange clothes and ate exotic foods. Now we can communicate with these same men and women who dress much as we do; we can taste their recipes, enjoy their movies, share their art, study their politics, hear their leaders, dance to their music. This is the man and woman of the "global village," where anywhere is soon to be everywhere.

Even now we travel from New York to California and have to remind ourselves where we are. We watch accents disappear, customs merge, differences dissolve, architecture cloned, and matching malls everywhere. Once we would show slides when we went to Europe or drop hints about travels around the world. Now millions are able to spend a vacation or further their education in foreign lands, while millions more find such travel routine and uninspiring. A man in San Diego is not a stranger in Paris, nor is a woman in Seattle awed by the excitement of New York. People everywhere are becoming a part of the global village which makes each city both self-sufficient and in touch with the rest of the world, and the horror of Somalia or Sarajevo will take its toll in time on all of us together.

Once, in primitive villages, man shared a closeness with every member of his tribe. There were, of course, quarrels and violence, anger and disagreements, but each was comfortable in the security of his village. They knew its language, understood its customs, were familiar with its traditions. Nothing in the village was strange to them. The men and women around them were of the same color. There were differences in personality and talent, differences in courage and beauty and health. But the differences were nothing when compared with the common bond which united them to each member of their

44

own tribe in solid rootedness which is ever more rare.

Now the world is fast becoming such a village, a global village beyond all boundaries despite the wars and atrocities that accompany dramatic change. And the bond which unites its members is more than language or color or custom—for these are only artificial bonds. It is human united with human precisely because we share a common manhood. No trivial difference can unsettle this essential bond of agreement despite transient attacks and even the most blatant violations. Differences are recognized, but they are of no great moment or consequence. People are gradually less afraid of differences. To be an American does not contain for me the emotion that once it did, the emotion that could move me to murder the Vietcong and to build the Communist into an unfeeling monster, the emotion that could urge me to hold myself apart from the rest of men even in an Olympic Contest. I am not passionately an American, though I truly love my country. I am passionately a human being. I share something with Americans, indeed, but I share something far more important with every man and woman and child and the whole universe. Such feelings have been a lifetime in evolving.

In the global village, political differences are not of great import. To be a Republican or Democrat is merely to share a misty and evolving political leaning; it is no longer to embrace a unique way of life or economic posture. And religious sectarianism only plays a superficial part. To be Catholic or Protestant or Jewish is only to describe an accident of birth or circumstances; it is only to admit one's past training and values, or perhaps one's restrictive bias. Such a commitment, no matter how deep and unyielding it seems, is only on the surface when compared with the depths of what we share with each other because we are human.

Thus to the thoughtful and visionary man of the global village, religious councils and conferences and ecumenical debates seem hardly worthy of genuine concern. The most liberal views of a multi-million dollar and media-deluged Vatican council startled absolutely no one in touch with reality with even one of its pronouncements. The enthusiasm of political conventions seems increasingly childish and unreal. The nationalistic pride that flows from the mouths of presidents and premiers seems archaic and ignorant when we call ourselves, "The greatest nation on earth". Who Cares? The man and woman of the global village are at home everywhere, nothing is foreign to them, nothing is occult or esoteric. Every person, regardless of the superficial differences which will always mark human beings, can be the brother or sister of every other. The member of the global village is a citizen of the world, a world beyond sect and nation, economy and symbols.

Such a world does not pride itself on the size of its factories or the strength of its armies, on the variety of its consumer goods or the amount of its gross national product. It is rather a world that is proud of the freedom and peace of its inhabitants, a world that finds gross and contemptible the system that permits the rich to select their food lavishly while the poor are starving and out of work. It is a world that does not permit some to be denied the dignity that is their due, not as Americans or WASPs, not as aristocrats or whites, not as socialites or literati, but as human beings, God's own creation. It will ever more emphatically and universally revolt in the face of such inequality and overthrow governments; it has taken up arms and burned draft cards, boycotted graduations and marched on Washington and Moscow, torn down walls and dissected the Soviet Union. It is a new world in which an evolving man knows that he can be the brother of every other man, despite the civil and religious wars still raging, that the hatred and bigotry born of separation will be dissipated, that the inequality born of distance and ignorance will be dissolved. It is a world in which we recognize how much we have in common with others rather than how different we are. This, not because of some great religious or political reform, but because it is eternally destined by our common sacred heritage as human.

46

It Is Destined

It is destined by some rhythm more powerful than religion
    or even economics
That the earth belongs to us all or none shall possess it.
What Christianity never achieved nor Buddha,
    What Communism never won nor Muhammad,
     Will finally ensue without prayer or sacred proclamation.
There is no good or bad, malice or virtue, only time and circumstance,
And the inexorable hand of a mysterious rhythm dictating
That art and love and understanding will flower
    Or dust will inherit the earth.
What nobility could never teach, survival's law will demand.
The exploiter will be pitied when exploitation disappears.
What man refused to share will finally be taken away.
Even as I write in the Manila Hotel where MacArthur governed
And returned to Corregidor to drive out the Japanese,
His very grave is silent, but the Kamikazes return
    to go in business with the Filipinos.
Today America salutes Peking and Taiwan curses her treachery,
But tomorrow China will host Hong Kong in mutual celebration.
Not because of virtue or even political compromise,
But because man is destined to live lovingly on the earth.
Or he shall not live at all!
Not because of Mao or Marx, Jefferson or Jesus,
But because a rhythm as obvious as water and land
    governs the destiny of man.
Lion will lie with lamb or both be devoured by Leviathan.
Men will not turn swords to plowshares, but swords will rust,
Not because man is noble, but because it is written in reality.
Churches never really changed anyone, nor did a poem.
Asia is no wiser than the west, man no wiser than woman,
Black or brown virtue no more enduring than yellow or white.
What socialism could not achieve or Iron Curtains,
    what democracies could not do nor kings and queens,
Will happen itself!
The Arabs will not be proud because the earth gave them oil,
Nor America because its soil is lavish of wheat and corn.

All will be as one whether they will or no, and death will
follow life like winter to spring and summer.
Thus it is written by man's own hand.

From Walk Easy On The Earth

Computers will help run this new man's machines and potentially can free him to be ever more human. Wisdom will direct our schools rather than faded traditions and childish discipline, and permit us to understand our world. Justice will direct our lives and enable us to enjoy the only life we have. No president will stop us by shouting and blustering, no policeman will stop us by guns or snarling dogs, no politician will stop us by idle promises, no Pope will stop us by token reforms and archaic excommunications, and no mad tyrant will long dictate to any least country in the world.

Such exaggerated authority still exists in some families. Parents insist that their daughter double-date until she is eighteen; they force a son to go to college, or demand that the family spend a vacation together no matter the ages and interests of their children. And if the youngster gets in some kind of trouble, suddenly they decide to play truant officer and private detective. These are the parents who cannot let go, who once disappointed cannot trust, who believe that freedom is a commodity suddenly purchased when a child leaves the family home. Sooner or later they are forced to make a choice. Either they must compromise and leave the maturing boy or girl the necessary freedom to make mistakes, or they must create some kind of physical or emotional imprisonment which only recreates the artificial bonds that have forever been totally destructive, and can finally be no longer because children, too, are people already.

The Church and the Temple have been such a dogmatic and controlling parent. So has my own government. So has the giant industrial complex which makes a free man punch his time card and ties him to a steel machine which promises to feed him if he will become an unprotesting slave without

48

ownership or stability. Freedom has been defined within the small circle of a religious or political tradition, within the framework of an economic or educational philosophy, so narrow and tight that only a revolution has been able to bring about change. The stubborn or helpless are cut off, or excommunicated. The poor and ignorant are starved or ignored. The weak individual is used and manipulated by the strong. The nonconformists are said to be in heresy.

Heresy is another relic from the outmoded past. It is the intellectual touchstone upon which some religious or political or social faith is made to rise or fall in the face of a common, projected enemy. A heretic is one who rejects some truth that a government or a family or a church believes in and has canonized. Often only words or symbols that have lost all meaning but fear and vengeance. In the case of the Christian heretic, it does not matter how fruitful and godlike a man's life. The Christian criterion of judging a tree by its fruits as Jesus insisted is not enough. There must be assent to a body of doctrine, which is rarely understood. The one who gives blind and meaningless consent is said to have childlike faith, not puerile dependence and irresponsibility. He or she does not wrestle with the meaning of a truth. They are not overwhelmed with the very idea of God or the significance of Christ's divinity, a doctrine which divided the early Christians for angry and volatile—even bloody centuries. They never think about the doctrine itself at any depth, but merely accept it without real awareness because no one can possibly comprehend what it means for God to be a man. Since such dogmas cause them no genuine concern, the religious body admits them as royal children obedient to meaningless history rather than to their own heart and deepest awareness.

It is no different with the political body. The patriot is the man who will fight in Vietnam or Desert Storm, who will pay his taxes, and who will build with them an altar of holocaust to murder helpless and unsuspecting men or to support a cold or hot war, or a defense program we cannot afford and support in false pride and arrogance despite national bankruptcies. To burn a draft card was heresy. To refuse to fight was a kind of treason. It was apparently not in keeping with the nation of Lee and Grant and Teddy Roosevelt. It does not matter if a man has maturely evolved beyond political theories that were founded on fear and exploitation and arrogance. He is expected to conform to the dictates of his president, his employer, his college president, his family traditions, his religious heritage in spite of his personal mind and conscience. This is how Fascism is born! By whatever name—even "family values."

The individual who rejects the truth which eludes his reason, or who at least withholds his consent, the one who questions the political system which says he is only permitted to be grateful for his right to vote, the person who despises the isolationism and nationalism that are called "patriotism" is heretical no matter what he does.

"Heresy" and "excommunication" in any discipline: church, government, education, family, work place—are coward's words. They have lost their impact and meaning. To be a heretic can well mean that one is finally alive and responsible, like America was a heretic to England, or Martin Luther King to George Wallace. To be excommunicated can well mean that one has at last made a mature and personal decision. How can one who behaves as Jesus be heretical? How can one who fights for Black and gay rights and refuses to fight a war be heretical? How can a godlike man who loves his neighbor be cut off from the synagogue or church, or a reformed Rabbi be dishonored in Jerusalem? How can a woman who treasures her right to honorable dissent be less a patriot? A life without love is the only heresy, a refusal to love the only excommunication, each forever subject to the wisdom of pain and time and love. I look for heretics among misguided racists and pitiable philanderers whose lack of freedom and experience has somehow shriveled them, not among creative minds that struggle with the problems of God and meaning and try to love their neighbors as themselves. I look for the excommunicated among the greedy and the bigots and the self-righteous, not among the priests who took a wife or the gentiles who married a Jew, or the white espoused to one of another race. This is the future, not the fearful past. We are one! And in reality there are no heretics or excommunicates, only fellow humans struggling to find their truth. And the most violent Fundamentalist has the same rights as I do, unless he acts on them contrary to the common good.

There is no such absolute authority as that which excommunicated people and called them heretics. It died somewhere in man's endless struggle to be himself. It only appeared in such monstrous forms as concentration camps and Communist purges, Chinese communes and uncivilized prisons, in a Saddam or Hitler, in Sarajevo or in jungle life among the beasts. To resist such authority, to wipe it out, is no mere challenge; it is a sacred duty in the name of mankind. And it is predestined by our very human energy.

I am not an anarchist, nor is the spirited age in which I live anarchistic. I do not reject the notion of authority or its honest exercise. I only reject the leader who treats me like an ox or a piece of concrete, who calls a manipulated republic controlled by special interest groups a Democracy. Maybe such a leader feels that we are not ready for the new freedom we demand. He will rant about gangs and revolts and other distorted and flamboyant symbols of unrest and change—as if past demands and docility were Freedom. Maybe he believes that man is asking too much. Maybe he thinks that religion and morality and patriotism will disappear in the face of the contemporary onslaught. History tells another story. Yesterday's heretics are today's heroes, yesterday's wild liberals, today's conservatives. It does not really matter what you think or what I think. Man is going to find out for himself what is true and eternal and free. Finally, after centuries, man sees the light and has a unique chance to look at himself without being cowed by religious authority or by the paternalism of an overprotective society. Some few see it decades or centuries before the rest, but soon enough that which is true and honest has to become real and universal.

Now men and women will take things in their own hands. Not simply today or tomorrow, but for ensuing centuries long after I am an obscure footnote in a dusty dissertation. Men and women ended the cold war, not America or Russia or insolvency, but those millions of brave men and women who were ready to die for freedom. They themselves tore down the wall, not the benign gestures of a free world. Mankind did it and is doing it still as we move beyond bloodshed and bombings, terrorists and murders to a Global Village. If it seems inhuman, it is, but precisely because authoritarian and arrogant nations and cultures denied us our human rights. We will make mistakes and pay the penalty within the framework of our own conscience, not in the courts where "heresy" and "excommunication" are frequent words. We will find authority enough in our gradual awareness of our responsibility to others, proof enough in our failures in the honest confrontation of friends. We will not pray away our loneliness in idle waiting. We will do something about it instead, even if our first clumsy efforts are exaggerations or even unjust, and at least attempt to find God and justice in the love and meaning that is our right.

This evolving new person is abandoning religious and political myths which have survived for centuries. He is not even asking for a professional evaluation of his revolutions. Men and women will not be talked out of their demythologizing by learned theorists or angry, dour commentators who hold them responsible for the increase in crime or the assassination of prominent and beloved men. We have slowly learned to believe in ourselves, in our own experience, in our own new and often slow awareness that every man is my brother, in our own conviction, born of the electronic age, that the inequality of the past can and must cease...because it is ignorant and wrong! And the senseless death of an innocent child in South Chicago is as immoral and hideous as the murder of JFK.

Men and women of the Global Village are aware of the crime in the streets. But they also know of the crimes of religious myths that have excommunicated and bound us in terror of eternal "hell," far more destructive to millions than a few gang murders. They know of the crimes of political myths that have starved the poor and murdered millions of Jews and Armenians, Irish, and Mongols, Kurds, Somalians, and Sikhs. They know the crimes of social myths that have deprived men and women of dignity and the right to work and read on their own. They remember well the tragic assassinations that made the world sad. But they also remember the soldiers, Vietcong as well as Americans, who died for a myth in Vietnam, the Black who died from the myth of white supremacy, the millions whose spirit has died with the crushing force of the religious and political and social myths.

This new human has appeared suddenly, but his roots lie deep. The philosophers have been forming him for centuries and revolutions have been freeing him for years. His discoveries have given him confidence in his own power and have taught him the value of his own experience. It is impossible to trace the ideas and events that spawned this new person, although everyone seems to be trying. I am not sure it is important to trace roots, only to recognize that he is here. We can give credit to the French and American revolutions, the industrial transformation, the discovery and use of nuclear power. We can speak of the disillusionment produced by wars and the resulting philosophies of phenomenology and existentialism that brought philosophy from the world of classroom concepts back into the world of man. We can give credit to the affluence produced by industrial growth and to the new leisure time that freed man from the fight to survive. We can praise the scientists, the historical and social critics, and the rebels—Jesus, Luther, Darwin, Kant, Marx, Nietzsche, Freud, Einstein, Ghandi, and their modern counterparts—who helped men and women to recognize their own dignity, their own capacity, who this very day help them to know that they are more important than any myth. Whatever produced him, a brand new person is here!

Once I Gave My Life Away
Once I gave my life away
  To parents who dressed their prehistoric wounds with my bones,
  To spouses who covered their own ancient scars with my flesh,
  To any wayfarer who asked my blood and knew
        what fragile artery to invade.
I gave my life away
  To faceless crowds and impotent powers hiding
        behind history's barricades,
  To bankers and jugglers, well-spoken whoremongers
        and seductive sorcerers,
  To bearded mesmerists and white-robed vampires
        who sucked away my soul.

Now I am ready to reclaim my life,
  To take the final test to determine
        if indeed I am, or fearfully am not,
  With the heavens as trusted allies, and rare friends
        who ask nothing of me but honest courage,
And promise nothing but the freedom to possess my life.

From Tears and Laughter of a Man's Soul

Men and women, with all the negatives and financial
fears, have never before had the freedom that modern life
permits. And beneath the surface of fear, confusion and
bloodshed, the results of this freedom, even at this early stage
of development, impress me deeply. I love the openness of
the young people, their ability to communicate directly when
someone will listen, their honesty and emotional involvement
in their world when inspired and motivated, their willingness
to listen or to engage in dialogue. They have taught me a great
deal. They do not live with the same fear and bigotry that
marked my life. I do not see them as less moral than the
young man I was, or less moral than the young men I worked
with at the beginning of my priesthood. Nor are they less
dedicated, less idealistic, less responsible, or less concerned

in this most confusing period of radical social and spiritual change. They are better able to be friends, better able to approach their parents and pastors and teachers who are not cloaked in their own buried fear. I am well aware of the sometime irresponsible among the youth who would rather protest than work, who would rather talk than act. There are the drifters and frightened rebels that the openness of new freedom always brings, the very sign of change. They are yet too immature to recognize the chance that they have, perhaps too proud or afraid to seek help, as yet too troubled and immobilized to make decisions or to have goals. They are the victims who must for a time live off the society they condemn or who receive support from the very parents whom they criticize. But they do not represent the new spirit among the young. They are merely the visible and media glamorized exception that permits the fearful and perpetual religious and political conservatives to believe that nothing in life has really changed, except for the worse.

There is only one kind of authority that this new spirit will accept. This authority does not demand as much and receives more. It trusts men and women! Yes, it trusts! It confronts and deals in the now, without relying on the outmoded conclusions of the past. It does not frighten or threaten others, nor make them guilty, it tries to love them.

Modern men and women will not only accept such authority, they will respect it as well at every level. They will respect the father who wants to know them, who does not smother them with alien goals that seek the honor and praise of the family rather than their own honest aspirations. They will not love a father or mother simply because they have given them life and physical sustenance. They demand of them kindness and understanding, honesty and respect, even if they seem to conform to resentment. They do not belong to their parents, they are not some showpiece with which they can win society's applause. They will not parrot their parents' attitudes or memorize their every principle. They will not be what parents finally want them to be, but what they have been called to be. They will hopefully, ultimately be themselves! They will not think their parents' work and responsibility harder than their own. Parents will not make them guilty by telling them how much they owe, nor will they successfully frighten them with punishment or economic threats. More and more, they will not be afraid to work, to struggle, to go it on their own.

They do not resent discipline or honest punishment. They resent arrogance and a refusal to be human. They do not admire parents for hiding their weaknesses or for refusing to apologize or admit mistakes. Nor will they in youthful maturity accept the rules which have no meaning, the laws which have only authority's signature to give them worth. They will not accept parents or teachers, priests or leaders as perfect, as infallible, as beyond question or recourse. They will not accept material comfort in place of friendship and personal concern. They will not be deprived of privacy or the right to choose their own goals as million of us were obligated to do. They will not be forced to pay homage to the social emptiness that masquerades as recreation and pleasure as we did. Nor will they barter away personal freedom for a traitorous family peace. They will make their own mistakes and pay for them. They will form their own principles and pursue them. They will live their own lives no matter what it costs in terms of a family relationship or an economic depriva-tion. They are themselves before they are anyone's child, and they will not give real love where they cannot find respect.

Nor will I. No churchman will tell me to bow before some ordinance that does not make sense to me, or to embrace some doctrine without obvious evidence. No president can demand my allegiance to a policy that offends my conscience. No father can order me to accept some principle which is contrary to my own faith. I am responsible to the dictates of my own mind and heart, and even if the cost shall pain me or kill me, I cannot do otherwise.

I will not define patriotism in the chauvinistic syllables of the past. Nor will I tolerate injustice dealt in the name of freedom. I know that my country is not all good, that its enemies are not all bad. I well know that election to an office assuredly does not guarantee a man's intelligence or honesty, that it does not of necessity make him adequate for his job. I cannot accept any economy geared to war, a national budget that makes little of poverty and much of destruction and death and the safeguarding of the power structure and status quo, that can launch its space ships while children starve and a nation lives on badly borrowed money. Nor will I accept the empty explanations for such horror or for some national commitment made in my name without obvious reasons—or supported by reasons inherited from a time when the nation considered itself invincible and omnipotent. I know that no such nation exists, and no scowling president will tell me otherwise as he sends us off to any war, calling self interest and greed: nobility and sacrifice.

Nor do I believe any society can be "great" if children anywhere are hungry, or if its sons and daughters are at war. It cannot be great if a black man is less than a white man, or if a growing abundance of material comforts does not bring a consequent growth of love and peace. A society is no greater than its compassion, its pursuit of justice, its guarantee of freedom and dignity for men and women and children. It is no greater than its humility, no greater than the poetry and art in the lives of its citizens. No authority can command my love; no authority can demand my respect. I am man, and I am free. Any authority must listen to man, know him, understand him, and merit his love. And in such an exchange there is beauty.

Once I could listen to the Church and its Pope and scrupulously fulfill every command out of warped loyalty. Once I could deny my inner feelings, my personal hopes, my weariness, my dishonesty, my disillusionment, my pain. I could hold another responsible for the injustice and horror perpetrated in the name of truth. I could hide behind the impersonality of a society without face or hands or heart. And I could call such docility "virtue", yet now I know it was only cowardice and an irresponsible attitude toward authority. Now I know that authority is only human, that it will listen when I demand that it listen, that it will respect me when I begin to respect myself and you. Now I know that when authority is absolute and infallible, it is only reflective of man's pessimism and immobilizing fear. Such authority will no longer move me. Nor will it move the men and women of the global village.

Lately

Lately the mountains look sadly at me
    Because I do not hear their eternal song,
And the patient palms frown when I ignore their whispering.
I want to lie on the moor, on the desert sand,
    And let the night cover me, the earth reclaim me
Because in the torment of spirit and madness disguised as wisdom,
I did not listen to the inner melody which directs all creatures.
    Who walk on the earth and flow from its core.
I would have made a nice bumblebee,
A superb peony, a wondrous apple tree,
    I've only failed as a man.
There is time to plant all over again
And as I live, to seem much more like a rosebush
Than a man, more like a brook winding its way through rocks,
    Than a conqueror stomping his way across the earth.
Watch the birds, the trees, the disappearing sun,
    the laughing dawn, the rattling and splashing waters.
They will tell you more of life than all the masters—
    Without ego or interference—
    Without pretense or projection—
Only in simple, rhythmic, pulsing, liberating truth!

From Loneliness To Love

Modern man, whether he knows it or not, is fighting against absolute authority of every kind. His cry is a battle cry. It is the cry of the man of the global village, the new man and woman who know even before they can express it. They know at some level that every other is a brother or sister, the very one who is determined to put an end to the narrowness and arcane religious and political mythology that have forced us apart. This cry, this battle has only begun to be heard as the Soviet Union comes apart, the wall falls down, and a world economy must replace greed and slavery based on fear and exploitation beyond all care or compassion..

Perhaps you think I am overly optimistic or I exaggerate. Perhaps you are trapped in your dreams by some current economic hardship and lack of real leadership. Perhaps you do not believe that we still have the determination and courage of our ancestors who came on slave ships and steam ships as baggage, and fought their way to some degree of dignity. We have faced poverty before, we have faced every kind of war and the threat of nuclear holocaust. We have survived tyrants and famines, the most vicious hatred and the most extensive greed and lust for power even in man's history. Now we face the greatest war of all. To discover that we truly all are one and that our love can embrace the world. Already to some, it is not a dream but a present reality.

My Catholicism gave sincere and token homage to this unity and love in deference to its leader, but it got lost in the competition for souls and power, projected definitions and interpretations, history and hostile laws and an earthly kingdom, or leaders who shared and often surrendered their power to kings and emperors. The monarchy became the very model of the Catholic hierarchy. Our founding fathers dreamed of human dignity as well, and created it in their separation from Europe and its traditions and kings, and in time fear and greed reduced their noble vision to an impoverished caricature, even as Christianity did to Jesus' intent. Lenin dreamed theoretically of an equality when the hearts and minds of men and women were still too terrified and self centered to give substance to his ethereal vision. Even Hitler had a dream, to decimate and destroy and sanctify Aryan supremacy in rivers of human blood.

Dream after dream, good and evil, dreamer after dreamer have fallen short from Assyria and Babylonia, China and Persia, Greece and Rome, but time is only of consequence if I choose to make it such. I can begin to simplify my life today from the greed and economic pressure I was taught from infancy in my own culture. I can scrape away the barnacles of my own bias every hour of every day as soon as I want. I cannot feed Somalia, nor halt Saddam, resolve South Africa or even liberate South Chicago, but I can begin to be a man of this Global Village a hundred times a day. To change, to grow, to transform my values and finally free my spirit. Millions of us already know that and feel it deeply. We do not see ourselves as lofty or superior, but as finally fortunate. We still struggle with the old ways, the false security and the comfortable "retirement" that ads scream at us every day. We hear the horror stories, the murders, the revolutions, the stalled peace talks, the greedy clinging to parcels of land, the refusal to surrender to others what was given to us.

So we make heroes of fleeting rock stars and outrageous media stars until we begin to recognize the heroism in ourselves and our fellows. The pope is a well meaning, trapped figurehead, whose very office and frozen structure of operation makes change almost impossible. So is the president. Each a victim of history's prison walls. The gangs will continue to kill, the murders and rapes will persist, the economic unrest will not be solved by realigning interest rates or past methods of postponing reality with more indebtedness. But meanwhile, amid all the blood and screams from the newsroom, a vital change is taking place at a very radical level, beyond country, beyond religion, beyond social setting, because "man is older than the state", older than the Church, older than the culture, and as he dispenses with religious, cultural, and political myths, he will continue to emerge in oneness. Some of us refuse to wait for our institutions to reflect what is already happening. They never lead! They always follow, and tell us where we've been, so we have already begun, and the Global Village is just a matter of time. It has to be. We feel we have no other choice but annihilation. And that is a choice we not only refuse to accept, but know from a deep inner faith that it will never happen. The entire cold war and nuclear buildup was but a fearful, faithless, dissipation of energy, money and courage, the most expensive illusion ever created by ultimate anxiety. At it's deepest root, a cruel joke of human cowardice and ultimate terror. No More! A new man has arrived to stay, a unique creation, worthy of the world and beyond all history's intervening and destructive myths. And whether he or she knows it or not, his name is Everyman!

I Feel Sad

I feel sad about my country lately
When damn near everyone I know
  Thinks it's okay to take money away from the disabled and the old
As long as we increase military spending
And are certain beyond all paranoia that we can take Russia out
  Faster and more completely than Russia can take us out.
My buddy Danny tells me that we're getting rid of the freeloaders
  And I know damn well he doesn't mean the rich people
    Who invest in feed lots they don't see or want, or
    Get oil and mineral and agricultural allowances
    They don't need or deserve.
I confess I've occasionally wondered about
  Some of the people I see with food stamps,
And I suppose I've bitched my share about welfare.
But I do notice that the most expensive restaurants are still crowded,
  The Mercedes are as common as VW's once were,
  Fifth Avenue and Rodeo Drive seem as active as ever,
While the aged and the poor seem shabbier and more defeated
  Than I've ever seen them in my lifetime,
  Too intimidated and nervous even to whisper of revolution.
I feel sad about my country lately
  Because it lost its morals somewhere between Korea and Watergate,
  And it lost its heart somewhere between this recession and the last.
Now the strangers buy our banks and the immigrants our fast foods
  And we take any dollar or ruble we can get
  To satisfy an appetite as insatiable as the fear that creates it
Content to build cheap barracks and call them homes,
Content to widen the massive gulf between rich and poor,
Content above all to defend a country
  With the expensive nuclear trinkets of a paranoia
    Bred of greed and fear and most unmanly men.
I never knew a brave nation could be so reprehensible,
  That a dollar could mean so much or a life so little,
And I am very sad.

From Maybe If I Loved You More

62

Chapter 3

The Death of Tribal Gods

M an, in the course of his life upon the earth, has created thousands of gods. These gods have reflected his fear and helplessness and hopes in a vast and mysterious world. In the more primitive cultures, man had many gods because his fears were manifold. The forest and the sea frightened him, as did volcanoes and thunderstorms, so did hunger and war and death. Since man had limited knowledge, since he was unable to conquer his fears by himself, he looked for support outside of himself. He created gods who, if appeased, would make him happy, give him children and preserve their health, provide him with corn and meat, and rescue him from the dangers that lurked everywhere. Since men and women had no idea of an unconditionally loving God who could only give to all, they appeased their gods with fine gifts, and arranged the gods into elaborate mythologies to pay them homage. They stood before their petulant gods as helpless children. The Greeks, for example, paid homage to Atlas whose shoulders supported the earth; they honored Poseidon who controlled the sea, and they relied on Ares to help them in war. In the East, men honored Indra, the warrior god who generated lightening from the clouds and was master of the cosmic waters, and Enki the Sumerian god of flocks and fields.

Man could say that he had learned of his gods from secret "revelations" or "sacred" traditions, but in reality the gods were created by the men who worshiped them and projected their own inner fears and dreams, their deepest hopes and secret self loathing. Each god was a reflection of the culture which produced him. Thus the Jewish god of the Exodus ruled like a bearded patriarch, not unlike Moses, and was the voice of wisdom and authority needed by a tribal people wandering in the desert. Later on, at a time of a new and self-conscious monarchy, the same god appeared more as king or sovereign. Similarly, in Egypt, the god Atum was fierce and powerful, as was the Pharaoh. In Rome the people transformed their emperor into a god. God was always a mirror of man.

Hence, to study the religious mythology of any culture is to discover the attitudes of its people, to know their hopes, their fears and frustrations, their self-image, their basic values, their environment. Even today, in the religions of primitive peoples, we find this to be true. Australian aborigines worship a black swan and a kangaroo. The Dakota Indians worship the Wakan beings, the spirits that breathe in buffaloes and trees. In Labrador the Naskapi tribe honors the Master of the Caribou. And even in our most sophisticated theologies, God today often still reflects the anger and vengeance of our own pettiness and unforgiveness.

But in the variety of religious mythologies, beyond the gross superstitions and complex rituals, there is invariably an underlying awareness of the true God of mystery. This God is described as a power, a force, a kind of meaning that reaches beyond culture and defies accurate description. At times it is only a yearning, a subtle but intense hunger, a feeble cry of hope. But however apparent, it is more than a product of the culture; it is a kind of longing for the God of mystery Who is not made by man. In Polynesia, for example, despite a variety of cultural myths, the supreme god of the Maori, named Io, was not reduced to any human image, nor was man permitted to make offerings to him. In ancient Egypt the high god was the "maker of myself"; in ancient India he was the ultimate resting place of the universe and could not be reproduced in art. And the Jews, perhaps unique in their religious genius, spoke of a spirit "hovering over the waters," its name too holy to be spoken, a being too complex and mysterious to be reduced "to a graven image." They were speaking feebly of the God Who is beyond all myth even as their later history paradoxically reduced him to the most banal trivialities and inflexible control of meaningless law and ritual.

And modern man still speaks only feebly of God. He can easily see through the cultural gods of the past and dismiss them. The gods of the Babylonians are dead; their god Marduk who built the heavens from the corpse of the dead god Tiamat is no more. Neither is the god of the Jews who "planted a garden in Eden" and created Eve from Adam's rib. Modern man finds little if any substance in the gods of some ancient culture: the god who is little more than a bearded Jew, or a kind of modern Pluto who rules the underworld, or a Byzantine king who glides solemnly through court rituals, or the god who is a sour Puritan critic. But he finds it hard to reduce into comprehensible words the universal longing of man for meaning.

Paul Tillich, whose final lectures on "spirit" I was privileged to hear, speaks of "man's concern for the ultimate," and Camus describes the "fundamental human problem" of deciding "whether life is worth living or not." Martin Buber looks for his God in the uniqueness of a human friendship which does not use or manipulate its beloved. Even Vatican II, in a moment of exceptional honesty, asks, "What is man?... What is the ultimate significance of human activity throughout the world?"

This is man, now as always, searching for the God beyond culture and human traditions, beyond punishment and human vengeance, beyond manipulation and conditional love. This is man struggling to cope with the inevitable need that can make of life more than a meaningless continuum in the course of time. This is man struggling to find the God beyond statues and ritualistic initiation rites. This God continues to live. He is the God Whom the Hindus call the "ancient Spirit," the high God of the Rhodesians, named Leza, Who is "merciful and does not get angry," the God of the Jews Who is "my shepherd," the Christian God who forgives "seventy times seven times." This God will never die precisely because He is God. He survives all cultures, primitive and sophisticated, because He has no nationality and is beyond all history. He can live in the global village which has been screaming for

Him in every fear and failure, every hope and yearning.

It is the man-made gods that, if not dead yet and many assuredly are not, are destined to die. Granted, they seem to flourish for a time after the culture that produces them has passed away. Man clings to them lest he lose all contact with the true God of mystery and meaning Who lurks under the mythological forms. They are old friends whose moods he understands, comfortable idols that he can placate and control. Thus the Jews returned to the sexual fertility rites of the neighboring Canaanites long after Moses insisted that Yahweh was the only God. The Romans offered incense to the "divine" emperor long after he was recognized as a mere human being. The primitive Indians in Mexico continued to offer food to the god of death even though they knew that the shaman consumed it. And the Christians in Europe and America still whisper magic invocations and plead for salvation like the most primitive of peoples.

But such man-made gods are bound to die, as they always have and prophets inevitably rise up to speed their death. Prophets are idol-smashers, assassins of man-made gods and often are killed or maimed in their essential reforms as was Jesus. The prophet Jeremiah forbade the Jew to "pour libations to alien gods." Mohammed struggled to convince a stubborn Arab world that "Whoever disbelieves in idols and believes in God has laid hold of the most firm handle." Jesus, too, came as a prophet and said to the money changers in the temple, "Take all of this out of here and stop turning my Father's house into a market."

Initially, people have resisted prophets and have consistently murdered them rather than change. But in time, the relentless prophets made their mark because they appealed to the deepest part of man, where he yearns for the God Who is not "made by hands," the living God of mystery and meaning. In acknowledging this appeal, historic man turned, partially at least, from his idols and moved ever closer to the true God, step by arduous step. He passed from the sacrifice of animals to the love of men. He smashed his golden calves, his totems, his charms. He drove out the sacred prostitutes and took away the witch doctor's powers. Then he was free again to feed the hungry, to comfort the lonely, to search again for the true God in pain and love.

While this reflection of idols has often been a gradual process, it's possible to look back at the past and detect periods when it was cataclysmic and widespread. Moses lived in such a time, so did Jesus and Mohammed. So do we. And while it may be interesting to explore ancient mythologies, usually they have no more significance than ancient art or architecture in our contemporary life.

Man can no longer hide in remote areas and pay homage to his witch doctors and priests, under whatever choice semantics. Life does not permit men and women to live as strangers and to honor 20th century tribal deities as the living and true God. In the past, man had time to shed his idols. He could evolve gradually into religious maturity with a minimum of pain. But today, the death of the man-made gods, long predicted and talked about is taking palace with unprecedented speed. This is not just another bit of idol-smashing in history's record, but the most complete and radical that man has ever known. Nietzsche wrote about it in the last century, theologians and journalists have described it in recent years. Even Tillich hoped that it would be gently evolutionary. But it is not, as arrogant and sophisticated moderns termed it a generation ago, the "Death of God." It is the "death of gods" who usurped His place, and created the kind of confusion and destruction we are experiencing even now in our revolutionary culture. A religious revolution, like a political one, is not serene and bloodless, and does not end with a clear treaty and well defined boundaries.

The man and woman of the global village are aware of their own individual power, of a personal God within, a Spirit Whose very reflection they are. They are ready to face the fear of the unknown and refuse to build gods that only reduce their terror to empty symbols. They know they can bring an end to war, whereas the cultural gods have only requested prayers for peace. They know they can ultimately create social justice, whereas the man-made gods have only asked people to be patient with their poverty and starvation. The global village has no privileged sects and does not need petty gods to sustain it. It has no magic beyond the marvels of man's creation, so it may enjoy, but does not necessarily need ritual or sacrament. It is a matter of choice and taste—a decision that reflects or diverts our union with God. Man now rises up to tell the priests of every culture that their sectarianism and mythology produce the very climate of fear and narrowness in which suspicion and hatred grow. He is ready to dismiss the traditions that made static and absolute a given period in man's religious history. He is not even waiting for the prophets; he is scattering the idols on his own, as are his children.

Becky's God

Becky's God is all thunderbolts and lightening sticks
Ready to zap sinners with cancer and rivers of molten lava,
Not missing a single adulteress or roving husband,
Keeping books on all of us like a compulsive accountant.
Becky's God thunders on Sinai and forbids Moses
    the promised land,
Robs Job of herds and flocks and enthrones him
    on a dunghill,
Opens the earth to swallow pagans and murders
    the eldest son of Egypt,
Decimates the folks in Jericho and introduced
    Samson to Delilah.

Becky's God killed Koreans and set fire to
    the villages of Vietnam,
Murdered the Kennedy's and snuffed the temptress
    Marilyn Monroe,
Cursed the Jew who killed His son, invented AIDS
    to wipe out homo's,
Made blacks to serve the whites and shopping malls for sinners.

Come to think of it, Becky's God seems a lot like Becky!

From Quiet Water

The men and woman of the global village would be embarrassed if I were to suggest they are doing a "religious" thing. They well may disavow all "religion," so angry and weary are they of its platitudes and superstitions. They are content to be doing the human thing, and that is to do the most "religious" thing of all. Whether he or she is a college student or a bank president, a housewife or a silent critic, they are prophets of the death of the gods and the midwives of God's rebirth. They do not fear to trust themselves. They do not look to an authority to grant them permission to be free. They are not afraid of the consequences of human behavior, and they will not accept the universal principles adopted by frightened people who claim to be unassailable or infallible. Thus, for example, the authority of the Pope is dying after centuries of development, and its declaration of infallibility in a 19th century fear of Nationalism replacing kings. The Papal office is obsolete. It is the reflection of a past culture which could not believe in itself, and feared the men and women who began to trust themselves fearlessly. A frightened, docile past needed a pope. Now his decisions are of less and less consequence. It is not merely a question of whether he speaks infallibly or not—this in itself is preposterous—but that he proposes to speak as a religious authority for millions. Why can he not simply be a gentle, holy symbol of our world unity, a respected, historic, powerful, expression of love and forgiveness available to all with compassion and love without judgment? A universal sign of peace and compassion—and not a lawgiver and moral critic of an often desperate third world?

Man now is not afraid to take an honest look at history. He knows that the Papacy was established by men, that it flourished under the protection of secular powers from Constantine to Charlemagne and beyond. God did not put

Peter and his successors there, Caesar and the Emperors did for their own purposes of universal order and complete control. Thus Peter was declared the first "Pope," and Scriptural authority was invoked to support his title after the political fact. In the fourth century, Ambrose of Milan could write, "Where Peter is, there is the Church." And a tragedy was cryptically codified. Early on bishops were supreme in their own churches, often elected by the people. What the culture had produced, theological arguments made "divine." Constantine, for example, supported the decisions of the great Church Council of Nicea in 325 with his soldiery to declare Jesus as the true God and not merely man—while thousands disagreed, and monks fought monks in outright primitive warfare. The Pope served the emperor's purposes as a kind of spiritual Caesar, the symbol of religious unity in the Empire. Christianity was the state religion, and that began its very undoing. A strong emperor, like Charlemagne, despite his multiple marriages, mistresses, and moral extravagances, made significant spiritual decisions. He determined the method of baptizing, ordered attendance at Mass, and supervised the liturgical ceremonies. When Leo III was elected Pope, Charlemagne wrote to him as if to an underling and insisted that he "conduct himself properly, govern piously, and observe the canons of the Church." Charlemagne appointed the bishops, supervised the Pope, and even decided intricate doctrinal questions.

It is obvious that the Church would have a different form if it had been founded in a democratic society. There would have been a representative form of government, not an infallible Pope who learned his leadership from an untouchable emperor. There would have been general religious principles and reasonable directions, not minute doctrinal codes and inexorable laws invading marriages and bedrooms. Or, even if the Church had developed in a monarchical era, it would have been a different Church if it had not attached itself to the Roman Empire. But the Church was the Empire's spiritual police force; it was the devoted teaching staff which dragged the barbarians into the world of culture, and it was the emperor's ally. It deserved an infallible Pope whose decisions were beyond all question. This is not to highlight history's decay, it is only to know the truth, and to realize that out of ashes and decadence God can emerge more fully.

Nor is it to deny the contributions the Church made to Western culture. It is not to ignore its art and libraries, its struggle to teach the illiterate to read and write. Nor is it to overlook the fact that much of the freedom and science we have today was spawned, at times unwittingly, through ecclesiastical leadership. Certainly it is not to overlook man's service of the God beyond culture, the God Who cared for the poor and homeless, the slaves and degraded, the God Who lurked under the mythology of an infallible Pope and brought men meaning and happiness, or a Vincent de Paul in Paris or Mother Cabrini in Chicago.

But it was this very God beneath the myth Who helped to prevent millions of men from rejecting papal authority centuries ago. The Church did give meaning to men's lives, it did build universities and feed the poor, it did support monasteries which were social and economic centers for the surrounding families, and tens of thousand of monks and nuns lived holy and dedicated lives. There were great spirits of every century, like Thomas á Kempis and John of the Cross, Meister Eckhart and Theresa of Avila, and thousands of devout pilgrims found God amidst decay.

But today, the god of papal authority is finally dying. The death rattles are now being loudly heard. Some of them are embarrassing. One such was Pope John Paul II's crusade against contraception in Mexico. Or much earlier Pope Paul's excitement when the bones under the high altar of St. Peter's in Rome were said to be the true bones of the Apostle after whom the church was named. To Pope Paul this meant that Peter was really in Rome, that he had come there as the first Pope, that every bishop who succeeded him would be another Pope. It meant to Pope Paul that he, the successor of Peter, had the same "divine" commission and the same infallible power.

Perhaps tomorrow he or his successor will find Caesar's bones mingled with those of Peter. Then perhaps he would have courage enough to bury them together—forever.

The Pope Recently

The Pope recently
Took the Bible a step further
And said that a man
Should not look with lust at his own wife.
Edna Mae O'Brien
Who would give anything
*   to be lusted after again*
Wondered if the Pope
Had discussed this matter with his father.

From Maybe If I Loved You More

The man of the global village does not know of any infallible men. One President made a mistake in Cuba's Bay of Pigs, another President made a series of mistakes in Vietnam, yet another helped to mortgage our economy. Nor is he interested in a twentieth-century churchman who wants to unearth Galileo and to free him from condemnation by the Church. He knows that Galileo was right. That is enough. He also knows that the Church has been wrong as often as any other human institution. The god of infallibility cannot survive in the global village, neither can the awesome god who attempts to intimidate men and women with past cultural forms. No such form has been more effective than the myth of purgatory and hell. It has frightened people for centuries, ever since the superstitious age which made it the focal point of Christian faith.

The myth of hell and purgatory, and, indeed, limbo, is a vital part of my Judeo-Christian inheritance. It created the framework in which the Christian myth of the afterlife evolved.

The ancient Jews spoke of a place called Sheol; its exact meaning is hard to define. In former times it was said to be a "bottomless pit" in "the depths of the earth," a monster with jaws that could not be satisfied. The idea of Sheol did not originate with the Jews, it was rather a part of the Semitic culture. The man who enters Sheol "will not ascend again," "shall not awake," "shall not see the light forever." Every man, indeed, went to Sheol. It was not, as in later times, a place of punishment, but rather a place of inactivity and immobility for everyone who left the "land of the living." Neither was it a place of happiness. Even the Jewish patriarchs did not want to go there; they wanted to continue to live because a long life was the only available reward. But, above all, it was another transient myth.

Later in Jewish history, some two centuries before Christ, there was a new note added to the concept of the afterlife. It appeared in the *Book of Wisdom* as well as in the *Book of the Maccabees*. There was mention of reward and punishment in the world beyond since the Hebrew notion of Sheol now seemed to merge with the Greek idea of Hades. By the time of Christ there were many theories about the afterlife. A new word had also developed, gehenna, which most likely referred to a garbage dump outside of Jerusalem where rubbish was burned. This was the word that was frequently used in the New Testament for hell. If Christ spoke of hell personally, and not merely in the dramatic reflections of the Evangelists who wrote about him a generation or two after his death, he may have used the word gehenna. Whatever word used, the whole concept of eternal punishment was vague and mythological, the product of the merging cultures of Jerusalem and Greece and Rome.

But it was in medieval times that the god of hell and purgatory became the very center of religious life. The medieval man was an apt subject for the most elaborate theories of the afterlife. An eclipse in 1315 made him fear the end of the world. The conjunction of Jupiter and Saturn precipitated predictions of all kinds. The plague of the Black Death in 1347 cut the population of Europe in half and sent man whimpering to pay homage to his magical god. Man was helpless before portents and omens of any kind; the fear of death became an obsession. Men and women spent hours meditating on the sufferings of Christ; sorcerers and witches became popular, the devotions to special saints who could rescue man from a fiery, Dantean kind of hell developed beyond control. Relics of the saints were prize possessions; the gaining of indulgences, to release charred souls from purgatory (a humane qualification of hell), was perhaps the most popular devotion and, as we all remember, became a focal pointing in Luther's revolt. Bands of penitents wandered through towns, lashing themselves till they bled—to atone for their sins.

In such a world the god of purgatory and hell could flourish, and the vagueness of Scripture and early Christian tradition about the next world could be built into elaborate systems. Dante could write of *Purgatorio* and *Inferno*; morality plays could delight the people when a god came down to rescue a soul from eternal torment. (Hence the so-called Deus ex-Machina.) And without one word in the Scriptures, the grotesque doctrine of limbo could develop as theological fantasy to reinforce the need for infant baptism and the reality of original sin.

Similarly, without any evidence that Christ said one word about purgatory, with scanty proof for any awareness of it in early Christianity, it could appear with full force. The great St. Augustine's attempt to prove its existence from a few verses in I Corinthians, Chapter 3, is an embarrassment. It modified the fierce concept of hell which had then developed. It gave man some chance to be "saved" despite the misery of his own humanity. The myth of hell and purgatory has lived until today to destroy lives, torment consciences, divide families, and transform God into the most despicable monster conceivable. Yet men still preach about it, Masses are still said to free tormented souls, the Pope is still granting indulgences to quiet "divine" wrath. Men still tremble at the final judgment at which Christ, supposedly, will appear to pass sentence on those blessed, or those to sear without finally consuming, forever.

But this horrendous, cruel god—like the god of papal authority—is dying, and his death is long overdue. Now, a mature spiritual person can focus on the horror of this world and will take his chances on the next. He knows of the hell of war, the purgatory of an unhappy marriage, the anguish of life. He cannot be concerned with the myths of another culture, with the god of fiery volcanoes and eternal hell. Such a god is too arbitrary to bother with, too obviously a myth to be worthy of theological discussion. He is dying and the man of the global village will put him in his grave, even as the "little ones" of earth still tremble and deny themselves life because of hell's fire!

Sorry For Jesus

Once I felt sorry for Jesus
But who felt sorry for me?
Together we walked to the hilltop
I cried till I couldn't see.
They nailed him fast to the crossbeam,
The nails went crunching through me,
I always felt sorry for Jesus,
But who felt sorry for me?

The women stood close to the soldiers,
Stood looking at Jesus and me,
The women stood there in their aprons
And swept all their tears to the sea.
The mothers drowned in their sadness,
The mothers bowed down by the limb,
They all felt sorry for Jesus,
But who felt sorry for them?

The men stood still like the mountain,
Stood staring at Jesus and me.
The men stroked their beards in confusion,

And wondered why this had to be.
The fathers were aching in silence,
The fathers bowed low by the limb,
They all felt sorry for Jesus,
But who felt sorry for them?

The world felt sorry for Jesus,
So they gathered to pray by the tree,
They all felt sorry for Jesus,
But who felt sorry for me?

Who felt sorry for me?

From Sunshine Days and Foggy Nights

Another prominent deity, the tax-exempt god, is dying too. Unlike the gods of hell and papal authority, he is defended by civil law and is doubly hard to dislodge. But like those other gods, he is the product of an ancient and alien culture. His roots lie in the privileged status that superstitious nations gave their priests. The Jews, for example, set aside an entire tribe, the tribe of Levi, to be used in the service of God. They were to take the place of every firstborn Jewish son who, according to their culture, belonged to the Lord ever since he was spared in Egypt. This particular tribe was then to be supported by the offerings of the people. The tribe did not have to work or fight; its entire obligation was to assist at the sacrifices and religious rituals. The ancient custom of tithing was based on this same root to pay for religion and priestly services. That it is still claimed as a "Christian" law is unhistoric and deceitful—actually a most profitable, theological lie post income tax.

The Christian cleric received the same exemptions as the Jews for somewhat different reasons. The Jews exempted the Levites because the Jewish nation was a kind of theocracy and the worship of God was an accepted part of their culture. The Christian priest was exempted because Christianity was adopted as the state religion. But even when Christianity is no longer the state religion, even when there is no state religion, religious exemption continues in our culture. It makes no sense to the man and woman of the global village. If they do not care to practice some formal religion, they do not see why they are obliged to pay homage through tax exemptions.

The Church in our society is a vested interest. Very often in the process of assuming a moral position, it takes a political stance as in abortion or birth control. Often the Church has its own schools which perpetuate its own myths and molds its own subjects. Such schools and such churches should not be tax exempt. (At times they were supported by racial discrimination.) This is to exempt household deities; this is to support the expensive bureaucracies that modern religions have become. This is not to deny the rights of these schools to exist. It is to question their privileged status.

There is a great difference between freedom of religion and the privileged position of the tax-exempt religious institution. Perhaps it would be different if religions were engaged primarily in universal works of charity rather than in the particular programs of proselytizing and "salvation." Why should modern man be charged for the private cultural hangups of religious groups? Why should religious ministers and priests be exempted from military service? We are not ancient Jews, nor are we medieval European Christians. We exempt religions from taxation, and yet we have nothing to say about how religions use their funds, even though I believe many churches use them well. Whatever the case, no serious politician and few honest Church leaders would reject tax exemption.

Yet recent scandals have highlighted the dishonesty which continues in Televangelism. We permit religions to exclude worthy citizens from their programs of charity because they do not profess the right kind of faith. Catholics can admit Catholics into their schools in preference to non-Catholics. Mormons take care of Mormons. We do not audit religious books; we know nothing of the expenditure of funds.

77

A religious group can erect a million-dollar church and ignore the poor—all in the name of charity and the tax-exempt god. A religious home for the aged or altzheimer victims can compete with a home that is privately owned and not have to explain why it charges as much or why it excludes people who cannot pay the entire monthly bill. A parish can operate an inferior school, hire teachers who are not qualified, and demand that its subjects attend; and society must reimburse the tax-exempt church for this religious act.

Increasingly, perceptive men and women see the tax-exempt god as a cultural relic. But no politician with a semblance of sanity would suggest a modification of this historic injustice. Men and women are anxious to see how long this god will survive if the coffers of Caesar are not opened to him. We rarely see poverty among the churchmen, nor hunger or need in the ranks of the clergy, nor do we see most of them rushing in vast numbers to assist the poor or to bring an end to suffering. There are, of course, wondrous and saintly exceptions. But, we see most making bank deposits to preserve their institutional myths. Many critics insist that if they have an adequate product, people will pay for it, but only as they require it and use it. It could terminate another artificial anachronism.

The god of the blue laws, too, is a cultural overlay still often protected by society's codes. As he slowly disappears, he is a relic of pharisaic religion and puritanical ethics. He is preoccupied with alcohol and gambling, divorce and dancing, and even Sunday rest. In New York a man could have a few drinks in a bar until four in the morning, in Phoenix the glass was snatched from his hand at twelve-forty, in Richmond he was not permitted to purchase liquor in a glass at all. This makes no sense to the man who could have breakfast in New York, lunch in Richmond and dinner in Phoenix. In Washington, D.C., when I was in grad school, we had to stop drinking on Saturday night at midnight, so we went a few blocks away and drank till two in Maryland.

The laws of gambling are equally childish and are

likewise a cultural hangover. Recently, they are beginning to change rapidly with lotteries and extended casinos, as necessity and greed outreaches history and piety. Virginia forbade horse racing, so its ranchers were content to raise horses for the nearby tracks in Maryland and West Virginia. Reno and Las Vegas became national shrines of gambling since so many states forbade gambling on cards or dice or roulette. Once such laws seemed to make sense to a solemn people who worshiped a puritanical, stuffy god. Now they are ridiculous and even Mayflower Americans with puritanical roots are licensing gambling. Such matters have nothing to do with religion or moral behavior unless it is to tempt man to break the law. The Mafia and the similar crime syndicates were supported by the blue laws. They supplied men with the alcohol and gambling that these archaic laws forbade. Each Mexican border town became an exciting "den of iniquity" for the same reason. These obsolete laws helped to create the numbers rackets, the "afterhours" joints, the "private" crap games. They have been an offense to any man of judgment, but they were, and at times still are solemnly enforced with the same childish zeal that produced them in another culture, under the aura of another mythological god.

Divorce laws reflect the same senseless rigidity. They are the product of the same archaic culture. In America they provoke a bitter battle between husbands and wives who are asked to appear in court as adversaries. It is not enough that they simply want a divorce. The blue laws refuse to face the fact that divorces will exist, as will gambling and alcohol, regardless of laws. The Catholic Church could not honestly permit divorce, so it created an elaborate annulment process which could make any marriage temporary, even after a previous annulment. After studying the process carefully, I concluded that it was the basis for an outstanding musical comedy—or Neil Simon at his best. Under the existing rules, I feel that Mary and Joseph's union could readily be annulled.

Not only is man reflecting the gods of religious authority who oppress him and the puritanical gods who treat him as a child, but he also finds a diminishing point to the ritualistic gods that reflect a dead culture. Once it seemed to make sense to dress ministers and high priests in special robes to symbolize their mystic power, and it still makes some people feel good. I prefer one of my favorite Unity ministers who wears a neat sweater and jeans.

The Book of Exodus in the Old Testament describes the vestments that were to be made for Aaron and his sons, the "pectoral, ephod, robe, embroidered tunic, turban and girdle." Each detail of tailoring was prescribed by law. The religious ceremonies were described in lavish detail; the position of the altar and the offering of incense were not left to chance. And Christianity was equally ritualistic. Even today, bishops appear in public wearing slippers and long white gloves. In my culture, slippers are for the bedroom or for the beach, and long white gloves are evening wear for women, but I may be simply registering a private protest. I would much prefer to see the pope in a simple white alb or cassock. I doubt very much that Jesus was costumed at the Last Supper.

The flowing vestments embarrassed me with their effeminacy and reminded me of a Shriners' convention or a fraternity initiation. I say this truly without mockery—but such accouterments are a "medium" that gives a distinct "message" about man's relationship with God. The stilted prayers and postures of the liturgy recalled an oracle at Delphi. Altars speak of Druids and bleeding lambs. Blessings and sacramental rites conjure up Macbeth's witches and dying Jewish patriarchs surrounded by their sons. I know some revel in this, but I only speak for myself. Such posturing is an eloquent exposure of how we see God by the very setting in which we honor Him.

The major religions still recite archaic prayers or change them for the worse; they still perform their outmoded liturgies with bows and gestures to honor the obsolete god of ritual that made sense in another era. Some time ago the Episcopalians revised their Communion service, and the Catholics offered alternate forms for the canon of the Mass. The revisions were merely a simpler and more elegant version of the same irrelevant invocations that came from another culture. Such ceremonies have no meaning now; they reflect another world.

Yet, I can well understand that such rituals can evoke warm memories of the past and can fill traditional hearts with nostalgia and that is surely their privileged preference as much as simplicity is mine. I can accept the fact that many people enjoy the elaborate ceremonies much as they might enjoy a familiar aria in an opera or a well-known scene in a favorite play. I am even willing to admit that for many men and women the mystique of the ritual has esthetic value and echoes the mystery and holiness of God.

But I know, too, that locked within the very rituals themselves is a description of man's attitude and approach to God. Rituals are eloquent expressions of how man must come to God in servility and according to formulae. They describe a man who appeased his god by passwords and magic signs. They describe a god who is outside of man, ruling like a Byzantine king or Jewish high-priest in some exalted heavenly court. They speak of a god who can "save" a man arbitrarily or send him to an incredible "hell." They well may have esthetic appeal to some, but they reflect most clearly the religious servitude learned in a culture when man was more docile in his slavery. My God lives within me and you, and I don't want to lose Him in ritual, symbol, myth, or costumes.

The Holy Man
The holy man made me uneasy
With his otherworldliness,
The guru in his flowing white garments,
Ascetically arrogant,
Fashioning his own words in wheezing, whining riddles,
Lest the symbols expose his cliches.
Suddenly a peanut-butter sandwich became complex.
  "You must have peanut butter,
  Which, of course, means you must have peanuts to butter.
  However, without the bread there is no sandwich,

Even if you have all the peanuts in the world."
The disciples groaned. The ladies smiled knowingly.
Someone coughed apologetically.
This is all very profound apparently.

Maybe I would have trusted him
  With a little mayonnaise on his moustache.

From Sunshine Days And Foggy Nights

Modern men and women increasingly refuse to grovel
before such a god, to bow and kneel in a superstitious kind of
devout subservience. They do not look for their God in frozen
prayers and in stuffy ceremonies. They do not seek protection
from wandering devils or ask blessings from "consecrated"
hands. They do not need to light candles or shake incense
unless they choose; they do not join in group incantations.
Modern man can often find his God in the simple, profound
search for daily meaning, in the struggle to learn to care, in
the commitment to be responsible to his brother. He wants to
talk to people, not to pray at them. He wants to love them, not
to hide from them in archaic rites or meaningless hugs and
handshakes. He wants to know men and women, not ignore
them in his concern for ritual or tradition. He is in search of
the God Who makes men and women free, and in his search he
is preparing hundreds of cultural gods for burial with solid
communities to take their place—communities which reflect
our current struggle! How many times have I gone to church
for solace and insight, the strength and courage to endure,
and left the crowd lonelier and more severed than before?
It wasn't real. The gods seemed starchy, distant, and even
oppressive.

Oppressive gods, I am glad you are dead. You are the
feeble creation of hungry and frightened men and women. You
starved them even as you fed them; you built walls against
their neighbors even as you spoke of love. You are the human
at its weakest, fearful, and most dependent. You are man's

intolerance, his guilt and anxiety, his dishonesty and prejudice, his heartlessness, his resentment, his childish fear, his pettiness and greed, his refusal to live in the present, his unwillingness to be responsible for his own acts, his jealousy, his insecurity, his inability to live with mystery and doubt. You are the symbol of man's rejection of himself, his deepest lack of confidence, his secret fear that he is not lovable in himself. Now you are dying or dead. Now men and women have piled you on an immense pyre to reduce you to the ashes of the ancient earth from whence you came. Soon increasing numbers will stand over you and all the world will know of your death. And I will rejoice, and so will free men everywhere, for in the death of the cultural gods is the birth of God beyond all archaic myth.

I do not reject all ritual and symbol, only when it gets in the way of my contact with God and my neighbor. Because it is familiar and comfortable does not make it effective or supportive. The opera on stage may be different. That is not my concern—only in spiritual community. And I want the climate, the atmosphere, the very air to reflect the union of God and man. I want to connect with God and my brother and sister at some real level. Otherwise, it is but a sterile repetition of a destructive history. As Nietzsche said so well, *"After Christ, came the Christians!"*

For One Unafraid To Be Himself

There is not failure for one unafraid to be himself,
No defeat for one who does what he can without
    sacrificing the private rhythm of his being,
A rhythm created over centuries and shared with life itself.
Failure is only a chance to begin again,
Defeat but a gentle warning to walk another road,
Loneliness an invitation to find a new friend.
A life built on sand and avarice is the victim
    of every earthquake or avalanche,
Every rise and fall of Dow Jones or a robot's dictation.
Wrap yourself in your own feeble being,
Warm yourself with your own fragile heart,
Defend yourself in peace and silence, and do battle
    with smiles and shrugs
And an awareness of eternal change.
Patience and humility are your impermeable armor,
Love and prayer your impregnable protection.
Your worst adversary is crippled with everyman's fears,
The most severe critic but a raconteur of his own story.
How can there be failure when the ocean still rolls
    towards the land?
And the night still embraces strong and weak alike
    with love?
The morning will come with its soft light
    to offer you a childhood again,
And the wind will sing the gentle rhythm that makes of
    each day a new adventure.

From Tears And Laughter Of A Man's Soul

Chapter 4

The Bible As History

*E*very major religion has had its sacred books which contain universal and inspiring truths; the Bible, the Koran, the Vedic books. Every major religion has had "sacred persons" in special contact with God. Gotama Buddha was such a person, and hence could say, "I am the holy one in this world; I am the highest teacher." Mohammed tells of a visit with the angel Gabriel, who appointed him Allah's apostle, and he speaks of special communications from Allah himself. Moses ascended to a high mountain and there "Moses spoke and God answered him with peals of thunder." Jesus, too, was in contact with God, and at the time of his baptism a voice from heaven was heard to say, "This is My beloved son in whom I am well pleased." In all of these cases, the special "revelations" from God were recorded in "sacred books."

Man could not question these books; he could not qualify them in the light of his own experience. He was asked to accept them as "absolutes" and to meditate upon them that he might find the truth. Once man was able to do this. For most of my life I did this. I could go to the Bible and reflect upon its teachings and stories and apply them to my daily life. I did not question the story of Adam and Eve as history, the murder of Abel by Cain, the transformation of Lot's wife into a pillar of salt. I believed that the origin of languages was traced to the tower of Babel, that Noah really built an ark, that an arm of the Red Sea literally parted to permit the passage of the Jews, that the walls of Jericho actually tumbled down with a resounding crash under the leadership of Joshua.

It was only gradually that I learned that many of the biblical stories were myths containing a deeper and symbolic meaning and that other peoples had a mythology similar to that of the Jews. I read the creation account believed by the ancient

Sumerians (2000 B.C.), and although it is primitive and mytho-logical, it contains enough similarities to the biblical account to put the Jewish myth in some universal perspective. The story of the flood among the Babylonians is obviously from the same remote source as the biblical story. And the Code of Hammurabi, dating from the seventeenth century before Christ, contains numerous similarities with the Jewish law and strongly suggests a common background. There's nothing wrong with any of this until some authority enforces cultural guides and interpretations as absolute truth to be accepted, or otherwise to endure punishment and massive condemnation.

For centuries man had not been able to put the Bible in any kind of context since little was known about the peoples of the ancient Near East. It was only after World War I that excavations were begun in earnest in this area. Some twenty thousand tablets were discovered on the site of ancient Mari, a city on the Euphrates, and revealed a flourishing life in the Mesopotamian world some three thousand years before Christ. There were important discoveries at Ur in ancient Chaldea, reputed to be the city from which Abraham came. Work was done in Egypt, in Syria, in the ancient biblical cities. Ancient languages were deciphered. People who were once a mystery were better understood. The religious world of Christ, long subject to the pious guesses in many areas, became much clearer with the discovery of the Dead Sea Scrolls after World War II. But even now, the work is only beginning as new texts are found and translated. I was privileged to spend a summer in the Nablus area (ancient Samaria) as an excited novice on one of the archaeological digs.

With these important archaeological discoveries, the work of biblical criticism became a most important science. The critics were hard on the religious myths that man had learned to accept as true history, and not "religious" history that had very broad boundaries when dealing with actual fact. The Exodus, which is the key to the Jewish nation, could now be seen as a tribal migration. There is hardly a mention of the Jewish Exodus in Egyptian history, as if the Jews had never been there or their departure was insignificant. The dates and circumstances are only guesswork. But the Jews, sparked by their religious genius, had turned it into sacred or "religious" history. Moses confronted Pharaoh, he inflicted plagues on the Egyptian people, he demanded release from slavery in the name of God by angelic swordsmanship and killed the eldest son of Egyptian families. Apparently the Egyptians were not awed or impressed, but this in no way dilutes "sacred history". When the Jews wandered in the desert for two or three generations, God was their leader. When water was found, it was seen as a miracle worked by Moses. When tribal laws were enacted to build a strong nation to keep the Jews apart for the dissipation of their desert peoples, it was reported that God had addressed Moses on Mount Sinai. The whole nation entered a kind of covenant with its desert God, and circumcision, a common practice among the ancients, became a religious rite to signify the pact, not a Jewish invention.

This is not to say that there is no factual basis for the Jewish religion. It is only that it does not now appear that it came from the direct dictation and "revelation" of God, but from the genius of a gifted and spiritual people. All the events of history were interpreted in a "religious" sense, and this is what is meant when we speak of "sacred history." Nations who resisted the Jews were seen as the enemies of God when they were only men attempting to protect their homes and possessions. The cruelty of the Jews, in destroying cities and massacring the inhabitants, became a kind of religious sacrifice to God called herem, a genuine contradiction to "Thou Shalt Not Kill!" of Mt. Sinai. A hailstorm that helped the Jews in battle was a kind of bonus sent from God, just as in another naive or angry contemporary culture Hurricane Andrew could be seen as a divine visitation on the sins of South Florida, or AIDS as a warning to homosexuals. The passage from tribal existence to monarchical government was interpreted as a refusal to trust God. Victories in war were given by God; defeats were inflicted for not following His leadership. Even monotheism for which the Jews struggled so long and hard, was not interpreted as a unifying political force, but a simple response to a revelation.

This is not to deny the beauty and truths of the Old Testament much of which I love, especially the beauty of the Psalms I recited every day for years. This is not to overlook the power of its myths and the spiritual heights of its prophets. It was Isaiah who wrote in the name of God, "I am sick of holocausts of rams and the fat of calves...help the oppressed, be just to the orphan, plead for the widow." It was Jeremiah who wrote, "I am Yahweh, I rule with kindness, justice and integrity on the earth." It was David who sang, "Yahweh is my shepherd, I lack nothing." The Old Testament rings with the fervor of a religious people and profound spiritual support and inspiration. But it also rings with mythology, archaic and superstitious ritual, narrowness and national pride, fierce cruelty and insane legalism. In a broad sense, it is a high point in the writings of sacred history. It is an immortal book. It is the record of the unparalleled religious evolution of the Jews. But it is not the "word of God," dictated as it were on Mount Sinai or in the desert.

I Cannot Answer

I cannot answer for all the others,
*   Nor understand their uncomplaining compliance*
*   With routine's demands and seeming boredom.*
I know nothing of age or settling down,
*   Or boundaries established be history or custom.*
Grey hair is no barrier or wrinkles,
*   Time spent or time remaining means nothing*
*   To a heart that requires freedom to live.*
In another life I would have carried my tent
*   Across the endless desert,*
*   And sailed my creaking ship across an unknown sea.*
Now I will wander freeways and crevices,
*   Hear strange voices,*
*   And make friends with whomever is at hand.*

It is not a choice I made but a destiny I inherited,
   Not a habit but an issue of blood and bone and madness.
   Stand back from life and observe it carefully.
   What makes sense and what is imprisonment?
   Who knows consistent happiness and who follows
      A path made by docile ants,
   Pursuing docile ants in prescribed procession.
   I have no idea where I must live or how,
   No blueprint made in Japan or heaven.
   Only a heart and mind that know
      What is true and what is false,
      What feels good and what feels bad,
And assuredly I will not speak for all the others
      Who have no questions and no answers.

From Loneliness To Love

Nor is the New Testament the "word of God." It cannot be understood except through the eyes of Jewish history. The men who wrote it were Jews, steeped in the law and traditions of their Jewish past. There is hardly reason for believing that God spoke to them directly; there is every reason for believing that they merely reacted with personal inspiration and fervor as religious writers to the life and teachings of Christ, to the religious needs of their own times, to the problems they faced within their own religious communities. Always they were individuals reacting as distinct personalities to Christ and Christianity, often in heightened or poetic consciousness. They did not write biographies; they wrote "sacred history," interpreting the events of Christ's life within the framework of their own Jewish experience. They did not hesitate to use common, borrowed sources in telling their stories and there are numerous other early "sacred writings" that were not accepted as scriptural by arbitrary rules of selection. Luke makes mention of sources at the beginning of his Gospel. Both Luke and Matthew borrowed heavily from Mark. There were two or three versions of Luke's gospel alone.

Mark in turn made use of an Aramaic version of Matthew and of material derived from the sermons of Peter. All made use of collections of the "sayings of Jesus" which were circulated before the gospels. Each wrote for a special audience at a special time. (I recognize and try to simplify a very complex and elaborate process.)

Mark wrote primarily to a non-Jewish world and stressed heavily the miracles that Jesus worked. Mark was a disciple of Peter and likely learned from Peter that the wonders of Jesus singularly impressed the Romans and would be effective in their conversion. Matthew, on the other hand, wrote to the Jews, and he stressed the fact that Jesus was the Messiah promised in the Old Testament. Thus in his work, we read that many of the events in Christ's life were seen as the fulfillment of some Old Testament prophecy, often by a very elastic connection. John the Baptist was said to be the Elijah who, according to Jewish tradition, was to return to the earth. Christ would be in the earth three days like Jonah was three days in the belly of the whale. The mothers weeping for their children slain by King Herod fulfilled the prophecy, by a deep strain of the imagination, of Rachel weeping for her children. Christ was seen as the new Moses who went up on a mountain with his disciples and was "transfigured before them." He also ascended a hill to reveal to the crowds the new and more perfect laws which would replace the commandments of Moses. Christ was the "son" of King David, the supreme prophet of Israel. It was all beautiful parallelism, but not literal history as we know it.

Luke, the most accomplished and human of the evangelists, emphasized heavily the gentleness of Christ and incorporated many of the "sayings of Jesus" and the personality of Mary. He also stressed Christ's role as Saviour and made Jerusalem, the holy city, the center of Christ's ministry. Jerusalem, with all of its traditional meaning in the life of the Jews, was the only fitting place for the new and supreme sacrifice, the death of the Redeemer, to take place. It was known as the "virgin city" even as Mary was the "virgin mother" (which had nothing to do with physiology) who gave birth to a new and undefiled covenant.

The gospel of John stands alone and was written some three generations after the death of Christ, long after many "sacred writings" which were excluded from the Bible. John, unlike the other Evangelists, is not expecting the reappearance of Jesus after a century so his gospel emphasizes the presence of Jesus in Baptismal water and consecrated bread and wine. John was much influenced by the contemporary literature which has only recently come to light in some of the Dead Sea Scrolls and more recent discoveries. Thus he made the frequent reference to the place of "knowledge" and to the struggle between "darkness" and "light." The Gospel of John is more subtle than the others and was written to a flourishing Christian community, but one that was suffering from the Roman persecutions as well. There is less emphasis on the physical aspects of the miracles of Christ and more on their deeper meaning as "signs" of spiritual healing from internal illnesses of the heart. Thus, for example, when he wrote about the multiplication of the loaves and fishes, his story became a complete discourse on the liturgical rite of the Eucharist which had assumed far greater meaning than years before. He discussed more thoroughly the meaning of baptism and contrasted it with the more feeble rites of the Old Testament. The actual story of the sufferings of Christ was abbreviated, but there is a long discourse on the hostility of the world to the Christian. And since John had witnessed the destruction of Jerusalem and its temple by the Romans, we see the ruined temple at the beginning of his public life rather than at the end as in Matthew.

Thus John and the other Evangelists were not biographers, nor simple chroniclers or objective historians. They were much more. They could "rearrange" historical details to fit their theme; they could emphasize aspects of Christ life which suited their own reasons for writing. They could inject their own personalities. They were sermonizers, inspirational and religious propagandists who for the best of reasons   wrote "sacred history" in order to establish the power and the authority of Jesus and to lend support to their own leadership in the Christian community. If persecutions were a threat to the Christians, they wrote about Christ's attitudes toward suffering. If there were Jewish converts who still insisted on circumcision before baptism, they wrote about the end of the Jewish religion.

There is no factual basis for believing that they had any special "revelations" beyond unique, creative gifts and plentiful borrowed sources. Similarly, there is no such basis for believing that Jesus himself was in any occult trans-human identification with God. More and more, the discovery of literature and religious customs contemporary with Jesus helps us to see him as a man—unique and a genius—of his own times in profound contact with the God-head within. But, the Roman historian Suetonius, the only non-biblical and non-Christian source that tells of Jesus, barely mentions in passing, a certain "Chrestus," and sees him as one of the many Jewish preachers and "wonder-workers." That's it—one, brief, contemporary, misspelled mention outside early Christian literature. Thus, the real power of Christ came after his death, even as Moses' power, of little consequence to mighty Egypt, took on new significance in sacred Jewish history. During his life, like Moses, Jesus was very much a man of his time, and to me that makes him all the more real, approachable, and a personal model. I don't need him as God. I need him as man, brother, friend to lead me to the finest limits of my own sacred humanness.

It is not unusual to read of miracles surrounding the life of such a gifted man in various ancient cultures. In fact, it was commonplace. The Jews had been waiting anxiously for a Messiah, a deliverer, since the nationalistic days of Judas Maccabeus two centuries before. There was a vast literature that sprang up during this period dealing with the messianic theme. The Jews had every kind of idea of what the Messiah would be, but generally they saw him as a man of militaristic strength and personal power. It was not unusual for disciples to gather around a given claimant and to attribute to him miraculous powers. But, Jesus was not a Messiah of the most popular variety, since he was a "peaceful" Messiah who had no intentions of overthrowing the power of Rome. He would suffer for his people and teach them, but his kingdom was "not of this world." Still, his personality and power attracted crowds and devoted disciples. His fame grew throughout the land and the stories about him grew as well. But he was certainly not "headlines" in Rome or Antioch or even Jerusalem.

The real creative and healing myth of Jesus grew in the New Testament. The story of his life in public was transformed into "sacred history." His birth was described in the mythological terms reserved for heroes and great prophets common among all peoples. He was more than Moses, who was found among the reeds by Pharaoh's daughter. He was born in a stable and seers from the East came to worship him. An angel warned his father that Herod was determined to slay him, although Herod could hardly be concerned about a Jewish baby born of peasant stock in a Bethlehem stable to a couple from minuscule Nazareth. He was forced to flee into Egypt, a most unlikely trip—a kind of reverse of the original Exodus. Every known event in his life was symbolic, filled with special meaning. This does not detract from the words, but it makes them "sacred" history that can lead us to great, spiritual truth and protect us from the literal fury of the Fundamentalists.

When Jesus visited the temple as a child, he astounded the doctors with his learning. When he was baptized, a voice from heaven spoke. When he began to preach, he was led into the desert by Satan and kept there forty days in hunger, like his people who remained there after the Exodus for forty years. He worked every kind of miracle to astound the people, healing the blind, curing the deaf, and raising the dead. Yet, despite his obvious wonders and the force of his words, most men did not listen to him. He was deserted in his death; he wandered through the streets of Jerusalem carrying a cross and no one came to his assistance. On the third day after his death, he rose from the dead and was seen by more than five hundred people, although one of his closest friends, Mary, did not recognize him when she saw him in the garden. Is that simple, recorded history? Or is it sacred and spiritual teaching to help us grow and become aware of who we really are?

Scholars now assert that most of his miracles were merely hearsay, or natural events, or spiritual transformations to which the people gave some mystic explanation. But most refuse to believe that his Resurrection from the dead is in the same category. Some years ago Dr. Hugh Schonfield, author of The Passover Plot, went so far as to suggest that the disciples of Jesus removed his body from the grave and made it appear as if he had risen. This, to me, compounds the problem, and goes to the absurd. Why did Jesus have to rise from the dead at all? Why in the light of what we know of "sacred history" would not the Resurrection of Christ be merely a powerful symbol of his genuine victory over death and the foreshadowing of ours. What would a physical resurrection accomplish except to make him more than human and to re-place the simple faith of his disciples with an astounding vision? To make him an impossible and unreal ideal! To make him unlike us!

It is an interesting experience to attend a lecture given by one of the modern Scripture scholars who believes in the Resurrection as a physical miracle. He will discuss the miracle of the changing of water into wine as a popular tradition and as a symbol of the transformation of Judaism into Christianity. He will talk about the miracle of the loaves and fishes and dismiss the physical fact with an emphasis on the word of God which feeds the starving multitudes. He will call the healings of the blind and the deaf literary devices that attempt to show the effect of Christ's teaching on hardened men. And he will support his reflection of these miracles with parallels from other traditions and with a discussion of the kind of literature that the Bible is. All of this I endorse, and it makes the Bible, not a book of fables, but a classical work of religious significance, that I love and revere.

But then, when he comes to the Resurrection, suddenly

the Gospel narrative becomes a physical fact. He says that Christ returned to strengthen the faith of his disciples, to provide them with unity and new leadership, that the evidence is overwhelming. I do not find the evidence overwhelming, especially when it is the written report of "believers." Nor was it necessary for the faith of the disciples if they were impressed with Christ's teaching about forgiveness and love. I much prefer to see the appearances of Christ after death as a mystical presence to his friends, something which I believe still occurs in Lourdes or Pittsburgh for that matter. Then he remains as human as we are, and at the same time I can celebrate Easter in the traditional way because I know Christ conquered death and sin and so will I. Alleluja!

The parables alone would guarantee him immortality; the beatitudes have been enough to inspire millions of lives. Sayings of Jesus have become household maxims; his equanimity in the face of death and his courage in the face of life have been a model for centuries. Paul could say, "If Christ is not risen, our faith is in vain," but if he was referring to the physical resurrection of Christ, I do not believe him.

I do not require that kind of faith, even though I have no special need to question Jesus' power of healing. Nor do I have to be knocked from my horse as Paul was and receive a special vision from Christ, though I have been upended several times to get my stubborn attention. I can believe in Paul's vision, just as I can believe in Christ's physical resurrection. But I find no essential need to do so. It has no significance or purpose, since I want my heroes as human as I am. What I do believe is that Jesus somehow conquered death; I believe that he gave millions of men hope that they never had before and continues to do so as I write these very words. I believe that his greatest miracle is the undying effect he has had on Western civilization, and that he has made an indelible mark on my own life. But for me to believe that he rose from the dead is to reduce him to a myth of sacred history, it is to confuse the symbol for the fact, it is to misinterpret the literary form of the gospels and the times in which Christ lived, thus to make

95

of him a mythical hero like others, rather than one as human as we are, our brother, supporter, healer, and friend forever available to us.

The Healing

The healing of the deepest wounds seems slow,
But time is of little consequence for all the joys that lie ahead.
So much time spent walking through life, going
where you never were.
Now, at last you are alive in each moment,
Taught by pain and the lonely separation from yourself.
Once you wanted it all, now you know that all
lives in each honest moment.
Excitement and exuberant echoes are no match
for serenity and gentle peace,
A contented heart, a trusted friend, and finally time
to look long enough to see.
It is a loving God Who hands you a custom cup to drink,
A brave and loving man who drinks it all and lives.
Take back the eyes that were blinded by hurry and preoccupation!
Take back the ears that were deafened by discordant!
Take back the words that only echoed in the wind!
Now you are your own, and patient healing will teach you
What no master ever did or could.

From Quiet Water

For centuries the Bible was accepted as a book of historical truth. Its fables were understood as fact. It was only with a study of the literature of the time that man began to realize that "sacred history" had none of the rules that we demand today. Historical criticism of the Bible is not very old, and Catholic scholars were forbidden to apply their knowledge to the New Testament until after World War II. It took them a long time to catch up with the world of scholarship, and to this very day, conservative and fundamentalist groups interpret each word literally and wreak wild and distorted havoc with a symbolic book like *Revelations*. (The Apocalypse) Now those who are able can begin to understand that the biblical writers were unscientific "children of their own day," and talented artists of "sacred history."

Even when the biblical critics began to reveal their conclusions, there was a tremendous resistance on the part of the people. They had learned the biblical stories in childhood; they had celebrated them on the major feast days of the year, and they had taught them to their children. The critics had to be cautious with their conclusions or they would be dismissed by the people. The Catholic critic had an additional problem. For generations Catholics had used the Bible as a kind of legal textbook to support traditional doctrines. They had sought out texts to establish the virginity of Mary and even her Assumption into heaven. They had looked for passages to make marriage a sacrament and to support their views on the last rites in the epistle of James. They had searched for a text to lend credence to purgatory and limbo, another to prove that the Pope is infallible and that priests had the power to forgive sins beyond the power given to each of us to choose another way of life or rectify mistakes. Catholics had reduced the Bible to a code of absolutes, and biblical criticism could bring the whole religious structure down on their heads, confusing and troubling sincere and innocent believers.

It has not been my intention to disprove the Resurrection or the physical miracles of Christ. No man can do that. That is not an area of proof or disproof. I have merely stated that I do not need to believe in the Resurrection as a physical fact, nor do I need to accept the countless miracles of Christ, even though miraculous healings still happen, I believe that they are the products of the age in which Christ lived and are characteristic of the type of literature that was written to reveal him to men. Nor do I have to believe that the Bible is the final word of God any more than the religious writings in the Koran or Vedic Books, as beautiful and inspirational as they are. I can only accept the gospels as the important religious experience of men who lived nineteen centuries ago and their reactions to the events surrounding the history of the Jews and the life of Jesus Christ. That does not defame these words to me, it elevates them, and unlike the Koran or other texts, they are the heart of my own personal culture and spiritual journey.

It is unfortunate that the Bible has been seen as some kind of "supernatural" invasion of man's religious progress. Those that see the coming of Christ as a "divine" visitation outside of the normal framework of history do man an injustice. History was ready for Jesus Christ. Given his own profound spirit and creative genius, there is an adequate explanation for his work and teaching in his own Jewish culture. Few of his ideas are so unique that there is not clear evidence of them in the literature of his Semitic tradition and in the religious fervor of his own age. This is not to say that he was not a man before his times. This is not to say that he did not possess unparalleled insights and holiness, and was the treasured model of what men and women are capable. It is only to say that the religious history and genius of the Jewish people could produce a Jesus Christ some two thousand years ago. It is my contention that this is exactly what happened. I do not believe that "God" should be given credit for what man can accomplish by himself in union with God. Nor do I believe that man would have accepted the teaching of Jesus Christ if he had not been uniquely conditioned by his own culture. Man listened because history and experience had made him ready to listen. The time was right. "The stars and planets were in place." Jesus was not a divine being superimposed on his own era. He was an extraordinary prophet of his own age and continues to make an impact in city and town when "your time" or "my time" is right.

This Above All

Walk easy on the earth without disturbing the sand.
Let others observe your footprints,
*   But like night and day leave no trace.*
Let your shadow move where it will,
*   Its magnitude decided by the sun.*

Do not love easily but well, linked in spirit and flesh.
Let your love be warm and generous,
   And like the sun do not measure your gift.
Let your friendship be enduring and loyal,
   Even as the mountains are not displaced.

Let no one judge you beyond what you actually do.
Thus you will not be judged
   By anyone harsher than yourself.
To judge another is to become blind
   And delay your own passage.

Do not try relentlessly to understand.
   Time itself will decide.
There will be stars enough when clouds and neon lights
   do not hide them.
Do not be sad. It has been written for you.
   Your joy will come when it is time.
But this above all. Walk easy on the earth.

From Walk Easy On The Earth

The whole idea of a "supernatural" revelation from God to man is a primitive and an artificial one denigrating the power of our divine gifts. Man does not need "revelation". It is a gift when human contact connects with the divine. He does not need God to speak to him in special visions or in mystic apparitions though it is not impossible. God did not have to appear to Moses in a "burning bush" or speak to him in "thunder" upon the mountains. Neither did God have to speak to the Jewish prophets or to Mohammed in some unique "Revelation," nor reveal Himself to Paul in the "seventh heaven." Nor did John require some ethereal transfusion of divine wisdom while writing the *Apocalypse* (Revelation). All that Moses offered men, all that John or Jesus provided, can be well explained by man's own progress in self-knowledge and the voice of the God within his own consciousness, at whatever level—the same voice Jesus heard perfectly, the same voice that speaks to us when we can listen. Man learns to know God as he learns to know himself. Assuredly he requires some special voices to make his own secret thoughts known; he needs some prophetic genius who can transform his own tenuous hopes and dreams into verbal form and concrete substance. He needs the inspiration of poets and evangelists, interpreters and philosophers, prophets and even seers if you will. But he does not need a dictated "revelation" from God.

God speaks in man's own struggle to be himself. God speaks in man's stubborn effort to translate his love for his own wife and children, his love for his own city and state, into a love of the whole world. God speaks in the struggle of the Black and Brown or Yellow for justice, in the effort of modern man to protest all and any war, in the rage of modern society to be free from institutions that have lost their meaning, to be free from traditions that have lost their roots, to be free from laws that only make it harder to love. He can speak in an atheist or a believer, "sinners" or "saints."

I don't have to believe that Moses had a "revelation," or that the Virgin Mary appeared to some shepherd children of Portugal or to Bernadette of Lourdes, but I do believe the people who experienced it —even as recently at Medjugorje, though the messages were in the idiom of the people who received them and not my own. I don't have to believe that God sent dictated messages to Paul of Tarsus or Jesus of Nazareth. I can also choose to believe that God speaks through chosen voices, but does not invade our world and interrupt its course. He speaks gently in the efforts of all men to be mature, to grow in wisdom and love. The source of "revelation" is the inspiration in man's own heart and mind, a universal divine force or energy that is the heart of the smallest particle of being. And the appearance of a special or unique prophetic voice means simply that man is continuing to grow.

It is unfortunate, too, that the Bible is viewed as some kind of absolute rather than an inspiring source of comfort for any and all. It is unfortunate that men have made it the ultimate vision in the religious development of man. Even though history bears witness to the various "kinds" of Christianity that have existed in every century, man still stands before the Bible as before some staid and megalithic vision of the all-holy God. To say that the Bible is only the record of a most important stage in man's religious growth as is the Koran is not to discredit the record or the man. I can read the Bible, as I often do, and be inspired by its pages. But I cannot go to it as though it were an unyielding oracle who related once and for all the breath and will of God in every minute circumstance of life. This is to make of the Bible a destructive myth, a pretentious idol, a barrier to creative and personal thought and the voice of God within each of us. When the Bible tells me that divorce is forbidden except in the case of adultery, it tells me more about first-century society and Jewish law than about Christ. But to insist that the biblical teaching on divorce is irrevocable is to deny all of the progress that modern man has made in his understanding of the spiritual relationship between husband and wife. It is to produce the very kind of quibbling that religious sects have engaged in for centuries, to create enemies and segregate their flocks. It makes the Catholic Church say that the "contract" of marriage can be annulled, because it's not a holy "covenant," then to describe the nature of their "covenant" so as to make it impossible for any but angels.

When the Bible insists that widows should not remarry, it helps me to understand the attitude of Paul when he thought the world was soon to end. When the Bible tells me that women should cover their hair in the churches and keep silence, it amuses me with its archaic customs and vision of women, and I would love to see it enforced at a feminist celebration. When it discusses the importance of sacrificial offerings, it relates to a Semitic background which I do not share. When it speaks of the "gift of healing" or the "gift of tongues," when it describes the suffering of "hell" or the manner of the Resurrection from the dead, when is discusses the Last Judgment or the cosmic phenomena at the end of the world,

I only understand a little better the kind of world in which the Bible was written, and the imagination and projections of the authors.

People will say that I do not have "faith." What they mean is that I do not have the docility to accept blindly the Bible apart from its environment and literary form. I truthfully do not want such "faith." It is not to Mark's credit that he could write of the miracles of Christ. He lived in an age when there was nothing extraordinary about a miracle. So did Peter and Paul and Luke. They could see signs everywhere; they knew nothing of science, nothing of modern psychology, nothing of medicine or chemistry, all of which are miracles in themselves, as we study and labor for even greater ones to wipe out Aids and Cancer. They lived in a world in which wonders of all sorts were the customary and acceptable panoply of a great man. They believed that Moses was a great man and that he worked miracles with his staff. They believed that he filled the land of Egypt with frogs, that he turned the waters of the river into blood, that he ordered the waves to engulf Pharaoh and his chariots. And in Christ they saw a greater man than Moses, a man who worked greater marvels. To such men, a miracle was no problem. Nor even now is it a problem among primitive peoples and superstitious children who escape modern acculturation. But it is a problem to me and to millions of modern men and women, and it has nothing at all to do with faith. I have experienced my own private "miracles" when I had strayed far from God or when I felt closest to Him. In His unconditional love it did not seem to matter what temperature my faith was.

I will not accept the biblical myth, but I will accept the Bible. I cannot accept the concept of "inspiration" that says that God worked with the sacred writers in some special way when they infallibly wrote down their account of Christ. I simply accept the sacred writers as great religious authors who offer me their first-century reflections on the life of Christ in accord with God's designs. I must distinguish in their offerings the kernel from the shell. I must determine what is a permanent truth and what is a cultural bias. I must compare their experience with my own and decide the direction of my own life, because as man I must be the criterion of my own truth or be nothing. Even if I am "wrong."

And when I see Christ beyond the biblical myth, his words and memory help me realize that I count. I count because I am a man, not because I am a Catholic or a Christian, not because I was baptized or ordained a priest. I count more than the lilies of the field, more than the birds of the air. It does not matter if I am wise or wealthy, uneducated or poor. It does not matter if my life is scarred with a thousand failures, if I am sentenced to the gas chamber or abandoned by my family. I am of value; I am worth the world. I am worth the ransom of kings and more. I am worth the life of a friend. Even if that friend is Judas.

I can go to the Bible, not as a court of law, not as a code of ethics that some angry man shakes in my face, not as an unswerving absolute, not as a textbook that some Fundamentalist uses to hide his fear or unawareness of the modern world or his own true self. I can go to it to get a picture of a man named Jesus Christ. I can accept the fact that he died and still lives, that I am alive and will forever be, and recognize that the only memory I can have of him is in the words of his biographers. I do not look to him for every answer; I reflect on the words written about him and find meaning. I do not care if they are inspired or special words; I only know they are important words that aid me in my search for God, and tell me what I can become through His power and inspiration. It was Jesus himself who prophesied that we might do "even greater things" than he did.

Jesus is not the only one who makes me feel this way, but somehow he usually seems to do it far better than the rest. And in my loneliness, the agony of my own search, I spend a few moments with his words. Or I converse with the Holy Spirit of God Who abides within my own consciousness. Jesus warns me of pinning my hopes on money or material success in place of meaning and love. Yet, he does not ask that I turn my back on the good things of the world. He does not overpower me, or make me feel immoral or worthless. I watch him weep at the death of a friend and know that he is like me. I watch him comfort a widow, give a blind man hope, a cripple courage, a leper dignity and respect.

He tells me not to fear the judgment of any man. He tells me not to pay homage to hypocrisy, not to be paralyzed by fear. He has no special powers beyond the great spiritual powers that belong naturally to man; the awe of his biographies has provided these supernatural phenomena. I could not accept him if the wind and sea obeyed him, if he rose from the dead or multiplied loaves. I can accept him as he is, sensitive and understanding, pragmatic and concerned, seeking out pain and loneliness and offering the healing of his own humanness and healing spirit. And his humanness is beyond all myth. And so can be my own or yours.

For the myth of Jesus, and the myth of the Bible, is as nothing compared to the reality. It takes no "faith" to accept a myth. It is not hard to believe that a man walked on water or another man rose from the dead. I do not necessarily believe it, but it would take no courage to believe. What does it matter if water is changed into wine, or if a storm is stopped in the midst of the sea? But it matters terribly if there is *"neither Jew nor gentile, neither slave nor free."* It matters terribly if *"those who mourn shall be comforted,"* if *"the gentle shall inherit the earth,"* if *"the eye is sound, the whole body shall be full of light."* Marvels do not matter, only love and hope, honesty and courage. And these are what a man finds when he looks beyond the biblical myth.

Life Has Its Beginnings
Life has its beginnings,
> *Each with its own special promises,*
> *Each a door opening to some new wonder.*

Each a unique melody fashioned in our hearts,
> *Each a personal adventure even as a time's beginning*

When darkness was dispelled and the sun and moon
   Were first appointed to guard
   the heavens and lovingly
To guide the day and night.
Such beginnings are a renewal of our very being,
A sometimes fragile gift
   That must be tended and loved,
   Nourished and understood,
Until all that can be, will be,
And life continues to be a joyful creation
Of promises and original melodies
   And endless new beginnings.

From Winter Has Lasted Too Long

Some time ago I made an appearance in court. I watched a man swear "on the Bible" that he should tell the truth. I was sorry that he had to pay homage to an old-fashioned custom and swear at all. But I was particularly sorry that he had to swear "on the Bible." The Bible is a book, granted a special and priceless one, but not a religious idol to be sworn upon. It is not a book to be incensed in Catholic ceremony or to be paraded in a courtroom. It is a book written for men, by men, with all the passion and love and feebleness of men. Man in his history has turned it into a creative and destructive myth. That is why he could be lost in the pettiness of its detail and forget that its only important message is one of love. That is why he could use it as a "holy" club to beat his fellowmen into line. That is why it could divide man from man and be carried by opposing armies as they tried to murder each other in a war. Day by day the Bible is becoming a human document, a proud record of man's religious past. Soon men and women will not swear upon it, they will only feel responsible to improve upon it, and will cease treating it as an oracle from God.

Our generation has a bible all its own, a bible that is being written every day in the struggle to bring justice to the

105

helpless and to end all war. It has its own psalmist in the song and poetry, the reflections and spiritual insights of our own time—as every other time. It can mean as much or more than the psalms of King David, *"Loudly I cry to God, loudly to the God who hears me."* The draft-card burners and the protesting college students were more meaningful and equally as prophetic as Ezekiel with his vision of dry bones, or the Jeremiah with his smashing of a clay jug to symbolize God's displeasure with His people, or the Hosea who married a whore to symbolize the Jews' unfaithfulness.

This is not to say that the Bible has lost its meaning; it is only to say that the Bible can be put in perspective and can be brought up to date. We can read about Job who lost his home and family and accepted his fate while lying miserably in a pit of ashes. We can contemplate his vision of the world, the new awareness of life's uncertainty that suffering brought, the utter misery that move him to cry out, *"May the day perish when I was born."* But every day I can see Job in the suffering of the Black, the homeless in a South Florida Hurricane, or the starving Somalians. I can see Job's frustration and anguish in the ghettos, in the crowded rooms, in the inferior schools, in the unemployment and poverty of the minorities. I can see the ulcerous sores of Job in the rat-bites on babies' arms and in the hopeless look in men's eyes. I can see Job's patronizing friends in the white supremacist who offer sophisticated theories and unenforced laws instead of help. I can also see a new and modern Job who is not satisfied to wait for God to restore his life. I see a Job who is ready to rage and revolt to win justice. Today!

I see Isaiah's call for justice in the throng of voices that refused to tolerate the war in Vietnam. I see Jesus' beatitudes in the extended arms of a Pope John Paul or a Dali Lama, in the quiet strength of a Martin Luther King. I see Paul's description of love in the dedication of the young to a life beyond the nationalism and self-interests of generations past. I see John's vision of "light" in modern man's new awareness that every person counts. I saw the agony of the passion of Christ in the assassination of a president and in the broken heart of a nation. I saw this same passion in a divided Germany, in an isolated Berlin, in the poverty of a village in Peru, in a deranged man who dissected bodies and perverted lives. I saw it especially in the senseless devastation of a tiny country called Vietnam and a Desert Storm that made no sense to me beyond macho display and self-serving indulgence.

In seeing the bible of my own day, I can read the Bible of generations past. I can respect the leadership of Moses, the courage of Abraham, the beauty of Isaiah, the wonder of Jesus, the gentleness of John. But I can also see the modern struggle to liberate man and to give him the dignity that is his due. And in seeing this, I can go to the Bible, but not as a religious absolute, not as a static description of a final "revelation" from God, not as a wall between sect and nation. I can go to it not as a myth that forbids me to reflect on the experiences of my own life, but as the religious experience of an earlier and special age that continues to grow with greater love and more impressive miracles. I can see its wisdom and beauty, and I know that even now I am sharing in its growth and development, beyond the myth of the past, beyond churches and temples, beyond prophets and sacred gurus, to the Birth of God forever renewed in creative forms of community, and future forms of spiritual assemblies that stagger human consciousness. Even if these new communities and assemblies are but two "gathered together" in God's Name.

No More Angry Gods

No more angry gods for me tossing thunderbolts like frisbees!
No more stone-eyed preachers threatening eternal lakes of fire!
No more bloody, atoning crucifixions to coat
    the innocent in guilt!
No more hostile words making Jesus the sacred bile of buried rage!
No more bibles spewing venom from rabid tongues
    of private fury!
No more bitter verses teaching frothing hate and gnashing teeth!
I want gods who can love and laugh from morning till night,
Laugh till the days skip and frolic, and weeks fall
    giggling over months and years.
I want to be saved from greed and avarice and good investments,
Saved from anger and fear, from courts and hostile words
That drain my life and leave no patch of ground to walk on
In a world grown dark and grey, where the news is
    beyond enduring!
Life was meant to be joyful, work expressive of the best I am,
God attendant to my needs, and angels to guide me
    from all harm.
Can I go back and do it again? Feel what I feel, and
    find love for whatever I happen to do or be?
I want to lead an army of laughing people across freeways
    and over the hills,
Rid the world of gloom and despair, loneliness and unkind words!
I want to form a parade that marches beyond sad stories and
    human tragedy!
Finally I understand that the man from Galilee knew
    a better way of simplicity and love.
A pity his spokesmen still turn joy and promises into
    the lot of a galley slave!
And more the pity he does not return to start again
And clarify!

From Quiet Water

Chapter 5

God: Loving Or Vengeful

O ne of the biblical myths that deserves very special attention is that of salvation. It is a core and central part of the biblical faith, and it pictures man as standing sinful and guilt-ridden before God, the helpless victim of "salvation authorities" and an endless parade of doctrinaire evangelists. Mankind is said by most to be born in sin and is prey to thousands of temptations and legalistic impurities that only serve to push him farther from his God. He is confronted with the inevitability of death. Only God Himself can save him through a variety of laws, trials, rituals, and especially, empowered preachers from the most sophisticated to the most banal and naive.

The salvation myth evolved from Man's awareness of evil in the world. Seeing no obvious reason for sickness and death, for murder, theft, and hatred, philosophers in every culture centuries before Christ have attempted to explain them. Even today writers ponder why "bad things happen to good people" and New Agers declare our own thoughts destroy us, even if we cannot seem to control our thoughts. Some, like the Persians, described two principles of creation, one a god of light, the other a god of darkness and this rational explanation has maintained some variety of currency for centuries. It's likely the origin of "original sin". Accordingly, man contained within himself particles from each god; his existence was a constant warfare between these two opposing forces. The ancient Babylonians actually pictured the serpent as taking away the plant of immortality from their hero Gilgamesh, thus leaving man to flounder in his own evil and ignorance. The Jews shared the theme of the serpent in their story of creation and picture Adam and Eve as being tempted by the cunning reptile who in other cultures often reflects healing.

But in the Judeo-Christian understanding of evil, man appears not only as tempted but as fallen. It was held that evil resided in the heart of man. The Book of Job is a classical treatise on the problem of evil. Job asked, *"Who can bring the clean out of the unclean?"* And the answer: *"No man alive."* King David said, *"My guilt is overwhelming me, it is too heavy a burden; my wounds stink and are festering, the result of my folly; bowed down, bent double, overcome, I go mourning all the day."* Jeremiah said, *"Well you know, Yahweh, the course of man is not in his control... Correct us, Yahweh, gently, not in your anger or you will reduce us to nothing."* Even problems of hygiene and sickness were somehow seen as evidence of man's impurity. A woman was declared legally "unclean" after childbirth and was obliged to come to the temple to be "purified." All kinds of physical occurrences - such as burns, boils, chronic skin disease, rashes and loss of hair - were to be "examined" by the priest. Certain animals were declared "unclean," for example, the pig, and to eat its flesh made a man legally "impure." Owls were also outlawed which I find a bit amusing.

And in the Christian tradition, the Apostle Paul said, *"...every single time I want to do good it is something evil that comes to hand...my body follows a different law that battles against the law which my reason dictates."* In the fourth century, Augustine, who fathered a child out of wedlock (appropriately named Adeodatus, the Gift of God), wrote in his Confession of his own helplessness in the face of evil. Luther, in the sixteenth century, described the "damned mass" (massa damnata) of his own corrupt flesh, and Calvin was forever suspicious of the evil contained in human pleasure. One of the most beautiful Christian hymns wonders if God can be concerned about a "wretch like me."

This is man in the Judeo-Christian tradition. Weak and sinful, he cannot find peace within his own heart. He requires salvation through the help of his God as described by his priests and ministers of every category.

From the earliest times, the salvation of men and women came from sacrifice. Sacrifice was the putting to death of a

110

victim to acknowledge God's dominion and mastery over all of life. The death of the victim was a person's way of admitting that he himself did not deserve to live and in the flowing of blood there was healing.

Some people, such as the Semitic followers of the god Baal, offered human sacrifice. In the ninth century B.C., a man named Hiel rebuilt the city of Jericho. He killed his eldest son and put his body in the foundation of the reconstructed town, and he placed the body of his youngest son at the base of the city gates. This sacrifice supposedly assured evil men of God's protection. The Canaanite neighbors of the Jews were accustomed to sacrificing children. Numerous Indian tribes offered the fairest maiden in the community to appease the wrath of God, and far more subtly and legally we have sacrificed the lives of our own children by the very destructive teachings themselves—a less obvious prolongation of human sacrifice.

Physical human sacrifice was forbidden among the Jews. The familiar story of Abraham, who took his son Isaac to the top of a mountain and was ready to slay him before an angel stayed his hand, reflects the Jewish tradition forbidding human sacrifice. Among the Jews, as among many people, animals were sacrificed to God in place of man. The kind of animal was determined by the culture of the people. Thus the Ainu tribe originally from Siberia sacrificed a bear; in the Deltaic rituals of Asia, a horse was offered, and one ancient Roman sacrifice included "favorable owls, favorable crows," a male and female woodpecker. The Jews, in addition, offered fruit, grain, and incense. But usually the Jews killed lambs, goats, and bulls. The key to the sacrifice was the shedding of blood since the ancients believed that life was in the blood. Sinful man owed his life to God; vicariously he offered the blood of beasts.

The ritual of the sacrifice differed. There was a holocaust in which the flesh of the animal was completely burned, a peace offering in which part of the flesh of the animal was returned to the man who offered it to signify God's approval, and a sacrifice of atonement in which man placed his hands on the animal to transfer his guilt to the beast, as in the case of the traditional "scapegoat goat" who was then turned lose in the desert to be destroyed. But the shedding of the blood remained the heart of the sacrifice.

And by this sacrifice, man was "saved." To be "saved" meant many things to many people, and still does. It meant that man was God's friend, that he was approved and worthy—no longer ritually unclean. Usually such salvation was temporary. Among the Jews it meant that he was free to be a member of the religious community and to pray with the rest of the "good" people. It meant that he would live long upon the earth, and, at a much later time, some maintained that he would know peace after death. To Christians it meant that he was living in the "grace" of God, that he was able to do a godlike work among men, that he would be spared the torment of an eternal hell and know the happiness of heaven as long as he avoided "mortal sin" or had it "removed" appropriately.

Sacrifice as the key to salvation explains Christianity's view of the crucifixion of Jesus as a sacrificial death, a theology that expanded and evolved when it was apparent Christ would not return a few years after his death as was anticipated. This sacrificial death motif was only natural since Christianity originated in Judaism. The Christians drew a special parallel between the death of Jesus Christ and the death of the lamb which the Jews killed when they departed from the captivity of Egypt in their celebrated Exodus, or Passover.

On the night before their departure from Egypt, the Jews were instructed to select a lamb (or goat) from their flocks. The animal was to be a one-year-old male without blemish, and the blood of the beast was to be sprinkled on the doorposts of the Jewish homes so that the angel, who would kill the firstborn son of every Egyptian family, would spare the firstborn among the Jews. (Hardly a godly act to murder innocent children.) It was the blood of the lamb that saved the Jews, and thereafter the firstborn son was said to belong in a special way to the God Who saved him.

Jesus Christ became the new lamb of the "Passover" from death to life in Christian symbolism. He became the "Saviour," the perfect lamb, the Agnus Dei, whose blood would withhold the wrath of God. He was without blemish like the lamb, he was born without sin of a virgin. Jesus Christ was the "first-born," the one who most perfectly belonged to God. By his death on the cross, the Christians claimed that he had opened man to the freedom of eternal life, although there was and is a vast array of theological opinions as to how this took place—each one seemingly absolute and infallible. Man would no longer be the prisoner of his own instincts and base desires, no longer the slave of his weak and "sinful" human flesh. For this reason, John the Baptist, in prophetic terms, called Jesus the "Lamb of God who takes away the sins of the world."

The sacrifice of Jesus Christ, however, was said to be a final one, and it put an end to any kind of imperfect sacrifice. Thus it is written in the letter to the Hebrews:

"...according to the (Jewish) law almost anything has to be purified with blood; ...Christ does not have to offer himself again and again, like the high priest going into the sanctuary year after year with the blood that is not his own...Instead of that, he has made his appearance once and for all, now at the end of the last age, to do away with sin by sacrificing himself."

In the same letter the author said, *"Bulls' blood and goats' blood are useless for taking away sins."* And in writing to the Ephesians, Paul said, *"Blessed be God the Father of our Lord Jesus Christ...in whom, through his blood, we gain our freedom, the forgiveness of our sins."*

The Christian myth of salvation goes on to assert that man cannot be saved apart from the death of Christ. Not only is man born imperfect and in sin, but he commits numberless sins during his lifetime and constantly needs to be restored to the friendship of God. By himself, man is helpless because a giant chasm stands between him and God. Through centuries of imperfect sacrifice, he could not bridge this chasm. Then, Christ came. The "perfect sacrifice" had come, and man would be saved by the shedding of his "Redeemer's" blood. Jesus was the "Bridge Builder."

To a Christian raised in the Jewish world of sacrifice, this made some sense. To the Roman even, who had read the legend of the consul Decius who plunged into the midst of enemy forces as a heroic sacrifice to the gods, this might have some meaning. To any man of the ancient world who stood before God as a helpless victim, who believed himself a hopeless sinner, who considered God an unapproachable and angry judge, the sacrificial death of Christ was a myth of some substance. But to modern man, it makes far less sense unless he has been suitably frightened and brainwashed from birth. To him, he is a voiceless victim of God's decree in the Bible. To me, it is a primitive "salvation" myth which portrays an angry father appeased by the death of his own son. It is a tale of unbelievable cruelty. It harks back to the Odyssey of Homer: *"But when with vows and prayers I had made supplication to the tribes of the dead, I took the sheep and cut their throats over the pit, and dark blood ran forth."* It sounds like a sacrifice to Rhea, the mother-goddess in Greek mythology: *"Son of Aeson, thou must climb to this temple...and propitiate the mother of all the blessed gods on her fair throne and the stormy blasts shall cease."* It sounds like the world of the ancient Persians: *"I will sacrifice unto Mithra, the lord of the wide pastures, who has a thousand ears, ten thousand eyes."* But in modern life, the only parallel would be some madness similar to that of the psychotic art student who killed a co-ed because he had been "directed by God" to free her from evil spirits.

I accept the fact the Jesus died, even that he was crucified. But I cannot accept the myth that his death was an atonement for my sins. The salvation myth as it appears in the New Testament is an interpretation. It is a primitive myth, in essence parallel to the salvation myths of primitive peoples everywhere, but it is more unbelievable and cruel than most myths. It rings of a world in which man could appease the gods of thunder during a storm. Now cats and dogs are frightened during storms; man stays inside and understands the natural phenomenon that is taking place.

The more sophisticated modern Christian theologians have come to realize that man finds it hard to accept the "salvation" myth. They have, of late, played down the crucifixion of Jesus Christ and emphasized his Resurrection. They have ceased, in many instances, to preach about the intense sufferings of Jesus and to make men guilty for the misery that they piled on their bleeding victim. They now claim that Christ is more a victorious Saviour than a suffering one. They insist that in his Resurrection he made all men triumphant over sin and death. Thus, it is not the blood of Christ that saved men, as the New Testament openly asserts; rather, it is his entire life and chiefly his glorious Resurrection.

These theologians admit, in effect, that the authors of the New Testament misinterpret the death of Christ, that their emphasis on his bloody sufferings was an exaggeration, a myopic vision that stemmed from their Semitic concepts of atoning sacrifices. They proceed, then, to quote Paul when he insists that *"Death is swallowed up in victory,"* and to soften his words when he says, *"Christ died for our sins."* Actually, they still pay homage to archaic myths, no matter how they refine them, when they speak of "salvation" at all. If I must pay homage to such a myth in order to be a Christian, then I'm not a Christian.

I do not need to be "saved" or washed in anyone's blood. What am I to be saved from other than my awareness that I cannot and will not be separated from God? I am His Son, cast in His very image. Thus, I am not to be saved from my humanity, the body that is mine, or the struggle of my own spirit. There are many thing that Jesus the Christ has to offer me: his concern for men, his indifference to material wealth, his honesty, his fearlessness in the face of opposition. I emulate his courage and admire his compassion for the suffering and the poor. He inspires me to get involved in my own world, and he helps to rouse me from my indifference to the injustice that enslaves the Blacks and other minorities and the neglect that oppresses the poor. He teaches me the value of the individual, the significance of a single human voice, the power of love, the absolute responsibility to share with the poor and needy that which I have in abundance. He is my friend and companion whose hand I often hold on my own journey, to whom I reach out at times of fear and despair. But he will not save me from my sins by his bloody, sacrificial death.

Those Truths

Those truths you seem so sure of,
   Somehow don't seem like yours.
And the words you spout so easily
   Remind me of how things were
When prophets told me what to feel and experts what to say,
   When the high priests decided what was real,
   And gurus knew the way.
Latterly I've learned to wonder
   To withhold my final belief.
Secretly I pity Judas, and admire the unrepentant thief.

From Laughing Down Lonely Canyons

I will not accept this mythical God-the-demanding-Father Who could treat His own son Jesus in unfeeling justice and demand his death on the cross to pay for my sins. Nor is the myth more appealing because He brought His son gloriously from the tomb. I cannot love such a Father or even be grateful for such a son in this borrowed and modified tale of archaic semitic theology. I did not ask him to suffer for me or even want him to. This is the arrogant Father-God of myth, the God Who dares to ask me to be perfect even as He is. My God knows that "perfection" is already mine and offers me the choices that lead me "home". Yet, this angry, mythic God is different. If He could send His son to Calvary, assuredly He could send me to "Hell." And for this I was to be grateful and to thank Him for my "salvation"!

116

At times man has had his bouts and wanted to be free from the God of "salvation." But this God has had the massive support of history and giant institutions with the support of trained minds and eloquent tongues. He has called intellectuals into His service to build Him into a giant rational system. He has had mystics who turned Him into mystery beyond all question. He has had businessmen who surrounded Him with mighty monuments and made Him a part of the culture, and in fear and sacrificial seduction, gold and silver were surrendered to keep the angry myth alive and housed in splendor. He has had dedicated men and women who described Him to unsuspecting children and who frightened adults. He has controlled men by guilt and fear and sophistry.

The myth of "salvation" became an elaborate one. Paul insisted that the Christian shared in the death and resurrection of Jesus through the initiation rite of baptism. In his letter to the Romans, he said,

"When we were baptized in Jesus Christ, we were baptized in his death; in other words...we went into the tomb with him and joined him in death, so that as Christ was raised from the dead by the Father's glory, we too might live a new life...Our former selves have been crucified with him to destroy the sinful body and to free us from the slavery of sin."

The atoning death of Christ became a giant reservoir of "salvation" from which "sacred persons," called priests and ministers, could draw "saving" drops of blood to cleanse man. Once Moses could sprinkle the Jews with the blood of a young bull to make them pure. Now the Christian minister can pour water on a child's head and wash him from the "sin" of being born through the power of Christ's blood. The ritual of baptism, a pre-Christian form of purification, was adopted as the Christian initiation rite to replace the more primitive circumcision ceremony adopted by the Jews. The cleansing water "poured" into man the very spirit of Christ, the "Holy Spirit" Who dwells within a man and makes him acceptable to God. All of this would make palatable sense if the ceremonial simply announced what is—our eternal innocence—and did not turn the story into an angry and controlling myth that destroys human lives.

Recently there has been renewed discussion about the value of infant baptism. The late Karl Barth, a noted Swiss theologian, long a believer in infant baptism, announced to the twentieth-century world that he found no support for infant baptism in the Scriptures. This reactivated an old argument. The pity is that Barth saw any need for baptism at all, beyond an attractive symbol of what already is, that the whole ritual cannot simply be put in perspective as a primitive and archaic initiation rite. This is not to put down baptism or any rite or ritual that give comfort and spiritual insight without seeing humans as sinful, tainted and defective. I can understand that man still baptizes his children because he has some regard for the ritual that admits them to the Christian tradition. I myself have done it hundreds of times, even after leaving the priesthood, and on two occasions for Jewish couples who favored the ancient ritual. I cannot, however, understand a man who can take seriously an obsolete sacrament that claims to wash away his sins with the blood of Christ and provides him with the beginning of "salvation" when he was never lost.

Gradually, in the course of Christian history, all of the religious rites were somehow related to the death of Christ. A priest was able to forgive sins in Confession because he had access through this ritual to the blood of Christ. The sacrament of marriage was said to give the couple special strength in their union because it united them in the blood of Christ. The oil of the last anointing was the oil made powerful by Christ's blood; bishops and priests derive their special consecration from the same blood. Even such a trivial so called sacramental like holy water, which men use to bless themselves, was some how indirectly powered by the blood of Christ, and it commemorated the original baptism with water. Every prayer reached the throne of the Father-God because the blood of the Son had penetrated the "holy of holies" and had made man able to be in touch with God. And every sacred rite set this sect apart from that one—all absolutely certain of their divine commission from the Salvation Army to the Roman Pontiff.

The Mass, especially, centered around the sacrificial death of Christ. It was no longer a meal shared by friends, the last supper that Jesus had while living on earth. It became the "unbloody sacrifice" of Christ on the cross, reenacting at every hour of the day, somewhere in the world, what took place on Calvary. There, man was permitted to eat the flesh and drink the blood of Christ in the ritual form of bread and wine.

Very important within the framework of the "salvation" myth was the notion that Christ had to be God, because only God could restore men to the friendship of the Father. Paul seemed to equate him with God when he said, *"Grace and peace to you from God our Father and from the Lord Jesus Christ."* At other times Paul seemed to deny this as when he spoke of *"God the Father Who raised Jesus from the dead."* Of the four Evangelists, John was the only one who, almost a century after Jesus' death, seemed to indicate that Jesus was certainly God. In the prologue to his Gospel, writing some three generations after the death of Christ and using the language of contemporary philosophy, John referred to Christ as the "Word" who was "with God in the beginning" and who "was God."

After several centuries of agonizing and fiercely angry and bloody theological quarrels, the Catholic position became that Jesus Christ is the unique "God-man" and in his very person he is "of the same substance as the Father." This was decreed at the Council of Nicea in 325 AD, three centuries after Christ's death, with the Roman Emperor ready to defend it with soldiers and arms. When such a dogma was accepted by the Catholic Church, it was easy to return to Scripture and to "discover" further references to the divinity of Christ (as Shakespeare remarked, "The devil can quote scripture to his advantage!") This doctrine lent support to the "salvation" myth since the God-man was human enough to suffer and divine enough to appease the Father-God. In a new way, he became the perfect victim in an elaborate myth that perforated human hearts with guilt and shame, rather than innocence and perfection at birth.

The third person of the Trinity, the Holy Spirit, also entered the picture. He had a kind of twofold mission, one to enter the heart and soul of the man who had been "saved," and another to direct the work of "salvation" in the Church as a whole. By the death of Christ, the Holy Spirit was unleashed in the world to take his place in the souls of men who had been washed in Christ's blood. He was the Spirit who united the Father and the Son, and his presence in a human soul would unite man with the mysterious Trinity. He was foreshadowed in the Old Testament when the first book of the Bible tells us that "the Spirit of God hovered over the waters." He was the "Spirit of sincerity and truth" Who would give men wisdom, Who could guide the Pope and bishops in their leadership of the Church if they listened, and would speak lovingly to the simplest and most abandoned of men and women.

So Often
So often I stand like a bashful child, speechless before those I love,
Wanting to tell them all that is in my heart,
But frightened by some distance in their eyes.
Thus, so much of life is lived all alone,
So many conversations with one's self go unanswered.
I would like to begin again, do it all right this time.
There would be no docile, frightened adolescent,
Smiling endlessly to hide his anger
Trampling on his own fears
Ignoring his private dreams
Fighting for some recognition that never came from within.
No one could push or prod me,
No one could intimidate or smother me,
No one could drive me to adore a God I didn't understand.
Strange! Even as a little boy I knew it was all wrong,
That life was far more than docility and duty and self-annihilation!
All these years spent reclaiming that child who was instinctively

wiser than all his teachers,
All these years spent trying to recapture what I surrendered
   to frightened preachers,

Until I can only ask that the loving, prodigal child who was lost
   will finally reappear,

So that life is the circle it was meant to be,
   That the child who flowered at life's beginning
   Will once more flourish at its end.

From Laughing Down Lonely Canyons

But no matter how theologically complex the salvation myth grew, no matter the subtleties that were added by the great minds of the Church, such as Augustine and Aquinas, man was still the helpless victim who could not be "saved" without the blood of Christ. He had to replenish the supply of the "Spirit" Who alone could enable him to love. When he was baptized, the Spirit came to him with abundant gifts, the Spirit who in reality had always been there and never left, because each of us is God's child, guided by His Spirit, whether we know it or not, or absolutely deny it. When anyone was confirmed, the Spirit was said to bring additional strength. When one confessed his serious sins, the Spirit could return to dwell in a sinful soul purified in Christ's blood. We received the Spirit when we were married by a priest, when I was ordained to Holy Orders, when we were anointed with oil at the hour of death. In a sense the image of Spirit is much like that of energy, and if we do not get lost in the mythological maze rooted in guilt, fear and separation from God, all of these rites can have positive, contemporary meaning.

But this mythological Spirit was often petty and temperamental. He would not come if the words of baptism were not recited properly or water did not flow on the skin, if a marriage were performed without the permission of the Church, if the oil did not touch the flesh. He would not come if the priest did not say the absolving words, or if the bishop failed to recite the proper lines in an ordination, or if the priest in changing bread and wine to the body and blood of Jesus omitted certain words. Protestants said he came in a way that was different from what the Catholics believed, and the Protestant concept of "salvation" was not as involved as that of the Catholics, but was often even more vengeful and inhuman depending on the minister's private guilts and personal projections. For a time Catholics seemed to say that Protestants didn't have the "Spirit" and Protestants retorted that Catholics only had the empty spirit of Rome. But lately the Spirit has been more ecumenical and Catholics and Protestants have acknowledged His presence in each other's sects and in the souls of "sincere" unbelievers as well. (It took a brutal battle with Rome by the admirable Jesuit theologian from America, John Courtney Murray, to give this "new" interpretation solid validity.)

But I do not believe in this chameleon Spirit who makes of God's unconditional love a mockery. I believe He is a way of man's giving credit to God for what man can do himself with his own Inner Divine Spirit by whatever name (force, intuition, power, light, Jesus, guide), who is always present. The traditional Holy Spirit, temperamental and rule-bound is a part of the "salvation" myth which makes man a helpless victim in a mythology of primitive content. I believe He is a historical gimmick that has forced men to cling to their separate sects and has made fearful men proud of their own righteousness. He is a way for man to blame his mistakes on something outside of himself, a way for even well-intentioned churches to bully men into believing that "salvation" rests in their consecrated hands. I do not believe He assists the Pope and bishops in their decisions any differently than our own Inner Spirit guides each of us in our decisions whether we pray or not, or that He brings some unique and complicated "salvation" to men. It is the Inner Spirit of each of us that brings "salvation." Many of the contemporary churches like Science of Mind and Unity, Quakers and Religious Science—most fundamentally American—have helped me and many other "orthodox" Catholics, Protestants and Jews to escape their angry and controlling traditions.

I find, however, that even though those creative and supportive religious sects—as much as an Ernest Holmes or Charles Fillmore, Mary Baker Eddy, or Emerson, have broadened my vision, —they too can create new forms of guilt and fear. Perhaps my "faith" is not strong enough, my "thought control" not rigid enough, or my "meditation" not effective enough. Ultimately, my "Inner Guide," or that "Quiet Voice within" is my primary authority and support, and I measure all I hear or read by my personalized spiritual judgment. Otherwise, a modern sect can be just as arrogantly orthodox or belligerently dogmatic as any ancient Cathedral or Temple. I humbly but firmly challenge the Church's orthodox position on the divinity of Christ, as perhaps I have already made clear. Man turned Christ into God only to substantiate the myth of salvation.

But there is another God in the Bible, another God Who does not deal in "salvation" or rituals or oils. He is the God Who trusts man, Who believes in him, Who warned against pettiness and legalism, Who cleared the temple of the merchants that made money from the sacrifices of the poor. He is the God Who is visible beyond the myth of "salvation" to which weak men reduced Him. He is the God I have learned to know since I threw my "salvation" to the wind, and knew only my separation from God in my own mind could make me feel lost.

Spiritual guides from a variety of sects have helped me in my painful exodus from the priesthood, and my private on going journey to an Inner Spirit and personal God. A television show by a Billy Graham or Robert Schuler might have said a word I needed to hear. Even a Jerry Falwell or Jim Baker on some occasion. Because I did not take their entire product, did not mean I couldn't find a word of personal truth anywhere. And it always seemed to come when I needed it — even on the sports' page of the *Chicago Tribune*. Thus I have visited Ashrams and Self Realization Fellowships, gurus, and Baptists, Mosques and synagogues, Mormans and Baha'i, Himalayan Institutes and Indian Shamans and Medicine Men because I know there is only one truth and I can separate "my" truth from that which eludes or offends me. Perhaps most of all, outside the Bible and the teachings of Jesus and the teachers to whom he has directed me, the book, *A Course In Miracles,* has helped the most during the last few years. At times, it confuses me, angers me, or makes the journey seem hopeless, but I return to it when I am directed to do so from within—as to this or that bible, book, article or teacher. It is the TRUTH that attracts me, what the wondrous Thomas Aquinas called "fulgor veritatis" (the lightening flash of truth") when your Spirit speaks to mine, whoever you are, wherever you've been.

Critical Voices

Critical voices rasping their religious wrath,
As if the appointed custodians and judges of history.
Now I no longer listen, my mind is fenced with
    "No trespassing" signs,
And only the gentle and kind of heart are admitted.
Once I would have borne the pungent, scarring words
    of the self appointed elect
Like the confused and helpless child I was.
Now I guard that child with newly developed sinews
    of my own spiritual being,
Recreated in freedom by God Who watched over me
    from the beginning,
Who finally convinced me that the child within was fashioned in
    His very image.
And the man I am becoming,
    After a thousand essential detours and delays,
    Ten thousands abandoned fears and private victories,
    Is ready to be what God had in mind at my creation.
And the critical voices rasping their religious wrath
Now have power to judge no one but themselves.

From Quiet Water

124

And once a man has been freed from the "salvation" myth, he can also be freed from the traditional Christian attitude toward human pain. It is natural enough for a man who relied on a suffering Saviour to give "sacrificial" meaning to his own pain as well. Thus, Christianity produced an endless procession of self-made martyrs who were able to wallow gloriously in their personal suffering. Religious writers and spokesmen helped them to understand that they must "carry the cross" and "walk in the bloody footsteps of Christ," as if anyone can truly comprehend the meaning of pain, save perhaps in looking back. But in the midst of terrible suffering, it is a great courage just to hang on, to cling to the flimsiest thread of hope that it will pass. Life was not meant to be a "vale of tears," a "solemn life of exile," a place of "bitterness and tears."

Such preachers and their faithful followers could tolerate pain because they believed they deserved it. They could explain natural disaster and wars as the anger of God, and could work hard because it was only right for a "sinful" man to live by the "sweat of his brow." They had a pat answer for every human problem, answering every grieving human being with a mystical kind of interpretation of the "will of God." Only death would end their pain and bring them their "salvation."

But now there is another kind of person who does not believe in the prejudicial and distant kind of "salvation." Neither does he find merit in needless human suffering, though we may learn much from it when it cannot be avoided. Such ones believe in life and health and happiness. They know that work is sometimes hard, but they are striving to create a society in which it will be easier and more fulfilling. They hope the computer will free us from work that has made humans seem like an unfeeling machine. They know that children die at birth, that young and promising lives are ended before their time. But they will not pay homage to some archaic attitude that speaks of "atonement" and "salvation." They will learn from people everywhere; they will transplant hearts or remake kidneys, conquer cancer and Aids and the horror of clinical depression, and struggle to end sickness, hunger, even war.

The suffering of the world is the suffering of our brothers. We cannot stand back and consider it with the detachment of the prophets of "salvation." We cannot classify men as "saved" or "unsaved," as "baptized" or "unbaptized," as "forgiven" or "unforgiven." No one is special, and absolutely no one is not! Each of us is a unique creation selected from billions of possibilities, unconditionally loved.

Assuredly, there is a "salvation" that man needs, but it is not the "salvation" that comes from the mythological interpretation of Jesus' death. It is what man gives to man by caring and what God gives to each of us in an unconditional, forever present love. It is what was not possible as long as man believed that angry "Fathers" and "Holy Spirits" would have to grant him permission to be free and human. It is the "salvation" that is possible now that man can look beyond the narrowness of his own nation, his own church, his own family, and be a member of the global village.

Man alone can save man; man alone will save man with the Inner Guidance of a loving God who belongs to all! We will not rely on presidents who, often with noble intentions, promise us peace and give us war, nor will we rely on parents who promise family loyalty and often unwittingly transmit bigotry, nor will we rely on priests or ministers who promise "salvation" and bind us in fear and prejudice and guilt. Man will rely on himself precisely because the God the churches seek, is already his Father, forever. Men and women will "save" the world, not in a year or in a decade, perhaps not in several generations, but they will "save" it in the new and even smaller world which can look beyond "salvation myths" and see men and women as all one —beautiful and saved— and unconditionally loved by the God Who made each of them unique and special by the very fact of their being. There is only salvation because there cannot be ultimate separation from God. This is what our faith and hope and prayer must

126

establish in our daily consciousness for true peace. Where there is fear, it is not from God, no matter the nature of the fear: health, age, finances, family, failure, loss of love, divorce, rejection by children or parents. You are God's revered and beloved child, and that means you forever dwell—even at this moment—in peace. protection, confidence and love. You have EVERYTHING YOU NEED, NOW.

In knowing this, the Re-Birth Of God beyond destructive and dividing myths will continue to unite us all in peace and joy—no matter the headlines and continuing rumors of war, poverty, and financial collapse. The only real reality is that we, each of us, is God's child and cannot be separated from Him no matter what we say or how we think. That, and that alone is our salvation beyond any historic or personal myth! Fear can still bring us pain but existence as God's child is the knowledge that finally and forever will quiet fear and assure us of true love and peace because GOD LIVES.

Walk Easy On The Earth

Walk easy on the earth:
    Each life has its own fragile rhythm,
    To be aware of it is to understand,
    To ignore it is to abandon oneself to sadness.
    It is to search vainly for the wholeness
        that only comes in surrender to what is.

Walk easy on the earth:
    Too much seriousness obscures beauty,
    Intensity blinds and distorts one's focus,
    Excessive ambition destroys true perception.
    It is not hard work or suffering that debilitates,
        but a loss of contact with oneself.

Walk easy on the earth:
    Anger clouds vision and rage shortens life,
    Laughter is the greatest gift of the free spirit.
    To laugh profoundly and often is to understand,
    To laugh at oneself and all of life,
        and thus to see clearly.

Walk easy on the earth:
    Love is waiting to reveal itself when it is time,
    Nor can one create it despite the most noble intent.
    Love is the discovery of one's own rhythm in another.
    Any other love, regardless of time or commitment,
        will only be doomed and painful.

This above all: Walk easy on the earth!

From Walk Easy On The Earth

Chapter 6

Dying Religions And The God Of Laws

*O*ne of the more obvious evidences of transformation in man's struggle to become civilized is the evolution of moral codes. In the Middle East, in 1901, a copy of the code of Hammurabi was found inscribed on a six-foot column of black stone. Hammurabi was an outstanding military commander and lawgiver who was the King of Babylon about four thousand years ago.

Justice in his day was often harsh and brutal. If a man was discovered looting his neighbor's property during a fire, he was thrown into the fire himself. The penalty for adultery was death, but if a woman felt she had been unjustly accused, she might clear herself by plunging into the sacred river. If she sank, she was convicted. There were laws governing inheritance, adoption, and the rights of holding property. Unjust accusations, always a problem in a primitive society, were treated savagely. And the so-called lex talionis, or law of retaliation, was strictly enforced. *"If a man knocks the tooth out of a man of his own rank, they shall knock his tooth out."* Or if a man caused the death of another man's daughter, his own daughter would be put to death. There were even times when a doctor's hand could be cut off if his patient died. The Code of Hammurabi, by our standards, was strict and even savage, but it provides us with great insight into the attitudes and problems of that ancient culture.

So does the law of the Jews. The more primitive a society, the more harsh and direct are its laws. The Jewish society, with its Ten Commandments and hundreds of lesser laws, was somewhat more sophisticated than that of Hammurabi, but for the most part, far less refined and sensitive than our own. The Ten Commandments were the law of a tribal people who required clear-cut rules and strict justice to maintain some kind of unity and order. They reflect the problems that faced a newly formed nation wandering in the desert for forty years. The very substance of the laws dealt with many problems that do not concern us today. Thus idolatry was forbidden because the pursuit of false gods would lead the Jews to mingle with other nations and to dissipate their own tribal spirit. Similarly, they were forbidden to take the name of God "in vain." There was a special reverence for God's name among the Jewish people. To give a person a name was in some way to have power over him. The God of the Jews, Yahweh, was not given His name by men, as were the gods of the pagans who *"have eyes and see not"* and *"who have mouths and do not speak."* Rather Yahweh revealed Himself to Moses as *"I Am Who I Am."* To the Jews he was the one, true God, and not a simple, tribal deity produced and named by men. In later years the name Yahweh was not even used in prayer, but was replaced by Adonai or Elohim.

The law of the sabbath rest, too, had special significance for the Jews. The very day itself was a sign of the treaty or covenant between Yahweh and His people. In the myth of creation, it was associated with the day on which God Himself rested. *"The man who profanes it must be put to death."* Any man who did any work on that day was to be *"outlawed from the people."* And not only did man rest but his animals and his field as well. This law, too, made sense in the simple existence of a primitive people whose life was uncomplicated enough to set aside a given day for rest, and whose faith was such that they could consider this day as consecrated to God. The so-called "Blue Laws" are a vestigial reminder of an ancient tribal law, many of which are still on the law books in more primitive or provincial areas, while the enforcers know nothing of their archaic origins.

The law demanding honor to parents was of unique significance to a wandering and often disgruntled people. The family was the most important social unit in the tribe, and disrespect to parents could lead, ultimately, to an undermining of overall authority. *"Anyone who strikes his father or mother must die."* Imagine! Murder, too, was a frequent problem in the tribal society. *"Anyone who strikes a man and so causes his death, must die."* There were no exceptions or refinements or time for testimony with prolonged trials and the modification of judgment. The word of a man was important, and there was a special commandment covering unjust accusations. There was no time for investigations, no time or capacity to comprehend motives. There was a special law forbidding theft, another forbidding adultery and the kind of jealousy that would lead to overt acts of greed and lust.

The very wording of the law and the detailed listing of the crimes tell us the quality of the people. A stolen ox was to be replaced by five more, a stolen sheep by four. Sexual intercourse with animals merited the death penalty. A "sorceress" was to be killed. There were laws demanding that the "first-fruits" of the field and flock belong to Yahweh, laws governing holy days and special feast days, tax laws, property laws, laws concerning the kinds of food to be eaten, laws declaring men and women "impure" for hygienic reasons, laws concerning menstruation and sexual defilement. And the people were warned that if they did not keep the laws, *"I (Yahweh) will let wild beasts loose against you to make away with your children...I will send pestilence among you...You shall eat the flesh of your own sons...I will pile your corpses on the corpses of your idols..."* There were no elaborate and sophisticated methods of crime prevention and detection. Only the severity of the law and the horror of immediate punishment could bend the stubborn wills and the fierce passions of a people strong enough to survive for years in the desert and to build a mighty nation.

Indeed the Ten Commandments are a high point in the history of law, and primitive as they may seem, they reflect the degree of sophistication that the Jewish people had attained through their religious genius. But at the time of Christ, the Jews had apparently become a very legalistic people. A vast tradition of law had grown up around the Ten Commandments and the numberless laws of the Book of Leviticus and the

Talmud, much as in the history of our country or the Christian churches. (The Catholic Code of Canon Law had 2414 entries with elaborate commentaries on each item.) Christ referred to the religious parties of "scribes and pharisees" of his own day as "hypocrites" and applied to them the words that God spoke to the prophet Isaiah: *"This people honors me only with lip-service, while their hearts are far from me."* He insisted that they had put on the people an intolerable burden of law, and he defied them when they objected to his works of mercy on the sabbath, or when they questioned his disciples' failure to observe the ritualistic traditions of cleansing after meals. The law had replaced love and often invested its original purpose as has occurred in every civilization and institution.

More that this Jesus qualified and interpreted the Ten Commandments in his Sermon on the Mount. He said he did not come to "abolish the Law" but to "complete" it. He did not look to the ancient law of Moses as an unchanging monolith, nor did he tolerate the human traditions that had grown up to subvert the very purpose of the commandments. Finally he summed up the whole of the law in two commandments as the heart of the Old Testament: love of God and love of neighbor. In fact, he insisted that the whole law of the Old Testament could be contained in a single phrase: *"You shall love your neighbor as yourself."* While the Christ thus saw nothing permanent about the Ten Commandments, his cultural spokesmen in later centuries transformed them into a sacred and permanent code of angry control and brutal projection.

As the law of a tribal people, the Ten Commandments reflect a variety of life that modern man finds hard to understand. While it is true they seem to safeguard some basic values that our culture shares with the more primitive and tribal ones, the laws that Yahweh is said to have entrusted to Moses have no literal binding force today. For modern man is not a violent tribesman; he will not resolve the complex problems of his personal conscience by simplistic principles of archaic law. Man often confuses laws with values and, when he does, he ends up a pharisee, a nit picker, an unbending legalist, and charismatic leaders like a St. Francis of Assisi or Pope John XXIII realized that they were destroying the Church. Thus in our society it is considered wrong to "swear." Historically, "to swear" meant to invoke God's name, or the name of some heavenly patron, in support of truth. If a man "swore" that his statement was true, he said, if effect, that he was willing to have God witness the truth of his heart. To lie under such circumstances would be frightening to a man who believed that God might suddenly invade his life and strike him dead or blind him for his prevarication. In the course of time, "swearing" came to mean any use of God's name in a profane way. Swearing was further extended to include any word that the culture found unacceptable in conversation, especially crude words about sex or the toilet. After several centuries, man had acquired a vast number of taboo words and somehow they were said to violate the commandment forbidding the use of God's name in vain.

When such words appeared in novels, they were said to be "bold" and "frank," even though such phrases were often used in daily conversation. And most of the same words are "beeped" off television in the name of some "moral" code, while the very "beeper" may well use the same words in regular conversation. Children are disciplined when they use these words. Men are often expected to clean up their language in the presence of women. This is not to say that many are not offended by an exceptionally vulgar use of language. It is only to say that this reaction has nothing to do with "religion" or God. When to use such language is a question of taste and social propriety, a matter of custom and breeding. I can share with the ancient Jews the value of proper language; I cannot share with him or with his puritanical commentators the law which forbids the use of God's name in vain.

Even the commandment forbidding adultery no longer applies. This is not to say that our society applauds adultery. It is to say that the complexity of human love in today's world cannot be handled by a simple dictum. We share with the ancient Jews a value for human love and the marriage bond. Some of our modern laws, indeed, still reflect ancient tribal law, as did the divorce laws in New York and other states, which permitted divorce only on the grounds of the "crime of adultery." But these are mere remnants of the past that have been reinforced in our society by the Puritan ethic and repressed guilt. They do not reflect the thinking of modern man. We do not put adulterers to death. We are more concerned about human relationships and the kind of loyalty and honesty that can produce a personal commitment. Adultery is a private matter, not something for public legislation or tribal law. Sometimes adultery is meaningless, at other times it is cruel and tragic. Often it is a symptom of great immaturity and the incapacity of a man or a woman to have a deep and honest friendship. Or it can be a reflection of a kind of addiction to sex. But sometimes, too, it is the beginning of great personal growth and the foundation of a friendship which later blooms into a lasting relationship. In reality, to say "Thou shall not commit adultery" is to say nothing clear and univocal to modern man.

The very idea of attempting to produce a responsible man through law is ridiculous. That was the whole point of Jesus' reform of ancient codes and barnacled traditions without any meaning except arrogance and authoritarian control. Law only produces a careful man and provides a framework for some sort of social order. Law, of course, has its place, especially in protecting us from the sick and uncontrollable member of our society. But law does not hold a nation together. Men and women do. There is no police force that could not be wiped out tomorrow by a thorough and organized civil revolution if men and women were not basically committed to peace and order. And the very reason that it is at times difficult to find balanced law enforcement officials is that some individuals attracted to such work are often silent tyrants or victims of abusive and tyrannical parents.

It is not law that makes a loving and concerned human being, and certainly not tribal law. There are thousand of criminals who live within the law. We hear of the clever ways of getting around income tax, the intricate ways of cheating the public in sales. Many of the most brilliant lawyers have been handsomely recompensed to make a mockery of the law, and the legal profession is among the most mistrusted and abusive in our society. For good reasons: to focus on law, it's interpretations and exceptions is to make of human intercourse a dangerous, dramatic, and irresponsible game. Frequently in our daily life we are exposed to "legal" violation of basic human values. Mechanics and repairmen replace parts that are not defective. Dentists charge for Xrays that are not needed, doctors make extra money on nonessential tests or on overpriced examinations. Almost every business has its money making gimmick that is strictly legal and strictly dishonest. In the ancient tribes it might have been enough to say, "Thou shalt not steal"—or to cut off the arm of the thief. Today we do not cut off the arms of thieves nor do we produce honest men by law. Some of the most law abiding people in our world are among the least moral and compassionate.

Of All The Professions
Of all the professions that are devious and dirty,
Let's say there are perhaps twenty-five or thirty,
I would say that lawyers somehow lead the list
Of professionals who really get me pissed.
The union plumbers often have a greedy way about them
And real estate developers will often double deal;
Car salesmen are thought to be duplicitous and cunning
But lawyers learn to steal.

I've been cheated by mechanics grinding more than valves
And I've learned that doctors practice usury and medicine;
I've been ill advised by brokers who can't advise themselves,
And I wish electricians had to take an oath to Edison.
Morticians make additions in the cost of man's demise,
Police and politicians have been known to take a deal,

The labor union tactics seldom come as a suprise
But lawyers learn to steal.

Thus our system leaves its victims in the cold
Whether wife or husband, worker or employer
Because anyone who's wronged is quickly told
"You'd better get a lawyer."

From Today I Wondered About Love

Modern society is too complex to be reached by the heavy-handedness of ancient law, or even modern law for that matter. But religious leaders still attempt it. For this reason, religious leaders are treated with a patronizing kind of posturing by sophisticated men and women. Clergymen are too unreal to be taken as seriously as other men. There are cute little jokes about ministers gambling or priests playing golf on Sundays. There are droll stories about bishops who had a bit too much scotch or nuns who were seen sipping martinis on trains. Television interviews with "religious" personalities have been most often cautious and polite, as if in open recognition of the naivete of the religious society. Even the late-night shows, which are most often open to honest, adult discussions about life, generally taper off into polite amenities and discreet questions when "religious stars" are being quizzed. An actor can be quizzed about his personal life, but it is an affront to ask a clergyman about his, or try to suggest to a Catholic bishop that his attitude toward divorce or birth control is the product of the Middle Ages. The religious official cannot usually be treated like other men because he is not like other men. He is the lawgiver, the symbol of tribal law in a society that has outgrown both his product and his approach. So he is very often treated with the deference that is offered to the old and senile or to the obviously neurotic. Before the recent "annulment" privileges in Catholic divorce law, there were cases stacked in Rome for a decade or longer seeking solutions.

Part of the reason that the moral focus of the religious institution centers on the Ten Commandments is the belief that law comes from God. Most religions maintain this, and even the more sophisticated religious philosophies, like those of Augustine and Aquinas, or of Calvin and Melanchthon, insist that the basis of the "natural law" is in the unchanging essence of God. I do not believe this. I believe that law comes from man, that it is always a reflection of his own attitude toward his culture. "Thou shalt not steal" reflects a man' own respect for his private property; "Thou shalt not commit adultery" reflects a man's own concern about losing his wife. There is no need for God to intervene and to impose His will on men through law. Law is from man, and one of the reasons that the religious institution has lost touch with the moral life of modern man is that it has not kept up with man's evolving understanding of the moral law. To point to commandments as coming from God, to speak of primitive "revelations" as if they were presently binding, is to speak in nonsense syllables to the man and woman of today. Thus only the very naive would be surprised that a televangelist was consistently stealing vast sums, or a prominent preacher was in bed with another man's wife.

With their emphasis on law, religious institutions have produced a type of man who can be recognized in the counseling framework as distinct and different. There is a kind of "religious" syndrome that he brings with him when, for example, he approaches a marriage counselor. In my experience I have found that he has a variety of expectations and prejudices that make it difficult to work with him. He comes with a special sense of hostile dependency. He has learned to believe that God will do things for him that other men have to do for themselves. In this angry dependency, he has learned to make unreasonable demands on other people or to expect more of them than they can give. His counselor is expected to be on constant call; his wife should not treat him "this way" because he has kept all the rules that he selectively imposed on himself for life. He listens to the counselor with great docility and attention, but manages to hear only what he wants to hear because he has legal ears and myopic morality.

He is aware of his own great suffering and often considers himself a unique and almost "chosen" kind of martyr devoted to righteousness and the law. His God is an "easy" one as I wrote in my poem Easy God, because he can be as easily controlled by legalities as any mediocre jurist. He believes that, regardless of what he does, "everything will work out for the best." He can say with a resigned smile that his pain will "make a better man" of him, though there is no sound basis for such an attitude, especially because he is not speaking from personal experience, but from easily mouthed religious cliches. Often he sees no need to change his behavior, though he has learned to admit readily, perhaps too readily, his wrongs without serious intent of changing them. He says that he has his "faults" while actually believing that they are not of much consequence when placed alongside of his virtues. He insists that he does "not want to hurt anyone," yet his intransigent devotion to law may well be destroying everyone who lives with him. I have deep feelings about this, because I encountered its abusive effects so often as a priest and therapist. Such hypocrites were the only ones in the gospel narratives that brought Jesus to the white rage of attack, calling them "whitened sepulchers" , pretty on the outside, but within "full of dead men's bones."

The "legalist" has the highest of goals since he is not satisfied with anything short of perfection. His drive for perfection makes him feel guilty and dissatisfied because he never really believes he has done a good job. Generally he imposes these goals on others as well, yet does not recognize his own fierce intolerance. Just watch, for example, the faces of the pro-choice and anti-abortion warriors on TV. Dialogue is impossible with any legalist, be it a rigid racist, angry feminist, fierce Christian, unyielding Jew, or "True Believer" of any kind. The religious legalist is seldom extreme about anything except his devotion to the law. He lives in a world of blacks and whites, disciplines his emotions with rigor, and controls his anger so expertly that only a trained eye and ear can recognize his rage. He is so "kind" that it is hard to be angry with him, so "polite" that it is difficult to be "impatient," so "sincere" that it is hard to tell him the truth, so "right" that it is almost impossible to penetrate his "holy" defenses. And all the while you can feel the rage and anger seething from within.

He is the man of the tribal code, the man who has turned complex moral issues into legal absolutes, the classic Fundamentalist. He is impatient of weakness, patronizing when he thinks he is forgiving, interfering when he sees himself as fatherly. He does not face life as it is, only as he demands that it should be. He does not really see people, he only classifies them and puts them in files. His life is a simple one; his responsibility is clear and well defined. It is a tribal responsibility that is content to follow an institution blindly and to accept devotedly its laws. And from this loyalty, he expects everything. This is the "religious right", the "fierce orthodox", the literal "scripture sniffer".

He is the man who looks no farther than his own narrow version of the golden rule. It has become his favorite motto, and when he says it, it means not: *"Do unto others as you would have them do unto you," but "Why don't other people treat me with the respect that my goodness deserves?"*

Or, "How can you expect any more of me when I have already given and suffered so much?" The golden rule is reduced to a legalistic measure that limits love. When applied in such a way, it subtly contains within itself a motive for good behavior. It means, "Treat me like I treat you" and becomes another version of "Virtue pays" or "Cast your bread upon the waters." It becomes a powerful philosophy of controlling people rather than loving them, and it does not tolerate honest anger and reasonable resentment. It says, "Be charitable" or "Be nice" when such behavior is artificial and false and manipulative. It reminds me of all the "religious" smiles that hide contempt, the "charity" that is submerged hostility, the devotion to law that is disguised arrogance.

The golden rule cast in this sectarian framework is the motto of those who live on the surface of life. It is the text of the comfortable, the shibboleth of those in power. The golden rule as applied by the religious sects has not worked for the black. It kept him smiling in his slavery and docilely shining shoes. It has not worked for the laborer who fought for his living wage when he got tired of waiting for his employer to "do unto him." It has not worked for the Vietnamese, or the Jews, or the slum-dwellers in South America. The religious distortions of the golden rule have made of it a motto of inactivity, the chant of the high priests of the status quo.

Of Martyrs

Emma Burns is a martyr and stays with Jimmy
Only because she feels sorry for him, her folks like him,
    The neighbors expect it,
    And he takes their two boys fishing every Saturday.
Emma survives by a furtive affair with Frank Harris
    Every other Thursday afternoon.

Jimmy Burns is also a martyr and stays with Emma
Only because he feels sorry for her, his boss likes her,
    The neighbors expect it,
    And she is teaching the boys how to play the piano.
Jimmy survives by a furtive affair with Frank Harris's wife
    Every other Wednesday morning.

The Burns boys are also martyrs.
    They hate fishing, but feel sorry for their father.
    They also hate the piano,
But don't want to hurt their mother's feelings.
They survive by smoking dope with the Harris kids.

Sin sure does have a way of keeping families together.

From Walk Easy On The Earth

Modern man wants more than a self-righteous version of the golden rule. He does not want the obsequious love of men who make of him a kind of investment in their personal search for "salvation." He wants honesty, not "charity;" he wants direct confrontation and genuine relationships, not the pompous niceties provided by those who claim to know what he wants before they talk to him and ask. Today's man and woman does not need this deformed golden rule. Honesty is his way of life, "telling it like it is." He will not blindly "do unto others as he would have them do"; he will speak to others about what is in his heart. He will reveal the price of his involvement, the depths of his pain, the cost of his struggle, the hope of his heart, the vision of his soul, the strength of his love. He is not afraid to do more than he would have others do for him; to walk that extra mile, to give his cloak as well as his coat as Jesus asked;, he is not afraid to demand more of himself than any man would dare to ask. He will not reduce his love to rules because religious rules have destroyed millions of lives, ripped families apart, and are the focus of most of history's ongoing wars.

Even now millions of men and women are "moral" without the churches. They learn their values from parents, from schools, from their involvement in life. They learn values within their own heart. This is what the churches have failed to understand: that man's goodness comes from within himself. The best one can say of any law is that it represents a stage in man's development, and the tragedy is that religious institutions have enshrined it and made it permanent. The larger the corpus of laws, the more immature the society.

A new kind of brotherhood now reaches beyond nations and families and religious sects. It does not talk of adultery; it talks of a good human relationship and honest communication between husband and wife. It does not talk feebly of "charity"; it can talk of a love that is not afraid of anger, that does not hesitate to reveal its wounds. It does not talk of "stealing," instead it asks a man to come to grips with his actual view of material things; it asks a man to be responsible for his brothers who are poor and hungry. It does not impose itself on man through law; it believes instead that man's goodness comes from his own discovery of himself. The "moral" thing is the "human" thing, and the "good" man is the one who is most really and humanly himself, and who truly believes that he is his brother's keeper—and his brother is everyone in need. There are no "bad" men and women, only weak and wounded people searching for love, or savagely destroyed and dissected by prolonged abuse. Today's world cannot deal with man in universal principles; it is bored with discussions about "situation" ethics versus "moral" absolutes. It knows that a man can only answer for himself; he can only be moral if he does honestly what he has to do. It realizes that men and women will have to make mistakes before they can know themselves at all. It knows that "morality" is only mythology until a person senses his own responsibility for what he does, until he is aware of his own place in the lives of those he loves, until he is "self-conscious" and personally responsible.

It is this awareness that has moved modern man to stop war. Not the churches or religions! They have blessed the participants via the same, one God. There is a "new" man and woman who cannot distinguish between brothers and sisters no matter the color or flag under which they fight. It is this same awareness that promises to give the black and gays and the aged and poor their freedom. It is a morality beyond all commandments, a morality beyond all law. It is not, as its critics say, too undisciplined to observe the laws; it is rather too human to find them meaningful. Jesus talked of feeding the hungry and clothing the naked, comforting the bereaved, while the lawgivers fight abortion and forbid sexual expression as if they are on a battle line. Most of all, with all their protests, closing clinics, banishing books, attacking films and gays and minorities, they change the mind of no one. They only act our their own self contempt and hatred. The laws imposed by religious institutions are monuments erected to a person too afraid to believe in himself. Today's man is too responsible to be bound by tribal law. Religious institutions ask conformity, docility, a dull response to an ancient view of the world. The new man and woman are not afraid to dream, to move beyond all law into the freedom and responsibility of human love. It is not that their love is too self-centered for law; it is too real to have boundaries.

Now Hammurabi is dead; so are Moses and the great prophets. Jesus, too, has died. The Evangelists who applied his words to the problems of their day are dead. It is man and woman alone who live, searching their own hearts for the honest answers to the moral issues of their own lives. We have outgrown the Ten Commandments that once bound a tribal people into a nation. We have outgrown the centuries of Christian legalism that forbade us to believe in ourselves. Now we have moved past the age of religious law into the era of personal responsibility. No longer can we ask God to make us human; nor can we blame Satanic forces of evil for our inhumanity. Now each has his own opportunity, beyond the moral myth, to establish that man can care enough to love his fellowman, and in this love beyond salvation schemes, no matter how long it takes, is the real Birth of God in each of us—beyond the destructive myths of privilege and separation that have only led, and will continue to lead, to chaos and self destruction. That's why Jesus said it all in five words, *"Love your neighbor as yourself!"* The rest is only conformity and control which obscures and denies what really is, and does not believe that "you shall be as gods."

This is not to make light of evil, to ignore the horror of a mass killer or a savage and maniacal murderer. It goes without saying that a society needs protection from its diseased and defective members. But morality is not based upon dramatic exceptions to normal human life, nor does the law itself make a man or woman moral. Morality is our contact with an Inner God-Self by whatever name. It is the result of time, effort and experience. We are born in beauty and innocence and sometimes lose our way out of fear and pain and abuse. But it is not the law which brings us back on center.

143

It is intimate and honest contact with our true self. Thus Augustine, paraphrasing Jesus could say, *"Ama et fac quod vis"* (Love and be free of all law).

The very notion of sin has been a destructive one because it produces guilt, which in turn produces greater fear and more guilt. It is common knowledge by now that the Greek word for sin in the New Testament, *"Hamartia"*, means "to miss the mark" or "to be off course". It is the result of a choice I made that is to my detriment, or yours, and I can forever choose again. There's a great difference between making mistakes because of inexperience, sudden passion, or a lack of knowledge, and "sinning" because I am "evil".

I heard confessions for almost ten years and I can never remember making contact with an "evil" person, or a "sinner". Many were much farther along the course of love than I am. "Sin" and "legalistic morality" have only produced frightened and repressed people, not bold and virtuous ones. To focus on "sin" is to miss the whole point of life. To be absorbed in "keeping the law" is to lose contact with the God Within Who guides me. Most of all, to attempt to impose my vision of "law" on someone else is arrogant and futile. That is why the "Abortion-is-murder" people and the "Free choicers", for example, waste their time in strident conflict. There is no respect, communication, or real dialogue.

The legalistic approach to morality is the reason that poverty still exists, that the rich do not feel compelled lovingly to share with the poor. It is the reason for war, when words can be distorted and turned into bloodshed without breaking a "law". The Second Vatican Council actually freed Catholics that needed freeing when it stated that one's individual conscience or inner awareness is the primary source of all morality—beyond any lawgiver. The Council really didn't need to say it, because it has always been true. As Science of Mind points out so beautifully, there is only one law governing every facet of the Universe and that law is God's unchanging Love.

Finally, the problem is one of trust. The rigid family

structure that does not permit mistakes creates buried resentment and frightened conformity. So does any institution or society that intimidates its members. "Committing adultery", for example, may be a mistake or a brave and courageous act. It may end a marriage or start a life. It all depends where love begins and fear ends, for love, truly is "letting go of fear" and that is the only law.

In The Center Of Your Soul
"There is quiet water in the center of your soul,
Where a son or daughter can be taught what no man knows.
There's a fragrant garden in the center of your soul,
Where the weak can harden and a narrow mind can grow.
There's a rolling river in the center of your soul,
An eternal giver with a rich and endless flow.
There's a land of muses in the center of your soul,
Where the rich are losers and the poor are free to go.
So remain with me then, to pursue another goal,
And to find your freedom in the center of your soul!"

From There Are Men Too Gentle To Live Among Wolves

The churches have been the enforcers and teachers of past morality, rather than breaking new ground and leading the way in moral growth and reform. It was not the traditional churches that brought an end to war in Vietnam, save for a few exceptional priests and ministers who supported students who burned their draft cards, ignited rallies, refused to fight and kill, emigrated to Canada, and suffered punishment and indignities as well. It was also those independent and select adults who saw the futility of war, the agony of young men dying for political arrogance or the standards of another era. But the churches only spoke out when it was safe and popular.

Nor was it the traditional churches that fought for the equality and dignity of the Blacks and other racial minorities.

Enlightened and individual religious leaders fought, but it was mainly the young who marched at Selma, whites as well as blacks independently of traditional churches. Most of all it was the brave and inspired blacks themselves who marched and protested consistently, who laid their bodies on the pavement and lives on the line. Often they were aided by religious leaders as individuals, and black churches were used for political assembly, but traditional churches stood apart from the "revolution" until it was more respectable, and many stand apart still with but token awareness and help.

Churches have felt they must play it safe. They tell us where men and women have been, not where they're going. Many fear to challenge the bias and ignorance of their congregation. This is not to ignore the courageous work of individual clergy or members who grow despite the faults of the structure. It is to say that in ending war, racial struggles, homosexual rights, women's equality, divorce, overpopulation, poverty and starvation, family limitation, the immorality of nuclear weapons, sexual enlightenment, and the destruction of the environment, churches have never led the way. I could almost understand this if the focus had been spiritual growth of its members and not to support the status quo. In many traditional religions, *"Thou shalt not rock the boat!"* is still the first and greatest commandment.

I say none of this sadly or even judgmentally. I think it is good that the churches do not do for people what they must do themselves. Just as when our government fails, finally we grow up, make changes and take matters in our own hands. So it is with the churches. If they help me, I attend. If I can help them, I try. But I know that morality comes from the hearts and spirits of individuals in touch with their own Inner Power. Traditional churches only reflect what we have become as a society. It is for that reason that churches must die, so that God is reborn in the integrity, compassion, and awareness of our universal oneness.

Paraphrasing St. Paul: There is neither Jew nor gentile, male or female, black or white, gay or straight, slave or free, rich or poor, good or bad, but we are all one in whatever image serves us best: Jesus, God, Buddha, Krishna, or the "holographic universe". And to the extent we live that way, we live a life of godliness, true peace and real joy—even as GOD LIVES.

Love Breaks Through

When it is time,
    Love breaks through
Like a fragile sprout of Spring,
    Softly green and tender,
Crawling sinuously from the dark tomb of earth,
Where first it died only to rise and live.
It appears almost suddenly,
    When it is not watched
And takes its place quietly
    Amid the assorted flowers and trees
    And miracles of life.
At such a moment, the lonely seedpod is forgotten
    And the damp, cold earth of dark incubation
Is but a vague and distant memory.
Love has arrived! Like Spring itself,
    Fragile, but rooted in destiny,
    Newly awakened from sleep
And ready to enjoy the cyclic rhythm
    Of each passing year.
To grow and flower, to rest and rise
As was destined when an unseen and loving hand
    First drew life from the chaotic heavens
And foresaw our special, springtime love.

From Quiet Water

Chapter 7

Love Taboos And Sexual Guilt

Some years ago, a reporter for a national magazine called and asked me to make a statement about the sexual revolution. I told him that I was not concerned with such a limited revolution, but rather with the broader struggle for men and women to become whole persons. He asked if I did not think that the clamor of priests to marry was part of a sexual revolt. I said "no," that it was an integral part of man's search to be himself. The reporter refused to understand, since my answers did not fit the preconceived thesis he had devised. He could see no farther than the greater sexual freedom in movies and literature, in beach parties and college life. This was not to him a symptom, a sign of a deeper, more significant revolt. So he dealt with bikinis and miniskirts, the decline of the Legion of Decency, and adultery in the suburbs. He gave us another hysterical article which established that man is rapidly going to the dogs.

Such a prurient emphasis on the sexual revolution was out of focus. Our society very often makes far too much of sex because the Puritans and celibates are still doing our laundry. Modern men and women are struggling, sometimes unwittingly, to put sex in human perspective, and they have had to shock a few tight-lipped judges to do the job. It is the critics of modern society who lack sexual balance, who angrily see AIDS as another "Divine" intervention to bring men and women to their knees. Many of us today have finally come to grips with our own sexuality after years of confusion and obsession, and even a period of freely selected celibacy can make sense. It is a previous society, with its whispers and prudishness, that made of sex a murky preoccupation. Ours has given men and women a chance to discover what sexuality really means as we grow from adolescence to spiritual maturity, and are still doing it without gurus or lawgivers. Just honest self awareness.

We are not satisfied with the sexual attitudes we inherited from the past, especially when a repressed celibate mentality or a disciplined libido dictated our orientation. We are not satisfied with the women who knew so much about being mothers that they forgot to be wives, or the men whose only passion was for possessions. We are not satisfied with the thousands of couples who married in blind passion only to calm down and discover that they had no foundation for friendship or marriage and didn't know where to go for help beyond fantasy, affairs, or withdrawal. We are not satisfied with the dull relationships that endured for the sake of the children, which is often a noble prevarication to cover up fear. We shrink from the "religious" women who held sex as a club over their husbands' heads and received "divine approval" for such blackmail. Nor do we accept the men who resorted to itinerant adultery or indifference, or lost themselves in pursuit of work and money. All of these are screaming for help and light, and it's available.

Today, perhaps, some are still confused, but such confusion is the sign of learning and progress. A person's search for a balanced sexuality is tied to his search for God. For a time, perhaps, we may hide or flaunt our sex until we are unafraid to be ourselves. Then, gradually, we can learn our own uniqueness in the closeness of marital love. This closeness is what we seek, this sense of being unique and special, that does not deprive us of being who we really are, nor isolate and imprison us from every other love. This is what God is all about; this is the focus of Christ's love. Man, the unique animal, can know symbolically that divine love is the complete giving and surrender in the symbol of sexual love, not a clinging relationship of two people who live with dissimulation.

Frequently I have counseled men and women who know none of this. Recently a woman told me that her husband is happy as long as she goes through the motions of sexual love twice a week. Probably she does satisfy some physical need and leaves him a little less restless at his work. But she does not reach him at the core of his own loneliness, nor touch her own, where God must speak to man. There is nothing creative about their sexuality, nothing unique or sacred. (This is not to imply that all sex must be existentially and spiritually grounded—sometimes it's just fun). But when she doles out her favors like a weary prostitute or a sex machine and thus soothes her conscience in her biweekly attendance at church, it is sad. The strange thing is that her husband does not seem to mind only because he doesn't know how it really could be. He gives to sex as little meaning as she does. He tabulates the encounters, times his orgasms, and measures his manliness by the quality of her physical response. He, like his wife, could find more depth and joy with help and personal awareness that seldom comes.

Frequently I see another kind of man who, in not understanding sex, will expect more of it than it can give. He is the one who must fantasize every little swaying hip that crosses his vision. Though married, he remains a drooler, a dreamer, a lifelong adolescent. If he is charming enough, he becomes the constant seducer, as does his female counterpart. If his mobility and income allows, he will engage in a series of futile affairs, hoping that each one in turn will quiet the restless appetite that no amount of sex will sate. Occasionally he learns from such encounters and then returns to find himself in the remains of his marriage. But more often than not, he continues to search, hoping that the next seduction will satisfy a deeper, spiritual need that mere carnality cannot reach. He, too, is often ready to learn, but rarely is there a suitable and professional opportunity to be taught without extensive effort!

I Wonder About Derek
I wonder about Derek
With all of his bachelor talk about prime sex and multiple orgasms,
*   Assorted beds and new stimulants, and freedom despite herpes,*
*   Of liberating love so available in chance meetings*

and vagrant arms.

I wonder about the loneliness in his eyes
   The emptiness of leave-taking in the morning
     As he heads out for new, exciting conquests and fresh appetizers,
Setting himself up for more excitement with the ensuing letdowns.

I wonder if sex is as good and satisfying as he says
   Or if he's just another kind of junkie with his fix
     That doesn't fix anything very long, but yearns for more,
And each startling novelty of strange flesh only makes love
     more impossible.

I wonder if sex has not become a hype
   To replace warmth and caring,
     A commercial to keep us confused about what life offers,
An obsessive diversion for those
     impoverished ones who never rest in the arms of a sunset
Or make quiet love, hand-in-hand, watching a bold moon
     disappear behind clouds.

Most of all I wonder about Derek
   His lonely eyes
   His restless energy
   His sadness in repose
And all his bachelor talk about "prime sex."

From Laughing Down Lonely Canyons

He is, perhaps, less likely to learn anything if his infidelity takes place in his head. He would learn more quickly how empty is his search if he were to experience the frustration of a fleeting encounter in some safe motel or borrowed apartment. He would have to make a decision, either to continue in the stifling narrowness of secret affairs, or to come to grips with his marriage and begin or end it. Frequently the churches and synagogues have helped to make of him a coward.

They have pressured him to remain in a marriage that can lead nowhere without extensive professional help they are not equipped to give. They hold his children over his head and make him feel guilty; or they promise him a meaningful heaven that will give fulfillment to a meaningless life. Or they even tell shrunken men and frigid women how insignificant sex really is, so much have they divorced it from genuine meaning, so detached are they from the thrilling communication of body and soul.

Modern men and women do not easily tolerate this. Even before they are married, they will likely know much about sex. He will not be an overeager boy on his honeymoon. Or if he is, he is taking a dangerous gamble that his marriage will last. This is not to say that there can be no happy marriage where virginity is a condition of the courtship. This is merely to say that marriage is an extreme gamble in any case. But whenever there is little more than sexual excitement bringing it about, the odds are often impossible without experience. And all too many "religious" marriages have been entered into to legalize the sex act. Even in our permissive culture today.

Most modern men and women, however, want sexual experience before marriage—despite the anxiety over sexually transmitted disease—so they will not be as naive and disillusioned as, possibly, their parents were. Nietzsche was not far wrong when he said that many laws of morality were merely the resentment of one generation for the freedom and wisdom of another. I find this very often true in matters of sexuality— the frigid and frustrated unconsciously impose projected rules on the young to make certain that they become equally unfulfilled and miserable, and marriage becomes a mere search for a younger prototype of mom or dad.

The lack of sexual experience or additively expecting too much has been a major factor in our high rate of divorce, which I do not intend as a critical comment. A high divorce rate can mean sincerity as equally as promiscuity—especially when lawyers have made divorce so inhuman and costly. Our rigid, religious rules of sex have forced many young people into a permanent marriage in the past. Today, youth is more apt to learn from a temporary relationship, or a monogamous series of them. The immediate presumption by the conservative moralist is that such temporary relationships must of necessity be irresponsible, as if we learn about sex instinctively. (But make sure we have cook books). Currently, however, there is abundant evidence to contradict this attitude. Premarital sex does not have to be promiscuous, and once people reach a certain degree of maturity, it seldom is unless other underlying pathologies are present. And even the uncovering of such wounds is beneficial and can lead to healing.

Traditionalists often have difficultly in understanding the value of mature and responsible sexual experience before marriage. The young man or woman who admits to "sins" of premarital sex is told that he or she has committed a serious wrong, and for years in the confessional, I was one who eloquently told them. There is little or no attempt to discover if the act was irresponsible and self-indulgent, which has it's place, or a creative effort to produce that personal closeness and complete understanding that can lead to commitment. What or who makes its wrong? More mythology reducing sexual, relational complexity to immoral ignorance and simplicity.

Most of us who are suitably alive and not repressively victimized have known "promiscuity" in some form or other, either in actual physical union or in the limitless world of fantasy. Few of us are so rigid and self-contained that our sexual frustrations have not been expressed in some obvious way with or without guilt. Yet many social critics are afraid to reflect on their own experience, to discover what it means, and honestly to share what they have learned. Modern man, in growing numbers, is not unwilling to reflect and to experiment. No matter what anyone thinks, premarital sex, even with AIDS, is a normal phenomenon in our society, and the modern parent or philosopher has to deal with it realistically or be classified as irrelevant or, as I think, irresponsible.

They must know that modern man is reflecting on a

154

problem much more profound than the sexual permissiveness that Puritan or celibate critics abhor. He is not simply preoccupied with sexual techniques in most cases, or the right to engage in sex before marriage. More and more he takes these for granted, or learns them. He or she may worry regularly if they are suitably equipped or decently endowed enough to be "good in bed". But they are also gradually more concerned with the kind of personal closeness and honest communication that makes genuine marriage and commitment possible. This is where our emphasis must be. What does it mean? What can it mean? Often they are not satisfied with the relationship that their parents had. They want much more. They may not want jobs that leave them little time for creative love; nor do they want a family so abundant that they will have no chance to grow both as individuals and as a couple. They will probably not remain in a dead marriage unless their guilt runs very deep; no church or familial guilt will force most to sacrifice their dignity and chance for love. So they prepare for marriage by reflecting on the kind of relationship that can bring happiness and personal fulfillment. Of course they are steeped in illusions until they have had the time and experience to determine what is real and possible. And no longer does a failed marriage have to mean a failed and discarded life, but a preparation for a better one.

So serious are men and women about marriage that frequently I 've heard them discuss openly their relationship in a counseling or therapy group. I've heard young unmarried couples and gay partners talk honestly in the presence of others about sexual encounters they had a few nights before. A young woman told how frightened she was, how tense and unfulfilled. The group was not easy on her. They suggested that she found it easier to have sex than to discuss with her mate how she felt. From the group, her mate learned that he related to women only through physical sex and three or four familiar and tried techniques. He discovered how simple it was to take a woman to bed, how difficult it was to reveal himself and to risk being rejected; how far beyond touches and techniques was genuine intimacy and spiritual orgasm. This couple discovered how inhibited they actually were, despite their seeming physical openness, how dishonest, how fearful of real communication, how ill prepared for marriage, or even a solid friendship. Most of all, they learned how truly lonely they were, focused entirely on one's self in an eagerness to please or fear of falling short.

In such a group there was no talk of church morality. There was little attention paid to the simple fact of physical sex. But there was serious attention paid to the way in which two people used each other dishonestly. This was the most moral talk of all. The responsibility of one person to another could not be reduced to a simple act of confession or a guilty request for God's forgiveness. It had to be faced, to be dealt with, to be included in a man and woman's picture of self. In the past, such a couple might well have been denied real, prolonged and intimate contact, and pushed into marriage before they were ready for real courtship. It could have been disastrous. Now, in an atmosphere of freedom, they were able to discover how little they felt of the unique closeness that can lead to genuine love, how important it was to be one's real self, and not a "pleaser" or "actor", perhaps for the first time since early childhood.

You and I
You and I could be the greatest lovers,
could abandon hurt to the wind,
Could make of life the paradise it was meant to be.
But even you and I have drawn the
shades on whom we really are,
Afraid that the very revelation will make
love and longing impossible,
When in reality, it is love's only chance.

From Mystic Fire

This is what man and woman want. Not the relief of physical tension alone, (though that has its place) not a series of dishonest seductions that offer momentary comfort, but the sense of being one's true self in a fulfilling relationship—married or unmarried—the sense of being loved in a unique and special way, of loving honestly and freely amid frailty and confusion, and not to live in frozen confinement and boredom. Man and woman are not asking sex to deliver more than it can, but they expect sexual love to make them know at some level that they are the beloved of God because they are the beloved of another god-person. This is "consciously or not", at the root of the revolution that has been going on, not a sexual revolt to glorify nudity or to enshrine human orgasm, although that will forever live on the fringes for the lonely and addicted, and was, in truth, a successful way to break down "religious" and "moral" barriers erected by compiled ignorance to free the healthy among us for sound sexuality. It has been a revolution that is bringing us through the sexual confusion of the past to the freedom of committed love and spiritual growth.

Such a revolt did not occur without innocent victims. It can unsettle relatively sound marriages. It might give new opportunity to individuals who want nothing but lifelong dissipation and fleeting pleasure, or it might finally stuff them with enough flesh to pursue spirit. It can wound the minds and hearts of the young whose parents have no love or understanding to give, but time and freedom is on their side. It will break up homes that might have survived with counseling and patience. It can hurt deeply the naive and innocent who trust too easily gracious words and empty promises, but it also can make them come of age. It will feed the sexual obsessions of the sick and immature and helpless, but at least there will be new opportunities for healing. It will profit the lurid publishers who exploit the weakness of the unhealthy and addicted, but eventually even such freedom and openness can produce much good. Men and women have never been so free before, and now we have the chance to discover what sexuality means even as some are injured in the throes of such freedom. We learn finally to lead with our honest words and not our speechless libido.

Despite all the new freedoms and openness, I doubt that any group has suffered as much as the homosexuals in their private fears, their massive confusion and self loathing, and often their inability to share their feelings with anyone. I never liked their expression "coming out of the closet", it was more like slowly emerging from the fury of a volcano and the teeth of a dragon. Nor did the traditional churches support the struggle of the gays in their profound yearning for understanding and respect. To this very day, the Catholic Church and various shades of Fundamentalists have not officially budged from St. Paul's fierce indictment of the "effeminate" or "homosexual perverts" in I Corinthians. This despite the fact that it is commonly known both by current surveys and personal testimony that many clergy are active homosexuals. The battle of the gays has been a brave and bitter one, despite the ongoing studies that reveal their sexual choice has biological origins. And even the psychological components, which we bandied about so facilely for years, blaming parental pressures and inept role models, can be as real as any biology, and must be treated with the one love that God has for all His sons and daughters.

In time, the traditional moral position will change, as it has so often in other now discarded dogmas, but it will come from brave social revolutionaries and the homosexuals themselves. Even a recent edition of a contemporary Catholic encyclopedia says: "These tendencies may be overcome by personal restraint and counseling." What arrogant ignorance! Rome calls it "serious depravity", and Fundamentalists use much stronger words. For once it would be comforting for churches to say simply: "We don't know!" But if we've learned nothing about marriage, sex, divorce, or homosexuality since St. Paul, it's obvious why traditional churches must die if God is to be born. The whole issue is insane. The gays are God's sons and daughters. There is nothing else to say.

I cannot call this complete new freedom and understanding of sexuality, however, a sexual revolution. It is much broader than that in and outside of marriage. It is the revolution in which a person is so determined to be himself that he will trample on any taboo, no matter how sacred or seemingly righteous. Our sexual attitude is one such taboo. My Catholic Church has enshrined it carefully with rules and definitions and very often enshrines it still in its historic celibate focus of the "higher state" of virginity and abstinence. Other religions, without the heavy legal hand of Rome, are equally as narrow in their attitudes and traditions without as solid and rational a foundation. One thing I liked about being a Catholic was that the same logic that kept you in could lead you out into freer air. Society itself, without blaming its viewpoint on God or history, is likewise inhibited in matters of sex. The sexual sin is the primary target of curious and bitter tongues. It provides the ultimate in office and neighborhood gossip or in selecting presidents or supreme court justices; it often ruins good reputations. Even the man whose own moral life is spattered with sexual affairs will suddenly become a pillar of righteousness in any theoretical discussion about sex.

It is often difficult in our society to have an honest treatment of sexual matters except when we are dealing with the very young. I know of more than one adult who has been carrying on a clandestine affair for years to be most vicious when dealing with reputations of young couples who are living together before marriage or a young priest who had a gentle lover contrary to Rome's dictations. As difficult as it is to discuss sexual matters openly in society at large, it was practically impossible within the religious framework and often it still is. There adultery is condemned quite simplistically without any awareness that the very hypocrisy of religious attitudes has been most productive of such affairs. Frigidity has never been a sin, nor has the selfish squeamishness that has for some made sex a chore. Many a Catholic woman has been able to sanctify her sexual distaste under the banner of holy rhythm and virtuous self-denial.

Other religious devotees have hidden under the protection of Puritan views toward the flesh. Prudishness, uninspired sex, and physical detachment were never listed as sins. How many sexy, married women were declared "saints" compared to all the nuns, virgins, and martyrs?

Religious discussions of sex have most often been unworldly and unreal. I recently interviewed a married couple whose religious counseling experience was not atypical. They had been visiting a "religious" counselor for several months. He was a good and sensitive man, but they could not talk honestly to him about their real sex life. It seemed indecent somehow. He was polite, made gentle references to sexual intimacies, but never got down to the basic moves and feeling of the couple in bed. This particular couple had a genuine problem with sexual communication that was destroying their relationship. They were having sexual intercourse far more frequently than either wanted it. Much of their sexual need was mere anxiety, the fear that he or she was being rejected by the other. Actually, their hypersexuality fueled by this fear, was perfunctory and unimaginative, tedious and repetitious. They had never learned to talk comfortably about it. Unlike this situation, the unmarried couple having sexual experience usually will stay far away from the "religious" counselor when they want solid feedback on the state of their relationship. They know that the religious domain is seldom in touch with modern man's view of sex. Especially in a morality designed by celibates.

Modern culture has slowly determined that sex is a creative part of a human relationship. And I can visualize the time when couples not wanting children, or past the child-bearing years, will very often, not want to marry. Strangely, the marriage bond itself can activate a kind of ownership or possessiveness that can tarnish solid relationships. And once you've been through a divorce involving the madness of attorneys and the often attendant greed/adversary components, it's hard to see a marriage contract as a celebration— even with prenuptial protections. Men and women do change, sometimes from total trust to fierce hostility even in the best circumstances.

Nothing which brings a man and woman closer together can be bad. And openness and honesty in matters of sex is an important instrument in bringing this about. I have never had much patience with committees on censorship of programs for decent literature, as if anything is not available to anyone who really wants it. In truth, I find *Seventeen*, with its subtle paganism and physical appearance obsession, its rampant materialism and superficial bonding, far more hurtful than anything Henry Miller wrote in his Tropics. Man and woman must be their own censor, and the tragedy of cheap eroticism is not the fact of its existence, but that so many people are forced to indulge in it independently of a good relationship. For me, it was a kind of compulsive fixation at very lonely and fearful times of my life—a stimulating distraction that often increased the loneliness. Most of us learn soon enough that erotic literature or entertainment, even obsessive sexual self-gratification, is not really satisfying. It may be a preparatory phase that we must go through, hopefully without guilt, or at times, it may be a permanent state for an individual who finds no more satisfying form of sexuality or no suitable partner. With a little imagination and warm memory, I can see no reason why it cannot be a loving and supportive act. Or perhaps, a temporary relief of tension. It is only tragic when religion turns it into a heinous "sin", and thus gives it far more attention than it deserves. Again, self gratification or masturbation is a matter of personal decision. We can know when it helps or hinders our spiritual growth, and it is not mine or anyone's place to decide for you. Spiritual growth requires "aware choices" and not "guilt-ridden" abstinence.

In any case, erotic literature and its attendant fantasies has been part of all cultures for centuries. I can remember studying ancient Chinese scrolls that made *Penthouse* look like *Better Homes And Gardens*. Thus, it is reasonable to assume that it will continue. No committees will ever wipe it out.

Nor should they even try. Trust in human maturity and spiritual growth is the only censor needed.

It is much the same with prostitution. The best a realistic society could do would be to control it and make it hygienic. Our "religious" righteousness gives it over to racketeers and forces a man to risk his life and health to indulge a momentary sexual need. Unfortunately, prostitution has its place even in the lives of some most refined and respectable people filling some need, and although the threat of AIDS has made it far less inviting, it is still widespread and will continue to be. Papers like *The Reader* in Chicago offer a sexual desert tray to satisfy anyone. It is uncomfortable enough that a man is forced to avail himself of such commercial sex, but there is no need to satisfy society's pharisaism by making it illegal. So the girls hustle on the streets of Manhattan or Vienna and Mexico, in countless ads in every large city, or they hail you on the way back to your hotel in Paris or Berlin or Anchorage.

I used to work in a parish in Michigan that was in the heart of a red-light district. It was adventurous to see men looking for the right girl without running into the police. I found it a ludicrous game in a sophisticated society. It was a simple failure to deal with man as he is, rather than as the churches and the Puritans would like us to be. One young Latin woman used to hang around the church in Flint, Michigan, and became a warm and devoted friend. She was supporting two little boys and when I last saw her, she was a gracious and beautiful woman. I'm not recommending her vocational choice for economic reasons and after several attempts, managed to find her a good, well paying job without revealing or judging her past way of life. Years later I wrote a poem about her.

Maria
Maria, lonely prostitute on a street of pain,
You, at least, hail me and speak to me
While a thousand others ignore my face.

162

You offer me an hour of love, and your fees are not as costly as most
You are the madonna of the lonely, the first-born daughter
in a world of pain.
You do not turn fat men aside, or trample on the stuttering,
shy ones,
You are the meadow where desperate men can find
a moment's comfort.
Men have paid more to their wives to know a bit of peace
And could not walk away without the guilt that masquerades
as love.
You do not bind them, lovely Maria, you comfort them
And bid them return...

But you, Maria, sacred whore on the endless pavements of pain,
You, whose virginity each man may make his own
Without paying ought but your fee,
You who know nothing of virgin births and immaculate
conceptions,
You who touch man's flesh and caress a stranger,
Who warm his bed to bring his aching skin alive,
You make more sense than stock markets and football games
Where sad men beg for virility.
You offer yourself for a fee—and who offers himself for less?
At times you are cruel and demanding—harsh and insensitive,
At times you are shrewd and deceptive—grasping and hollow.
The wonder is that at times you are gentle and concerned—
Warm and loving...

From Men Too Gentle To Live Among Wolves

The strange thing is that we blame our prudishness in sexual matters on the young. We protest that we must keep prostitutes away from our adolescent boys, that we must free drugstore racks from the kinds of magazines that will stimulate our innocent girls. We claim we are afraid to be honest about sexual matters lest the young overhear, and any new sexual freedom is called a threat to the love and beauty of youth.

Yet it is my experience that the young have no great difficulty with sex if they are given a moral climate in which they are permitted to be open and honest. I hear them frequently discuss their doubts and misgivings about their sexual adequacy, the futility of promiscuity, the intimacy and closeness that are obscured by sex, the dangers of pregnancy, and their fear or rejection of abortion. They are not afraid of self-denial, and they do not always seethe with uncontrollable desires for sexual gratification. Such caricatures are more often the projections of the middle-aged commentators who reveal their own frustrations through their advice to the young, and the resentment that they lived under a far different code or are living in a sexually starved marriage. Again, Nietzsche's reflection that such resentment is the source of moral codes makes a lot of sense.

There are always the outspoken "rebels" on the fringe who use freedom of any kind as a mask for self-indulgence and irresponsible behavior, but so what? Life will teach them or it won't. Laws will have no effect. There have been "hippie colonies" that are composed of the inadequate looking for some concrete way to get even with overprotective parents and other "colonies" that are models of human relationships. There are college rebels who are not rebels at all, merely children who hide behind their student status and reflect their domestic rigidity. But beyond the extremists and the exhibitionists, there surges a mighty revolution for honesty and closeness, for deep personal friendship, for an open and realistic attitude toward sex that my generation never had. They will be heard despite the protests of their parents or pastors or political leaders. They will not accept double-talk, hollow rhetoric, or moral principles that do not make sense even to those who spout them.

Modern men and women do not worship sex; they strive to learn to put it in a proper place as is evidenced by the new attention paid to sexual harassment and abuse. They do not see it as a reason for a marriage, but often as a good thermometer of the kind of relationship that a man and woman have. They may question the twin beds of their parents, the almost sexless lives many of them may have adopted in late middle age. They may resent the self-pity of their "overworked" mothers or the over-involvement in business of their "important" fathers, or they may perceive and understand. They want to find themselves, and they know that such a task will demand a deep understanding of the mystery of sexuality. I found the Hatha Yoga of India to be an interesting focus on sex in a human context. Many people want to experiment responsibly, and we who lead them and teach them must be honest enough to be of help as we gradually understand our own sexuality.

There are millions of unmarried people in our society who were taught a warped and distorted view of sex. They are not beyond help, but traditional churches have largely refused to deal with them in honest and open terms or have not been invited or trusted to do so. Many people are beginning to find themselves through modern literature on sexuality, in therapy or counseling groups, or in small groups of friends who will react honestly to each other. They are a part of the revolution to be persons and to discover the meaning of sex.

So are those priests and nuns who only chose celibacy and endured it in their religious service because of guilt or Church rule rather than personal choice. Hundreds have left their religious communities and thousands more will follow. They now know there is no essential connection between religious service and celibacy, and it was not observed for centuries in the Church. But the present pope seems adamant in opposition to change, upholding not God's law but an angry ancient tradition. Many of them, like myself, buried their sexuality or turned it into a defensive kind of zeal to promote their religious institution. They asked Christ or the liturgy or the dedication to their work to provide them with the fulfillment that can only come from personal love. Many of them, like myself, will marry or not marry and will begin to understand at another level the meaning of giving and love. They will discover how vain and self-centered we have often been, how apart from the realities of life and how terrified of closeness to anyone. We learned to work, to keep busy, but many of us have had great difficulty in learning how to slow down enough to care and to be lovers. Some, in learning about sexuality personally, will discover that the celibacy they considered a self-denial was often a fearful and selfish insulation from personal love. At first, they may be confused by sex, as is any adolescent. At least, I certainly was. They will very slowly begin to understand it and to know its beauty when it includes compassion and involved concern, when it is at a deeper level a total, god like communication. Or at other times just plain fun!

When I left the priesthood and later married, I received many encouraging letters and many hostile ones, each of them reflecting what life had taught my correspondents. Some hated me because my dedication as a priest seemed to give them some reason for the life of misery and bitterness they had known. Some warned me that I was expecting too much from marriage and discussed the experience that they had found in passing from illusion to reality. Some loved me and told me how beautiful was the joy of a happy marriage. But a surprising number told of the meaninglessness of sex. They presumed I was leaving the priesthood for the kind of sexual freedom that a layman's life provides. They revealed more of themselves than they intended, because if sex meant so little to them, it was because they had found so little of personal love and open, honest self revelation or so little understanding and help.

Now I know something of sex myself. It is not always as wild and violent as my priestly fantasies imagined. It is not usually the endless seduction that I foresaw in priestly adolescence. It is far more. Sometimes it is a chance to get close to a person I love and receive the love I feared I did not deserve. Often it is a chance more honestly and perfectly to be myself, my moody self, my despondent self, my worried self, my happy, joyous, serious, and boyish self, my sad and frightened and even angry self. No act of sex is the same. Each has its own meaning, its own special history, at times its own eloquence, it's own place or even indifference, but it is a unique avenue to intimacy, a precious road to union, a special opportunity to possess and to be possessed. But most of all it can be a genuine contact with God who designed it to tell us something of our union with Him, even though hundreds of writers throughout Christian history considered marriage an "inferior" way of life to virginity.

No wonder modern man will not fear sex or smother it in taboos. How senseless to search for God in the Scriptures and to ignore Him in the intimacy of human love. Fidelity takes on a new meaning, the awareness that I can be so unique and special that no one else will do. Or if I stray, it does not have to terminate an honest union. This is God's kind of love, the kind of love that can make a human heart know why it wants to live forever. It is hard to be sexual for long without being close. Any little barrier is enough to prevent proper fulfillment. Sex without closeness usually will not last. It is asking too much of sheer physical pleasure to have the permanence that only love can give. Yet, the physical is very important, despite the sincerity of love. Even generous and well-meaning sex can grow dull and rotely lackluster. It must remain creative and alive no matter what it takes. This is not to say that periods of celibacy, even for lay men and women cannot be a source of growth and power. Or that freely chosen celibacy cannot be a treasured and loving way of life. It is only to say that human sex is God's gift.

Now I am a part of the revolution, and know that I can continue to grow as a person, unique and special to another human being, unique and special to the very Universe and its Creator. Now I can ask about my own sexuality, and speak of it, and experience it as it changes and grows mysteriously more profound. Now I can be involved in the mystery of human love, the very special place where a man discovers profound truths, far beyond orgasm or new techniques.

Now I better understand the tears of the woman who came to me and told me that her husband had been unfaithful after eleven years. There seemed no way to comfort her, no way to bring her peace. With time she could hide the hurt, perhaps she would even stop referring to it in angry arguments. Usually, as happens, it might mean an end to a relationship or a painful reminder she would find hard to forget. Actually it did not have to mean what she feared, and often letting go and forgiving is the only way to peace and greater growth. Something was lost I grant. At the time I considered it a hurt pride or humiliation. Now I think I understand a little better. She lost that sense of being unique and special to a spouse, but love is deeper than that and can move beyond it with God's help. So can she. Now I can hope, too, that by her husband's compassion and concern, by a new degree of closeness, he may ease her pain and hold her in his love and she will have the courage and good sense to move on in this new and deeper love, untroubled by a detour along the way. If it remains a detour, an unforgiven and unforgivable "crime", then I believe it best that the relationship ends. Where there is no forgiveness, there can be no love. And where there is no love, there is no marriage. For this is what life is all about, to find God in the unique and privileged love of man and woman, wounded, tried, and made whole to move beyond the myth of human perfection to the reality of honest, understanding, free and forever forgiving love! I don't think it possible without God—by whatever name beyond all the limiting and limping myths to the God Who lives!

A Friendship Like Ours

A friendship like ours is without pretense or barriers,
Where no word is without consequence, no pain
    without compassion,
When time means nothing and distance is as
    insignificant as astral travel,
Where a single word can sometimes say all there is to say,
And love grows organically each passing day,
Where misunderstandings are impossible
    and words have no currency,
Where a chance meeting is enough to last a lifetime,
And heart speaks to heart in a single contact.
I have known good and gentle men and women for a lifetime,
Have been bound to them by blood and debt and
    every circumstance,
Even lashed together by work and space
    and passionate concern,
Yet few of these could invade the privacy of
    my inner being
No matter their power or brilliance, beauty or wealth.
But you were destined to reside there, my friend
    by eternal edict,
Because even before we met,
You were already there!

From Laughing Down Lonely Canyons

170

Chapter 8

The Myth of Death And Hell

I remember a sermon I gave one dark, angry Sunday on death. I mingled the dire warning of the *Apocalypse* (the Book of Revelation) and its burning pools of fire with the threat the Virgin Mary made at Fatima in Portugal to a shepherd girl. The church was as quiet as a sunset when I spoke. It was the late Mass which usually attracted the more alive and restless of the flock. But this day no one coughed or stirred. Assuredly no one slept.

I insisted that life has little meaning, that it is only important to be in God's friendship at the hour of death. I warned the man who was flirting with an "immoral" friendship that death would come upon him "like a thief in the night." I told the greedy businessman that his mounting income would not frighten away the angel of death. I described the final moment, the awful agony of a man who suddenly discovers that it is too late to repent. I described the instant awareness that all of life was but a preparation for the moment of death. I told of the horror of the guilty man gazing into the piercing eyes of Christ. I spoke of the impossibility of recourse, the despair of knowing that for a handful of pleasure or a moment's diversion a man would face an eternity of torment. I described the torment, the pain of fire, the loneliness and regret, the awesome and unthinkable reality that such misery would never end. None of what I told them had any basis in the gospels or solid theology. I had merely borrowed from the fearful and hostile imagination of Christian history.

I could feel the fear mount eloquently within the walls of the church. I could see the revolving consciences of the weak, the worried and frightened, the scrupulous housewife, the very best and most sincere. It seemed that I alone stood within the church without sin when actually my own spiritual life was

171

confused and twisted. Hence my need to project. I spoke of the availability of confession, of how easy it was for a man to be freed from his sins and to reform. And at the end of my sermon I spoke of the man who hoped that there would be a priest at the moment of death to forgive his sins and send him to eternal peace. I described the man's vacillation, his foolish procrastination, then his sudden and unanticipated death. It was a vicious, unchristian sermon. But most of all, it was a lie.

The silence in the church was almost terrifying when I concluded. During the remainder of the Mass the guilty were reflecting markedly on every shred of their lives. It was not fair. They knew nothing of the scriptures, that the very concept of hell and purgatory was developed well after Christ with varied opinions by the most eminent interpreters of the faith. St. Augustine's "proof" of Purgatory, based on a few verses from Paul to the Corinthians would have been thrown out of court.

After Mass more than fifty people asked if I would hear their confessions. During the week, I received calls from college students who promised to break up with their girl friends and from young married couples who resolved never again to practice birth control. My whole sermon was but a powerful projection of my own deepest fears—with nothing to do with any reality of a loving God. I had frightened the congregation, terrified some of them, and the response indicated that my sermon had been effective. The "sinners" came to repent of what, in reality were not sins, but more historical Christian distortions that made of sex an endless obsession. They came not out of conviction or love, but to avoid an encounter with a sudden death that would drag them screaming into hell which deep in my heart I with ever greater certainty knew could not exist. Christ never used the word!

Once, long ago, I would have shared their fear, and the priest would have been the most important person at my deathbed. I had been warned by numerous critics of my Modern Priest book in past years that I would be whining for a

172

priest when it came my turn to die. An old lady in a bookstore told me this, a priest wrote it to me in a letter, a columnist said it in print. All insisted that I had given in to pride and lust until I no longer listened to God. I would grow more obstinate with time, and the moment that my soul left my body, I would face an angry and unyielding God. There would be no time left for mercy, only for the decree of justice that would sentence me to hell. There I would endure the physical torment of endless burning. And this from a God I was taught to love? The letters did not offend me, nor the people, but the vicious distortion of the love and hope that Jesus came to share. Life, at times, was hell enough, and from this experience evolved a theological concept with no basis in truth, the product of personal guilt and profound self contempt. This is much of what passes for morality.

But now I no longer believe in such a God or hell. It contradicts the very existence of God. One has to choose, either God (by whatever title of Spirit, Light, the Force, or Energy) or hell! To incorporate both would deny all rationality with no basis in theology or sanity. I, who once preached so violently of hell, do not believe in it. It is another one of the terrifying, decadent myths that man has fashioned through centuries in his personal fear and private effort to control man. It has worked with utter efficiency. Once it bound me and prevented me from being honest with myself. Sometimes it kept me awake at night as a child, more often as a man when I first violated my celibacy in adolescent innocence at thirty. It made me run to God in fear, scrutinizing my every act and intention, and denying the very heavenly humanity that came to me at birth. At times it made me calm and peaceful when I could say that I had carefully jumped all the hurdles that this angry, obsessive, God required. But then soon again the anguish would begin. Most of all, it guaranteed that I would not have a personal relationship with God but a dedication to fear and law. What else was possible?

The fear of hell made life's joys seem of little consequence.

The whole of life was gathered in death, wherein a gangster could find pardon and a just man could perish beneath a sudden and violent temptation. It was not important to do anything of consequence in life. One could be quite successful if he lived quietly without jeopardy or unnecessary risk. The best way to live, with such a view, was to avoid "occasions of sin." That sounds simple enough, except the occasions of sin are more often than not the occasions of opportunity and involvement. It makes for a cautious and fearful life, and provides a ready-made excuse for not facing up to oneself. Essentially, it is irresponsible and as inhuman as hell itself.

Yet, if man believes in the kind of Dante's hell that Protestant and Catholic preachers have so vividly described in pulpits and on TV, there is little wonder that he hesitates to take a chance. I have had hundreds tell me that the fear of hell made it impossible for them to oppose their church. Everything human tells them that their church's view is simplistic or even wrong. (Even the word is never used in the gospels despite the English translations.) And yet, they fear to move. They are not afraid of death alone. That fear would be violent enough. They fear the decayed and immobilizing myth of hell, and like little children, alone in bed at night, they make of every shadow a witch, of every noise the sound of a dangerous intruder. Think of it, if perhaps you have never been brainwashed by this horror tale. You could be crossing a street or riding in a car, and suddenly, you are torn from time and are in eternity. You are actually convinced you will face an angry God Who will not listen to a thing you say. Some may have had that experience with a parent or teacher or the law. But now, in an instant you are sentenced to eternal pain beyond which the sickest mind could not fathom. You have heard hell described in sermons and have read about it in spiritual books. You have heard dramatic tales of men and women who compromised sin, and just when they thought everything in life was smooth and comfortable, they landed in a never-ending pool of fire which burns eternally without consuming. In such a context, only atheism could be logical!

Within such a framework, life is of little consequence, save to prepare a man for death. A marriage can fail, children can hate parents, a world can be at war, blacks or gays can march angrily in the streets, children in Asia or Africa can starve, the economy of a nation can be threatened, a best friend can be torn away. None of this really counts, only an eternity matters and man and woman must do everything to escape hell as I described in detail in *A Modern Priest Looks At His Outdated Church*. Most of all, the entire focus of this twisted spirituality is on one's individual, single actions, not on one's goals and dreams and glorious vision of love and service.

Some Few Walk Easy
There are some few who walk easy on the earth,
Passing from childhood to wisdom without a usual turbulence,
> *Too aware to be young*
> *Too alive to be old,*
Contemporary and companion of every life
> *Beyond discrimination or explanation,*
God's gift to His world
> *To make the lonely laugh*
> *The neglected come alive*
> *To stir spirits and warm hearts*
> *To enrich the discordant parts of all the rest of life.*
Such gentle ones make a lasting mark on every life they touch
Without trying or preaching, judging or seeking,
Merely by their presence on the earth.
> *A shade tree by a favorite stream*
> *The morning sun on a damp meadow*
> *A green hill mirrored in a quiet lake*
> *A sugar pine silver in the moonlight*
Until the morning comes and they are gone too soon,
Leaving us in darkness and unspeakable sadness.

From Walk Easy On The Earth

175

There are millions who have been bound in misery by the nauseously sick myth of hell. I do not laugh, I weep, and I remember how hard it was for me to escape the sting of its wrath. It frightened me for years and kept me cowardly and hesitant, and robbed me of innocent joys and noble goals. Now, thank God, that sordid myth and vicious misery are at an end. Recently, I was on a plane, and the turbulence was violent and extreme. We were forced to land several hundred miles from our destination. I am sure that everyone in the plane believed that death might well be at hand. A few years ago, I would have recited carefully my *Act of Contrition*. I probably would have announced that I was available to hear confessions in the forward cabin. But now, I made no pretense to pray. I was frightened, and I found myself wondering what lay beyond this life. I had no idea, nor have I now. But I know it is not the concocted "hell" of Christian history assembled like the brew of MacBeth's witches. I was really quite ready to take my fateful chance with the rest of the men and women. I felt I had been honest and had done the best I could. I believe in the mysterious God Within Who gives joyous meaning to my life. I cannot believe that I will be punished at my death, and thus give Birth To The God that reflects man's self hatred as an omnipotent Hitler might.

I must confess, however, in that brief encounter with the possibility of death, I did not really think of God. I merely wondered. I have no clear picture of the world beyond as once I did. I do not accept the carefully refined rules of admission that once I preached. I do not pray for the dead, though at times I chat with one of my dead brothers, or my parents—sometimes feeling I have made some connection and I doubt that any of my friends will spend time praying for me. I have abandoned the mythology of death that was imposed on me—with its fires and devils and gnashing teeth—and have found no new one to take its place, save in the pain and suffering I have felt and seen on earth in gargantuan doses. That's the hell Jesus promised to relieve.

And yet I, like every man, somehow have to deal

with death. I sense my weakness, the impatience of relentless time, the fact of death and aging on every side. I read that a friend, a business associate, or even a stranger of my own age has died. For a moment I shudder at the thought that I, too, will die. Perhaps death is in a way harder to deal with now than when I had the clear outlines of the Christian mythology of death. Then, at least, there were rules, hard and at times impossible, but always clear and definite. There was a way of dealing with death, a kind of requiem ritual that I could perform. I could appease the anger of God, pay my debts with prayer and sorrow, ease my guilt with ceremonial and tribal law. Now I am obliged to give up my idols and childish games and to face the reality of my own death as part of life beyond all myth, increasingly believing that it is but a new and wondrous extension of consciousness.

Society is of little help. It has given death to the undertakers who have learned their trade in the shadow of the church. Often they were trained to be as oily and unctuous as witch doctors; to play on people's guilt in new and sophisticated ways. Some have made death into a kind of public parade, with their bronze caskets and limousines and private chapels of satin and saccharine. I detest such work and the mockery that this culture makes of death. Death becomes as artificial and vicious as the friendly atmosphere of one of Europe's tourist traps, or the glitter of our own Las Vegas. Many seem like paid vultures who hover over bodies and bury them in expensive plots before the living are able to decide anything for themselves. They have not improved the mythology of the churches. They have only borrowed it and made it worse. I would not give them my body, nor will any man a hundred years from now. I would rather my ashes ride the independent wind or my flesh feed the hungry fishes of the sea in gratitude for the life we share. I hope my friends will miss me, not pray for me, will long for my presence, not join the parade that professionals have planned to make money at my death. I hope they will comfort the few that loved me most. And most of all, remember my joy and laughter, and mad antics of living.

Now I have no clear mythology of death, nothing but faith in the God of meaning that I try to love. I believe that death is not the end of life, but I know little more than that. Especially I cannot accept the "hell" that was manufactured from mingling the Jewish concept of Sheol (a shadowy lower region), gehenna (a garbage dump outside of Jerusalem), and the Greek Hades which like Shoel bespoke the underground region of the dead. The evolution of "hell" is a totally different story which has nothing to with God and His Scriptures, and everything to do with repressed human guilt, anger, ancient myth, and self-loathing. At the same time, I cannot accept death as the end of everything. It makes no sense. It interrupts the order of life that I seem to experience. I see an old man who has struggled to find himself for eighty-five years. He has discovered the peace and beauty of life. He has mastered the man who once was restless and impatient, greedy and lonely, young and impulsive. His anger has cooled into tolerance and love. His wrinkles tell the story of a thousand struggles to give to loved ones and to wring meaning out of life. This man is not one of the disgruntled old, whose pain may have twisted them into bitterness despite their personal effort. He is loving, warm, talkative, reflective, and free. His eyes twinkle with a joy that a young man can never know, and they shine with a purity that only comes with the innocence of age or infancy. His smile is radiant and honest. His hand upon mine is warm and real. He does not boast or hide; he expresses in his whole being the wonder of a human life and its eternal existence.

But soon he will die. I can accept the death of his body. I have watched it grow wearier with the years. But his spirit seemed to grow more youthful and free. I have witnessed this ineffable beauty in men and women hundreds of times. I cannot believe such a spirit will cease to exist. It does not represent an end, but a beginning. It needs to be freed from the body that struggled with it, that fought it, that gave it weariness and pain. But the spirit has won out; the man or woman's eyes and inner beauty reveal that, as did a final look into my mother's eyes. For this reason I cannot believe that life is at an end. I do not know what happens after death. I do not know if we will be transformed in new and responsive flesh, nor do I believe does anyone else. But I do not believe we pass from existence, not when our whole life was a journey to be free, not when we are far more spirit than flesh. Not when young and innocent lives are snuffed out before they've really begun.

And in my own existence, I see my body grow a bit less vigorous even as my spirit grows a bit more free. And yet, I know death comes, and when it comes, I trust it will find me more loving and fulfilled than I was the year before. The longer death waits, the greater the chance I have to become the kind of man I want to be, the kind of man I know I can be. If death ends my struggle, if there is nothing after death, then my quest for freedom of spirit might still make as much sense to me as it now does when I look at the world about me. I see all of creation, plants and animals, stars and space alike, gathered to serve and to challenge man, to aid him in his struggle for freedom and love. I see man as the interpreter of all creation, the healer, the searcher, the hopeful, the curious. I see man fail and abuse his dignity; I see him wound his fellowman and lose his vision. But I see him rise up again and struggle on to be the free and loving spirit that is his destiny. I see all of history as an evolution of men and women from primitive life and primeval fears to the fullness of joy and freedom beyond race or nation, sex or personality to oneness.

Apartment Four Upstairs
Today I wondered about love
    And saw an old couple returning from the market,
    She with her varicose legs
    Like splotches of grape jelly on bread,
    He with his swollen, arthritic knee and emphysema wheeze.
They paused at the bottom of shaky, white steps

And grinned when he handed her the grocery bag.
  She went first, painfully, slowly,
  He followed, stiff hands pushing her rump.
At the top he gently goosed her.
  She shrieked at bit, he coughed,
They laughed and disappeared inside apartment four upstairs.

From Today I Wondered About Love

I do not believe that the man I struggle to become will be reduced to nothingness. Or will return to resolve some lopsided Karma, as do many of my associates, because I think each of us does the very best we can. I can try to accept the gradual dissipation of my body, its quickening response to infirmity. The quieting of my physical powers only serves to simplify my life and make me find meaning in more essential and less distracting ways if I am able. With the passing years, I am less inclined to ask a new experience or travel to bring me happiness and peace, though I continue to court my share of fantasy and wild adventure. I know that I am becoming a person in possession of himself, a person who can be a friend, who can learn the joy and fulfillment that comes from love. And when I sense my growth and know that I am not quite the restless man that I once was, I will not believe that death crowns my life with nothingness. Somehow I believe in a life that endures forever, and I have no human evidence but the power of my own experience with life and the experience of those whose vision matches mine. To me that is evidence enough! And I have my faith which has dissolved all doubt. Proof does not seem possible or required, but I do believe that Jesus conquered death as a symbol of our own conquest, but would never try to "convince" anyone else.

I see and accept life's lesson, that as I lose my capacity to live with the fullness of my body, when my work is complete at whatever age, I gain the opportunity to live with the fullness of my spirit. And if I reach the point that my brain and body are too feeble to bear my spirit without senility, when I have

180

reached the point that I am no longer useful to myself or to anyone else upon the earth, I do not want to be kept alive as some barely pulsating vegetable.

Even now I usually have no real desire to be twenty again. I have learned the lessons that the twenties had to teach. Life means more now that it did then, even though my breath is not as even, my face is assuredly not as fair. I have learned something of the futility of money and fame, the enervation that comes from business and speed, and am still learning. I can usually accept life's pain without deep resentment, accept its opportunities and excitement without running in endless circles. I can almost let myself be loved and have learned somewhat to love. I do not have to have everyone like me, though I would prefer it, and I can accept the fact that I do not appeal to some. I do not make friends easily, but I need the friendship of a chosen few. I have learned to avoid the pressure of superficial social friendships, that I can avoid gatherings that only make me less myself. I can disagree with more dignity and less anger than I once could, and I can increasingly accept an opinion counter to my own with some semblance of openness and peace—and yearning to know.

All of this my life has taught me, and yet I know how far I still must go. I know the shyness and fear that prevent me from growing closer to those I love. I know the impatience that makes of work an obsession rather than a joy. I know that I am too often preoccupied with trifles and miss the beauty a sunset or a landscape was meant to give. I know the ambition that still pounds at my temples, the rising anger and fear that restricts my freedom and makes my spirit narrow. I know moments of jealousy and self-pity, hours of discouragement, depression, and emotional fatigue. I know how often I demand that others be as I, how frequently I am insensitive to the needs of loved ones close at hand. And yet, I know that I will grow to the maturity of spirit and the fullness of heart that is my destiny as a person. I know because the past gives me courage, and at present, the future seems to give me time.

And yet, I do not know clearly what lies beyond my death.

I believe that somehow, I will continue to live. Yet, I cannot give evidence for my position, only an intuition and my abiding personal faith which seems beyond all question. There is, as yet, no adequate physical evidence. And so I live my life, not in fear of death, but in the hope that I can become a person more loving and human and at peace. I believe that I am somehow more than the dog or cat I love, more that the ducks and geese I have studied and admired. I am a man whose very words and breath can give hope and meaning to others. I do not have to kill to show my anger, because someone cares and will listen. I do not have to strike out, because I know the power of someone's human love. My pain is of concern, my voice of significance, my presence a need. The longer I live, the more meaning, the less diversion, has my life. This speaks to me of an eternal life wherein I shall only fulfill the life that I have initiated here at another realm of consciousness.

But this life counts, not like the Monopoly money that earns me heaven and rescues me from the hell of man's in-verted imaginings and incarnate perverted nightmares. It is my life, the destined life that I somehow believe will continue after death. It is here and now that a person is being made, a personality is being formed. I do not know if death will terminate my work or blot it out, if it will repair the damage that I have done and give universal pardon or a blanket kind of peace. I do not know if I will still have to live with my fears until love conquers them, live with dishonesty and pride until I can really be myself, live with occasional loneliness until I can be a better friend. I do not know if I will have a body, though I would like to enjoy the pleasure that it gives in life. I only believe that I will continue to exist in joy and fulfillment. I believe it only because the inner logic of my spirit reveals it to me. I believe it because I share what is to me the single most important revelation of Jesus Christ and has lifted me from my own despair at the loss of one I loved.

For me, Jesus is the prophet of life after death. Many Jewish prophets were skeptical and offered little more than the preachers of evolution who describe immortality in terms of a species or a race. They spoke of a people that would continue and prosper no matter the ravages of time, and never spoke of hell. They built a society that respected its forefathers and loved violently its children, but they made no clear and consistent assertion of an eternal life. Jesus, sharing the faith of the later Jews who believed in an afterlife, did that, not by the glory of his Resurrection, but by the power of his own vision and his faith. I do not find it necessary to believe his body truly survived the grave. It rings too much of magic and of myth. If he walked again after death, those who saw him would have no reason for any kind of faith. They would be faced with a fact that a man had survived death or with a fancy that their imagination had played an impossible trick. There would be nothing of faith. And yet I believe they felt his presence even as many still can... as I once did in a chapel in Sedona, Arizona.

There is, however, a place for such faith. Jesus, the Jewish prophet, had a new vision inspired by the deep religious experience of his own life. His vision of love was hardly new, only a reformed and expanded version of what man had already heard. Nor was his vision of peace a new one; it was just reemphasized and made practical. But his vision of life after death was revolutionary in its impact, and it said in clear and unmistakable terms what the majority of the earlier prophets had only hinted at in shadow. How paradoxical and tragic that the "hell" about which he said nothing has battered so many lives.

I do not think he came back to astound his Apostles in some upper room, though how can I deny it with certainty? After his death, I do not think that he spent forty days here on earth as some kind of special friend from a twilight zone. I believe he died and was buried and somehow entered a new life without appearing to anyone save in mystic communication that is not uncommon here on earth, to support timid faith with fact. He preached the reality of an eternal life because he experienced within himself the purity of an undying spirit even as can we. No longer would his followers have to blanch or turn ashen in the face of death. No longer would they have to pay homage to the pagan superstitions surrounding human death. Even the Jews were not permitted to touch a corpse, a kind of concession to the pagan environment from which they were spawned. But from among the Jews came Jesus, who took the vague longings for an afterlife and the misty faith in an undying spirit which his culture accepted, and transformed them into a personal vision of life after death, but never hell or even purgatory.

It is this vision that I share, this faith that I embrace. It is not simply a faith in Jesus, but a faith in his vision of life. The fact of death becomes the very spark of faith. Death confronts me and makes me ask myself: "What does life mean?" And from this frequent confrontation comes the human impetus to my faith. It is a faith that includes more than life after death. It makes of death a source of strength and not an avenue of weakness. Eternal life tells me that nothing on earth is more important than the power of love.

I did not experience this when I lived with the traditional religious mythology of the afterlife which I probably never really believed deep inside. Then I did not really think of death at all. I only imagined that I did. There were too many props, too many religious supports, too many theories that stood between me and my death, too much time. Now I live with a sense of death, and yet I live without the morbidity that such a sense of death can include. My thoughts of death are more often real and positive than before.

I think of death when I look at the ocean or when I ride on its waves in search of fish. I see the vast expanse of water and know that I came from this ocean through the wonder of evolution and the majesty of life. I am aware that I am a part of all of this, that the struggle of my own spirit to be free is the struggle of every living thing to survive. I have a sense of death when I see the grandeur of the mountains and know that the power of these formations are a fierce monument to the determination of nature and its human lord. I feel my death in all the fossilized forms that have died to give me life. And even though there are times I resent aging with its attendant human bias, I somehow know at moments like these that I am part of a seething, violent battle of one reality to transform itself from mute beauty and revolving forms into the power of an ever more conscious, ever more free and loving spirit in a kind of universal hologram. It is then that I rejoice in my life with its new awareness of the strength of human love. It is then that I sense the very power of death as a kind of entrance to a new and more exhilarating kind of life for everyone! It is then that I see the futility of a life that is lived in search of an earthly paradise or for heavenly rewards.

My sense of death mocks me or others when we hide behind material symbols or squander a desire for immortality in marble monuments. It smiles at the man I met today who sees himself as exceptional and important because he has showered his wife and family with expensive trinkets. In reality he is still a prisoner, as helpless as a mountain, built by forces he cannot control, and he has turned human love into emptiness and an expense account until he understands how truly beautiful he is all by himself. He has kept his family at a respectful distance by enshrining his own success and by giving those who want to love him everything except his time and personal attention. He pays for men to show him kindness in the most sophisticated clubs. He has everything but peace and joy and honest friends, and I believe he already knows it, and soon will change. The signs are all there, and like me, he may require a rather dramatic and "crippling" reminder of his real self.

But my sense of death questions, as well, the "religious" man who lives his life in the hope of some reward from the legendary god of the heavenly myth, and who lives his life in fear of an eternal hell created by the darkest fears and hatreds of mankind. Such a man often stands apart from life, he feels out of the mainstream, that he is not ultimately responsible, a cut above the rest of us and that there is always a way out. He does not have to be committed to love, to the struggle for the personal freedom that makes man truly human. He seems content to earn merit badges and to be rewarded by some eternal and omnipotent boy scout in the sky. He can hope for mercy at the hour of death as the TV preachers promise; he can await some final liberation that turns him into the loving man he never had to become in life. He can stand apart from men, carefully tucked into his own mythology. He may never have to know the ultimate confrontation of the man who refuses to turn his fear and uncertainty into a hierarchy of gods and choir lofts. But he may never know his strength; he may never know his commitment to life. He may never know the power of his freedom and the depths of his love.

And when I listen to his preachers tell about his vision of an afterlife, I am hard pressed to know whether I find heaven or hell more distasteful. His hell, indeed, is awesome and resentful. It is the revenge that a child might seek against his playmates, revenge learned in a sudden burst of anger and fantasy. It is a native's superstition, a helpless savage's fear of a boiling volcano, a weak man's desperate threat to keep the strong in line. But his vision of heaven, perhaps, is almost as disturbing. It is stuffy and effeminate, dull and meaningless, childish and superstitious. It is the promise of a finicky mother who will not let her children dirty themselves in the streets of life. It is the pledge of an old maid who makes a fetish of everything she fears, and who imposes her prudish rules on everyone she meets. It is a dull scene, an endless afternoon in grandma's parlor where the rewards are as meaningless as the punishments.

My vision of an afterlife is more like that of one of my closest friends who does not believe in such a life at all, than that of the man of the religious myth. This man who does not believe in an afterlife can recognize and pity the artificial existence of the rich man I have described. Assuredly he recognized the sterility of the religious myth. Often he is more involved in life than all the rest. Often he needs no convincing about the power of human love. Actually, I have numerous good friends who do not share my faith, who honestly believe that death is the end of every spark of their human life. Nevertheless they are in search of a life meaning and love. Even as I love them and respect their attitude, even as I reexamine my own position and compare it with theirs, I treasure the intuition that I have of a life after death. (And know I'll see them there.)

I have no capacity to describe this life. I have no need to defend it, no eagerness to impose it on anyone else. I am well aware that in the future I may lose this intuition entirely. But presently I have it, and I believe that it enables me to put my life in better perspective than ever before. Not necessarily better than other men. But better than I ever could. I find it harder to ignore the sufferings of others; I cannot dismiss the hurts of my brothers in the world while I pursue my own "holiness." I cannot confess my "sins" or ask pardon of God; I cannot add up my virtues or clip my spiritual coupons. I am a part of this one dynamic force called life; I am not its victim but its molding spirit. I have the capacity to love and to be loved and to share in the liberation of all creation. And when I love, really love, I somehow love forever.

I Want To Die A Careless Man

I want to die a careless man
*   With my yellow legal pages scattered on the floor,*
My desk covered with ashes and unfinished thoughts,
*   Borne away on the wind of an idea,*
*   Not far from one who loves me and*
*   Understands enough of my madness to stay until the end.*
I have not learned much of life,
Each evening a new mystery to wonder about,
*   Struggling somehow to stay alive*
*   Among so many satisfied to survive.*
Tonight I have no time for prophets or profit margins,
*   I do not worry about the failure of socialism,*
*   Or the vandalism on buses after school.*
*   Nor do I care what the President thinks.*
I would like to watch a flock of ducks

Circle a swamp three times before landing,
Eavesdrop on coyotes at the edge of a forest,
And hear church bells across a quiet valley.
Most of all I would like to die a careless man.

From Winter Has Lasted Too Long

I know my vision is vague. It can be no other way. I am not dealing with physical phenomena or historical myths. I am dealing with the distant depths of my own experience of the meaning of joyfully living my life amid great challenges and at times intense fear and pain. I believe that Christ's vision of eternal life, when shorn of the myths that men have attached to it, gives me additional strength to resist the emptiness of flattery and power, the prison of emptiness and greed. It tells me that there is no power on earth that is immortal, that there is really nothing to fear save my own thoughts. Yet it does not deny the meaning of life, the meaning of the present moment, the impact of present responsibility. In fact it highlights the present moment, because this is all I have of life. It tells me that only love survives the grave; it says that there are tragedies worse than starvation or poverty, more terrible than war or murder or unloved children, as much as they seem to crush our human spirit. It does not make light of these, but it is conscious of the emptiness of a life without meaning, the loneliness of a life without friends, the bitterness of a marriage without love. These are tragedies that do not need to be; they are not tragedies that make the stomach ache with hunger, but they do shrivel the spirit and desecrate the soul. Even as I ache for the injustice that smothers the oppressed or the misery that destroys life in Africa or America, I know as great or even greater pain in the tragedy of a life without love. Such a life has no meaning at all.

I cannot say for certain that if I were to lose my faith in an afterlife I would feel differently about life. Perhaps I would be equally as involved in life, equally as determined to grow in love, equally as concerned with my brothers and sisters in

188

the global village. Perhaps I would be satisfied to know that my efforts to do the best I could would help to free the men who would live after I had passed from existence. Perhaps it would be enough to know that the only immortality one has is in his children, in the creative force of the love he tried to give. Perhaps this would be the most unselfish vision of all. But this is not my vision. This is not my faith. I believe that I will continue to live after death, and currently this gives great meaning to my life.

I have never known great poverty or real hunger. Nor do I care to. I have never known the personal anguish and terror of my city under siege. But worse than even these must be a life without meaning, a life that could have been but was squandered for a fleshpot or for a surrender to power and prestige. To have had a chance to love, to grow, to know beauty and to have friends, and to throw all of this away for emptiness and gilded ashes is the greatest tragedy of all. It does not take wealth to suffer such a tragedy, sometimes a penny or a handful of praise and power will do. But it always takes pettiness and a narrow spirit, vanity and the inability to love. And it always offers a thousand invitations to change! And perhaps at some level which I cannot see or measure, everyone really does change—from the religious fanatic to the most greedy or murderous wretch alive. God loves all of us the same, unconditionally, and tells me not to judge lest I be judged. That takes real spiritual growth—never to attack, accuse, condemn, or withhold forgiveness. But that is our destiny.

So much of life is conditioning and cultivated taste. Once we thrilled to hamburgers, now we may turn up our nose when the filet or salmon is a trifle overdone. Once we enjoyed a picnic, now a trip to Bermuda can leave us restless and bored. The rich long for the simplicity of the poor, the poor pine for the opportunity of the rich. The young need money, the old need energy and time. The salesman needs another customer, the executive needs another business. The poor man can't buy what he wants until next year, but neither can the rich man—so much of his money is tied up in property and stocks.

Christ offered a beginning answer in the power of love and in the victory of death. The religions often turned his vision of death into a mythology that helped them to control men and make them frightened slaves. The morticians turned it into an expensive farce. The Great Society and greed turned it into a deadline, toward which the empty must race to know every comfort and pleasure the economy provides. Christ turned it into a sign of victory—man could learn to love before he spent an eternity becoming the person he had begun on earth to be. An empty man needs no fire to punish him for his lack of love. It is punishment enough for him to have more time to be himself, time to endure his own restlessness, time to love when he has no capacity to give himself. Hopefully, eternity will offer him an additional chance to learn if such is what some of us may need. Or more likely, wipe clean our slate at the 12th hour—who knows? Certainly not me!

In Christ's vision, life takes on new meaning; death is the door of its victory. Life's battles are of consequence, the battle to make a friend and to keep one. The battle to win love and to give it, the battle to conquer vanity, pride and selfishness, and to know the victory of a spirit free enough to love, to judge no one.

Such a vision does not answer all the mysteries of life and death. It does not tell us, as the mythologies attempted to do, what is the significance of the death of a child, or what is the meaning of a tragedy that snatches away a young life before its time. It does not tell us where we will go or how we will live or in what form we shall be. It does not tell us why terrible and tragic events afflict good and loving people. It does not assure us that we will have communication beyond the grave, that we will know again our loved ones. It is a feeble and incomplete vision, a human and uncertain one. It stands before the mystery of death with wonderment, but not with terror. It faces death with a sense of expectancy and excitement worthy of a loving God, but not with the religious fantasies that in reality forbid a man to contemplate his death. My vision just is. I live with it. Presently it gives me courage, it offers me strength, it provides me with meaning and a sense of hope and victory. Or as just before my beloved brother Bob died in his prime called it "the greatest adventure."

Perhaps there is a new symbolism to replace the trappings of death that have made a travesty of life. Perhaps the symbol of victory is the only one that Christ attempted to provide. Jesus seemed to know how to live and to be a friend. He seemed to know the joy that accompanies such an experience. Money could not corrupt him, nor could prominence or power, nor could flattery or a more exotic loaf of bread. He could enjoy a vacation because he had a friend, and he could enjoy his work for the same reason. Death made him tremble, but it did not take away his life. It was not an end, but a beginning; not a tragedy, but a victory, an eternity to be the person that he had become.

I am not yet ready to die, but I am more ready than I was a year ago, because I am a little less greedy, a little less restless, a little less vain, a little more a friend. I feel I need more time; I hope I get it. I want it. Lots of it. But I do not require time to rush to confess my sins and to receive the pardon of a well meaning priest. Nor do I require it to make atonement or to escape the mythical fires of hell. I want time perhaps to be a better brother or a better friend. I want more time to make sure that I can enjoy the simple beauty that is life, the everlasting wonder that is love. I want it to prove that neither money nor power nor vanity can make of me a fool, or terrible fear and pain cannot erode my spirit. Such a struggle is not easy, and it takes time, reflection and honest friends to tell me what I am, and what I can become.

When I was married, my wife helped me to understand much that the priesthood was not able to teach. I learned something of the difference between the freedom of love and the narrowness of over-possessiveness and control, even as she learned from me. I learned what is love and what is merely self-consciousness and fear. She did not accede to my every demand, nor did she permit me to get away with the things that the priesthood so glibly allowed. I gained a new and unaccustomed responsibility to care, to consider, to be concerned about the needs and feelings of another, who is as important as myself. My divorce or yours was not a failure, but the termination of a loving step along the way. We always have a new chance to love and let ourselves be loved, to admit our weakness and loneliness and need. And to learn that in such an admission we are not less attractive but more lovable. I need time for all of this, time before the victory of death. I need time to listen to my friends, who lately have been able to deal with me somewhat more honestly than before. And I am better able to care more than I ever could even without their presence.

Perhaps there will not be enough time for everything. I do not know. But I am not as afraid. I have no way of proving my intuition that I will continue to live. All I have is a resolute faith, a powerful hope. So I cling to my vision that death when it comes will in no way be defeat, but the door to a new kind of life, and when it comes, I will have had just the right time to be ready to spend eternity becoming the person I have begun to be, forever aware that GOD LIVES.

When The Pain Is More Acute Than You Can Bear

When the pain is more acute than you can bear,
And you are convinced that no one in the world suffers as much,
When the morning is as opaque as night and the dawn
    but a discordant alarm, announcing yet another bitter struggle
    to survive,
When a bird's song to the day or the serene murmuring of a dove
    cannot draw your mind from feeding on itself,
Clinging like some wretched scavenger to drain out joy and wonder,
When the soft light of daybreak cannot distract or
    the gently shimmering of the locust leaves cannot inspire,
When even the shrill cries of summer children are but
    screams that echo is some mad corridor of consciousness,
Know that you are not dying, but preparing to enter
    another level of life,
A level beyond avarice and fleeting fame, beyond
    servile dependence on opinions or words of praise,
Beyond power and mastery and control, beyond jealousy and competition,
Beyond lust and greed and insatiable ambition,
    a level where joy flows from simplicity and love,
From some rhythm shared with trees and flowers and circling planets.
Then all the pain is as nothing, rather a choice
    and heavenly messenger sent like some ancient angel of the East
To announce a more profound and solid way to self-esteem and serenity.
Thus pain is not an enemy, but a friend who promises
    to take you where peace abides,
Who leads you beyond bitterness to abandon specious and empty pursuits,
    hollow and ill-founded hopes, destructive and untimely dreams,
Until you walk in the world freer and more joyful than ever before,
Less anxious and less frightened of death, one with life,
In an harmonious accord,
    Bred of suffering, of annihilation,
    Bred of emptiness and frustration,
And leading directly and inexorably to a true and genuine,
    An eternal and purified self.

From Quiet Water

Chapter 9

From Myth to Maturity

*E*ven though we have long been in the midst of a religious revolution which is freeing man from the myths that held him captive, religions, on the surface, continue to thrive. New churches are being built even as others are shut down, men and women are still preparing themselves for the Christian ministry, experimental liturgies are being worked out, New Age churches are expanding, thousands of babies are baptized, "real" Bibles are still being published, as well as new dramatic and controversial books about the historic Jesus.

And yet, a new generation is moving rapidly away from the religious mythology, and the process will continue ever more rapidly. Those who speak of institutional religion's strength and renewal are myopic and frightened. Pope John Paul II can sound as sure of himself as does our President when he promised to balance the budget or end war. Each sounds as certain as did the university administrators who once asserted that the student riots and protests of the 70's were born in immaturity, that they were filled with irresponsibility. All sound as confident as the white supremacists who shouted that the Black must take what he gets. They were not aware of the mighty avalanche that is in the process of "renewing the face of the earth." A spiritual revolution from within, the Inner Spirit of Man not simply new politics or new religions based, however creatively, on the same old format and authoritarian structure.

The religious institution as we have known it is already dead at its roots, and so are its gods. But it is difficult for the man who took the religious myth seriously to escape it. One of my neighbors, Frank, is getting old. We often talk about religion, but he finds it difficult to change. He looks back on a life that was made meaningful by the sacrifices he offered to God. When the budget was strained, when he worried about a house payment, when his job was in jeopardy or his children were sick or in trouble, he turned to God. Sunday was a special day of prayer, and morning and evening were times to ask God's blessing or to put oneself in His care. For years Frank survived an unhappy marriage by calling upon God. When his children turned out well, he attributed it to God's guidance. When Frank heard talk of the death of God or new biblical interpretations, he was confused or deeply hurt. So we usually talk about other things because Frank and I are friends. Frank is happy in his way and approaching the end of life. There is no need to unsettle the myth that has provided him with such important help as it did my parents and million of others. We let go of our myths and illusions when it is time, and it is not for me to attack or destroy a religious faith that guided Frank's whole life, as it did that of thousands I loved.

The poor, too, have not known what to make of the new religious attitudes. Their life has been a physical struggle to get ahead, sometimes to stay alive. They are the Hindus who cling to their myths as they starve to death or hear their children cry for food. They are the South Americans or Eastern Europeans who pray to the Virgin in their wayside shrines and wonder where the next meal is coming from. They are the Indians who live on beans and rice, who resist acculturation, and who bury their still born babies at the base of a cactus plant to guarantee another child. They are the miners in West Virginia who were trapped for five days in a sealed-off shaft and were brought to safety with the praise of God on their lips and a promise to be more devout. Such men and women must cling to their myths since life has been cruel and unreasonable, often without hope, and their myths have been integrated into their lives.

The uneducated, too, do not understand the critical discussions about Christ and the Church. They were never permitted to think about their religion or to reflect upon the truths that they inherited from their parents or were not really interested. They learned of Jesus through the religious institution and were taught to believe that the Bible is beyond all question. Such people learned never to challenge a teacher or a doctor, never to question an authority or to evaluate what they read. They hear secondhandedly of The Lost Books of the Bible or The Historical Jesus, and they are dismayed. The uneducated may be wealthy and successful in their jobs; they may be executives and salesmen and the mothers of many children, but they know little about the history or the evolution of a religious institution, nor its demise.

How do you speak of this present new awareness to a man who has no sense of history? He does not know what you are talking about so why try to change his mind? He will change when it is time. He looks at you and believes that you have rejected God. He can only speak of what he learned as a boy, of what his parents and religious teachers told him. He trusted them, and they were most often good to him as were many wonderful nuns and priests to me. To speak to him of religious myths is to assert that his friends were deceitful. He is the docile victim of the Establishment. He still may view communism as a monolithic monster that is waiting to wipe him from the face of the earth. He believed that he must fight a war in Vietnam to preserve freedom on the earth. He was proud when his son joined the Marines in The Desert War. He still listens to the President with a degree of confidence because he does not know where else to turn. He finds it hard to disbelieve that America is the same country and that it is in the same world that he knew as a small boy. And even more, when he views religion, it arouses the same kind of blind and unthinking loyalty.

But more than a lack of education, or poverty or old age, it is finally fear that prevents a man from escaping the religious myth. The fear is of many kinds, but at its root is the fear that life has no meaning without the mythology of the institution's God. It is a fear that resists information, that can ignore facts, and overlook evidence. It can bind a theologian, a college professor, a lawyer, a Pope, a traffic cop. The fearful still wait for the Pope's or a contrived Jesus' permission to be human. They are baptized to enter heaven; they confess their sins to find forgiveness, or pray to God in order that He will hear and change the rhythm of life when he already loves them unconditionally. They look to the Church, the Bible, the past. They bless, they circumcise, they anoint, they come forward in revivals and convert, and they look for "salvation."

Such fear is hard to deal with. It lurks everywhere. It has kept a nun in the convent when her restricted lifestyle or service lost its meaning. It forces a mother to have children she doesn't want even if she is losing her husband and tearing her marriage apart. It brings a man back to church even though its liturgy bores him and its sermons make him restless and angry. Only fear and familiarity still draws him. Fear also makes parents feel guilty and unworthy unless they indoctrinate their children in the myths that were transmitted to them in their own childhood. It forces parents to cut off their own rebelling children and to live as self-pitying martyrs for their faith. It forces sincere bishops to hide behind their office rather than to listen to bolder bishops and their own priests who know the truth and are ready to accept women priests and a modification of celibacy. It permits a priest or a rabbi to live in mental and emotional seclusion from the realities of the world, unaware that if the guilds and monarchies died, so can the churches.

I do not mock such faith, I pity it. I know how hard it is to escape. I have read men's letters by the thousands, begging, "Let me be free!" But often they do not know what to do. For a time I thought the institution would help them. I thought that the Pope would hear the cries of the people, that priests and ministers, who saw beyond the myths, would rise up everywhere and tell the frightened people the truth. Some do publicly and they are silenced. I thought bishops would be able to say, "We have not given you God but human traditions. We have no keys to heaven or hell, we cannot save you or set you free. We have none of the certainties that we once claimed to have. We are no different from you; we are only men who care about other men." The South American bishops seemed ready to say this at Vatican II, so did the bishops who had suffered from the Communist oppression, so did the bishops who had lived among the poor and starving. So do a group of American and European bishops! So do the three or four rabbis in all of Chicago who even now will perform "mixed" marriages. So do the Reform and Conservative rabbis who have lived with the narrowness and hostility of the Orthodox tradition in Israel and elsewhere. So do the ministers who had seen the Bible built into a savage and angry club to beat the little ones into line.

But then very often their fear and helplessness takes over. Many religious leaders have not trusted man. They feared that his spiritual revolution would be too extreme, that his protests would be too dangerous and irresponsible. They were afraid to go to the very roots of Christianity or Judaism in promoting reform. Only the exceptional clergyman of any sect or denomination has stood up to be counted. They have not the freedom or opportunity, even when they have the enlightenment or they are afraid to abandon their myths, so they try to update them with "new wine in old wineskins."

Catholics brought guitars to Mass and demanded new hymns when the people wanted relief from divorce, anti-birth control, and sexual madness. The nuns fussed about religious habits and the priests talked about the married clergy in the future. Reform rabbis travel to Israel and demand that the Orthodox give them equal status. Liberal Protestants water down their doctrine in the hope that the partial freedom they offer will keep men going to church. But meanwhile, many leaders like Pope John Paul II seem to grow more intransigent than ever as if the mature and growing spiritual transition is an enemy. The World Council of Churches, despite its ethereal and meaningless discussions of poverty programs, continues to bicker about religious differences in a world that is rapidly abandoning dogma entirely. Liberal rabbis are afraid to pursue the course that their "reforms" should lead to: a faith beyond Judaism, beyond temples and traditions, to rest simply in man and his traditional celebrations stripped of all archaic and petty traditions. Christian leaders fear to take the step that will lead them from "faith" in the historic system called Christianity to a genuine and substantial faith in the human person proclaimed by Christ. The religions of the world are content to refurbish and modernize their myths. Or they reenact them under the guise of New Age Dogmas and guilt that only seem liberating for a time because they are new, but equally as accusatory and cruel. The form and structure is often the same in what can be an exciting period of transition.

Wings

I let you take my wings away
*   And chirped appropriately like a jungle bird encaged,*
Entertaining on command and singing sometimes sweetly
*   For my supper like a frightened nightingale,*
But serenading not half so well as when I soared
*   Freely in the trees, and loved you*
*   In the solitude and silence of my fondest flying.*
Why did you never understand?
*   There is no cage large enough*
*   No captor powerful enough*
*   No chain strong enough to hold me.*
I would die before I would finally surrender!
Even a bird cannot be possessed, and if freedom is his birthrite,
*   So much the more it is mine,*
And neither he nor I are swayed when even the mountains
*   Are content to be captive.*
We build our nest where we are,
*   Lost only without the sun and sudden rain,*
*   Desolate only without the moon, or the hissing*
*   of a wind rattling October leaves.*
We have known such joy all by ourselves
*   That no melody could contain our rejoicing.*
We can fly even without wings, sing even when strangled,
*   And outlive any zookeeper,*
Even those who were appointed to love us.

From Tears And Laughter Of A Man's Soul

One does not update a myth. One either lives with it and remains a religious child, or one abandons it and begins to be a man. But the traditional institutions will not abandon their myths, not because they are stubborn, as I once thought, but because institutions are only people, and millions of these people are afraid. The longtime refusal of Rome to admit the divorced and remarried to membership was not only the decision of the Vatican, but the terror of the very little man in the institution who feared that his life might have no meaning if Christianity were demythologized. So the priest clung to his celibacy, content to wonder about it; the virgin clung to her "purity," content to resent it; the faithful clung to their dogmas, content to profess "faith" in meaningless words. And when the Church does permit divorce, it now surrounds it in elaborate lies and new verbiage like "covenants" rather than binding "contracts", and annulment rather than divorce —so as to save face and keep its members children. The Church is not the militaristic structure I once imagined, but a congregation of often frightened men who fear that their house will come tumbling down and bury them if they trust men and women, tell the truth, and permit every sort of dissension which already exists anyway. No two people worship the same God. Why can't they simply inspire, and when they don't know, say so! Hence thousands find a home in *Science of Mind* or *Unity* congregations which offer freedom of belief, and are usually as effective and dependent on the charisma of their leader.

The priest is often afraid to look at his life and to admit that his service may have become largely pointless in the real lives of his flock. The rabbi is often afraid to take honest stock and to recognize that he has been promoting an archaic tradition which could have contemporary meaning. The minister is often afraid to reexamine the "salvation" that he has offered men and do a reformation that has some genuine meaning. The faithful are often afraid to reassess their lives and to admit that they have wasted their time in the pursuit of mythological gods. To escape the myth would mean to them that they had spent energy in vain. The Catholic would be embarrassed because he spent years defending the Church's position on birth control and sex, and perhaps even walked angrily out of social events or lectures when the Pope or the power of prayer was under fire. The Protestant would be chagrined because he has talked for years about the power of Jesus and the strength of Christian morality which seems no greater than that of the unbeliever. The Jew would be humiliated because he boasted for centuries about the cultural contributions that men made, not because they were men, but because they were Jews and "chosen". All of the sects would lose the security blanket that gave meaning to their lives, status to their persecutions, support to their personal emptiness, and to their egos.

Even men who stand on the fringe of the religious institutions, who have been hurt by it or who have been rejected by some official excommunication or spiritual death, are often afraid to let go of the myth. Lonely and discouraged priests, suffering people rejected by their family or parish, little people who have been made to feel that their lives are a failure, still ask that the Church approve them. The "little ones" want the Pope to change the laws, (hence the excitement about the marriage "annulment"), they want the priests to vindicate their wrongs, they want doctrines that hurt them to disappear.

Such a demand is only ignorance and fear. It is the Jews asking the Catholic Church to remove references to their people in the story of the Crucifixion. It is the Protestant asking the permission of the Catholic Church to marry a girl in his own church. It is the Catholic asking an official annulment to receive the sacraments after a divorce or remarriage. It is any man or woman asking for an endorsement outside of oneself, approval outside of their own hearts and minds. Such approval is vain and useless. First one must accept himself before he can belong to anything. Otherwise he is only living in a kind of dependency in which men and women lean on each other's loyalty to the system so they do not have to face their personal doubts and fears. Each priest or minister or rabbi who leaves his institution shocks its fearful members because he withdraws another voice from the mob, a voice that helped to make the mob sound mighty and fearless. Actually he just grew up and moved on.

Even the bold reformers; the laymen who walk out of Church, ignore an "excommunication," or reject an archaic code of sins; the few bold priests who challenge bishops and voice their protests before cheering liberals; the hierarchies that qualify papal statements and dilute papal authority by courageous and abandoned documents; the theologians who face heresy trials and resist censorship—all of these are often in a sense postponing their freedom and trying to repair a building that has been condemned. So are the reformed rabbis who confront the monolithic orthodox, so too the ministers who gild their decayed doctrines as if they deserved discussion and debate. They want the institution to agree with them, to tolerate their point of view, not realizing as clearly as do the frightened conservatives that the very essence of organized religion is under siege. A dozen Catholic Bishops could start a powerful church independent of Rome and its mythology, but in months there would likely be new divisions and authoritarian battles for power unless freedom of individual conscience were honored.

Perhaps it takes courage to challenge the Establishment, unquestionably it takes personal pain and long-endured outrage. Often the challenge is a respectable cloak under which the reformer can hide the depths of his total disillusionment with the Church. Protest can give meaning to membership in Church that has lost its true reason for existing. But when the protest is over, there is actually nothing left of significance in the cultural relic, the religious institution.

The free man does not look to the Church for approval, he does not look to anyone save to the honesty of his own heart. If he has the courage to pursue his personal integrity no matter what it costs, no matter where it leads, and no longer to demand that the institution give him dignity before God and status among men, he will know the loneliness and joy of beginning freedom. He will have divested himself of the intellectual and emotional confinement of the religious myth even if he continues to enjoy attending the religious services and community support, while accepting what makes sense and gives strength and love as thousands do without anyone's permission.

Many priests and ministers cling to their churches because they need a job. I can understand them. I left with $500 and a Volkswagen. It is hard to reenter the world when your training is in theology, when your advanced study is of no value in the workaday world. It is especially hard for a minister or rabbi who has children to support. It is hard for any man who has struggled for years to gain some prominence and prestige, to get a job that marks him as successful and hard-working. For such a man to fear unemployment and loss of retirement is understandable. I am not even saddened when such a man hides his real reasons for remaining in the religious institution and makes himself sound noble, because he is. Many priests cling to the religious institution because they fear their families as I did; many people cling because they are afraid to disappoint their parents or a spouse. I can easily understand them, but I am saddened if they rationalize their stand, even as I respect their right to do so. It is not easy to start over, nor to pursue the power of one's dignity as a free man—no matter how noble it sounds.

Many priests say that they remain within the organization to "reform" it, and often I believe them. Perhaps they are right if that is their honest choice. Many times I have considered that option for the sake of the people. Many say that a man who leaves the religious organization can no longer help it. He has lost his effectiveness. No one loses effectiveness if he or she follows an inner light. I mistrust such heroic reforms, whether they move a man to leave or to stay within the institution. I did not leave because I sought to "reform" the Church, or to be an "example" to anyone. I left because I could not then be a part of what I saw as a dishonest organization. I respect, but sometimes question the man who says he remains within to assist the Church in its renewal, or to serve the helpless men and women who have no place else to go. I wonder perhaps, if men and women really need his help, and if maybe that is the final illusion. They have the spirit of God within. They only need honesty. They will survive without self-designated heroes who sacrifice integrity to assist them. There are thousands of married couples who have raised their families and would make ideal priests and bishops. The necessary training could be done in a couple of funyears.

Nor does a man lose his "effectiveness" if he leaves the religious institution out of honest conviction. A man or woman has no genuine effectiveness short of personal integrity. I believe the Catholic Church is an institution still trapped in the eras and chains of history, even though I attend from time to time to celebrate my own culture and history without the hangups. It often still has the feeling of "home" for those of us who have abandoned its myths. I also believe it can still cripple many and enslave them; I believe it still substitutes myths for reality and prevents many from reaching maturity and personal responsibility. I could not be a part of it in any orthodox and traditional sense. It is still doing harm to many, it creates bigotry and divisions among people, it prevents them from being brothers, it claims to be divine and infallible, it claims to be uniquely in possession of truth and "salvation." It is true that more and more people can take what helps them in the Church, and ignore what they see as false. This is assuredly an acceptable option. But is does not exempt the institution itself from honest reform which these very selective members are in reality demanding.

I cannot be a sincere part of any church when they are reflections of past mythologies that substitute fiction for truth; or even new ones that are only more subtle and dangerous in their certainties. I do not believe that God made any special revelation to the Jews, nor that Judaism is any more than a powerful historical development. I do not believe that it teaches anything of consequence that is not known to the rest of the world, even though I well understand my Jewish friends who celebrate its historic feasts with dignity and joy. But there is nothing truly religious or spiritual we do not share. I believe that its orthodox insistence on remaining a sect apart can only create new divisions and continued hostilities in the world. I cannot be proud that Freud or Einstein or dozens of great philosophers happened to be Jewish. I can only be proud that they were men.

Nor do most of the Christian sects attract me. They are only variations of the same theme: man's helplessness in the world. They only force him to look for strength outside himself; they only make permanent the boundaries that divide man from man. They are refinements of a more primitive mythology; they are palliatives that prevent man from facing up to life. I find it hard to be called a "Christian" (whatever that means) when it might separate me from my brothers who are not of my faith. Nor would I comfortably be called a Jew in any religious sense, since it would segregate me from the rest of the world. I will be called nothing but a man, and that cuts me off from no one of any color, creed, sex, or position. Why are they a "Church" at all? What do they ultimately agree on except their humanity and their attempt at honesty?

"Church" can be is a loaded word, when all it means in Greek is a "gathering". There is no real evidence Jesus ever wanted a traditional church. *"When two or three are gathered together in my name, there am I in the midst of them."* Why must churches be affiliated with the past? How do they differ from any group of men and women who, regardless of their background or their traditional faith, sit down together and try to be friends in a spiritual climate. Why must we put our spiritual relationship in some archaic framework; why must we reduce the magic of personal contact to a self-conscious formula? Why must we adhere to the ancient Christian forms or new ones rather than simply be together as men and women looking for new and honest ways to assess and transform our values, and seek personal peace and spiritual growth? Why is prayer more than a simple, honest chat with God—

even an angry one when we feel it? Or one of joy, gratitude, or a petition for help in real word and sentiments?

I Don't Pray So Very Well

I don't pray so very well
*   With all the levels of divine contact newly devised*
And all the assorted certainties of those who know
*   Far more about God than perhaps He does Himself.*
I'm still in the back pew with the publican,
Struggling to believe, pushing through today's pain,
*   And worried about what's in store for tomorrow.*
I hang on to simple things like a Father Who never
*   Gives a stone when I ask Him for bread.*

Some of the greatest gifts I received were when I never asked at all,
When a loving, unseen hand took me safely along
*   Some precipices I'd not like to walk again.*
God is still a mystery to me and my faith is probably
*   As weak as any man's alive.*
But I never quit believing in love and joy and serenity,
Knowing that somehow I am a favored son
*   Whether I deserve it or not.*
Our relationship keeps getting simpler:
*   I picture the kind of man I really want to be,*
*   And in bits and pieces He gives me the help to be it.*

From Tears And Laughter Of A Man's Soul

If man needs spiritual "community," as most of us do, we will find it when we need it. We will find it in a few friends, in a good marriage, in an intellectual, spiritual, or a social interest, in a neighborhood that has learned to care or in a church that loves and trusts. We will not have to create it in some obsolete liturgy or in some semi-ritualistic program unless it is truly our choice. Ritual itself, when bereft of guilt and historic chains, often is most appealing and helpful to me and many others. The man of the global village, with or without ritual as he chooses, will learn to be a brother without the obstacles of past, outmoded religious frameworks. He will not have to know whether a man is Jewish, Christian, Catholic, Protestant or New Age before he knows how to deal with him. He will know that he is human and that will be enough in a genuine community.

Sometimes I even balk at the word "community," not only the religious communities that I inherited or the "experimental" communities that propose to take their place, but the political and social communities as well. The very word almost contains within itself a contradiction that modern man detects. "Community," the Greek koinonia, the Latin communitas, centers in what man has in common. The Christian had his koinonia with other Christians, the Jew with Jews, the WASP with WASPs, the American with other Americans, and, of course, the white with whites. But the very sharing, the very "community" was at most, an official act of segregation by its laws and dogmas, and therein lies the contradiction. Man does not need false communities any longer. They assert that he can only share his humanity with a few, with those of similar faith or background, education or temperament, when in reality he is increasingly one with the world. He is not alien to any man; he can find his "community" wherever he is. Racial and religious differences still exist, as do national ones, but they will have no substantial meaning in the future.

Political parties, for example,are obsolete communities. There are "hawks" and "doves," "conservatives" and "liberals" within each political camp. It well may make a difference which man is elected, though not to me, and certainly not which party. Political parties are relics of "communities" which had a meaning in a world and in a time other than our own and are particularly inane in our society except to provide two candidates from which to choose. When Ross Perot challenged President Bush, he did not really challenge the party. He merely reflected the party's disintegration. "Religious" devotion to a political party is dying with religious institutions.

And the struggle of the Black is a dramatic symbol of the destruction of past notions of "community." The Black knows that he has not been equal, that he is still not free. He also knows that freedom is his right, and he is ready to dispel the myth of the white "community." However, he can never again rest until he is not a Black but a man or woman. The Black Power advocates attempt to repeat the errors of past "communities." They tell the Black that he is an Afro-American, who should be proud that he is black, that he does not need the whites. But that only produces, self-consciously, another division, and perhaps necessary for a time. They cannot dismiss the white man or ignore his help, not because he is white, not because he is in power, but because he too is a man. Maybe the Afro-American is like the Irish-American phase of my ancestors, but I am not proud that I am white; I never think about it. Nor will the Black of the new world ultimately be proud that he is black. He will not think about it once he is free from the bitterness that white men in America created by enslaving him, no matter how long it takes. Ultimately, there is no room for a white "community" or a black "community" in the global village. The Black and Brown, Red and White and Yellow can be proud together that we are men and women in the "Rainbow Coalition." It has to be! And it will be!

Liberated men and women will learn to find "community" wherever they are because they know that they have something in "common" with every other man. I fondly remember the old Chinese "communist" seamstress in Beijing who sewed two buttons, refused my money, and kissed me on the cheek. Somehow, for me, that said it all.

The New Churches will not really reform the traditional religious institution. Nothing will. The mythological religious institution is destined to die bravely. It has lived its life and done its temporary work for good or ill. The new churches will not replace it or renew it. It is not doctrine that has held the ancient Church together, not law or faith, but the fear of men and women, lay and clerical, to trust themselves.

This is not to say that New Age and updated churches" are

not necessary. This is only to say that many of them are a kind of "halfway house" for those not yet ready to trust the God Within. I try them all at times. They might well be the good and essential communities that can help incipient rebels to outgrow the traditional Church and enter the world. But when they are all finished with their "reforms," they will have abandoned the authoritarian Church. There will no longer be "New Age" churches at all; they will simply be an honest gathering of men and women who recognize they have more in common as people than they have as Christians or Jews. And all of us will feel welcome in any honest setting that suits our taste, and does not propose to dominate or contradict our Inner Spirit of God. They might not talk of Church or even, perhaps, of community, but of people. They may not talk of any law except love for one another and honest concern. They might not talk at all; they might prefer to do something for their families and their country, for their poor, their sick, and their war-torn. Then they will have escaped the myth.

They will discover that the world already knows and approves the important values that Christians and Jews have set themselves apart as specialists to teach. The lasting truths that the prophets spoke are already heard in bars and in supermarkets and are read on "subway walls." The essential truth that Jesus taught is already known to children and their parents; it is already shouted from the housetops by men who never studied Christ. What separated Jew from Christian, Catholic from Protestant, is only what separates Russian from American, German from Frenchman, black from white, and white from black, man from woman, straight from gay: prejudice, pettiness, greed, fear, lack of communication, ignorance, pride, painful memories. It is not dogma, not Jesus, not morality, not faith. Thus the religious institution, as a religious institution, has outlived its usefulness. Only men and women can help us now to transform religions into real love.

Jesus has been demeaned and institutionalized long enough. Now he is ready to be what he really was—an inspiration and ideal for all men that choose him. His service is no longer uniquely the boon of Christians. The Jews speak of love as well as he does, and they practice it equally as well as those named "Christians." So do the Oriental sects, so do men and women who have never known the religious institution. Jesus is humble enough to stand in the background and let others do what he himself proposed to do. He is not looking for a credit line. He is honest enough to cease being a Saviour, and institution, a myth. It is the institution itself and its frightened or angry members who are afraid to abandon the past and escape the myth. Jesus was willing to admit that we might do "greater things" than he did.

For this reason I have no great interest in ecumenism. It is merely an exchange of myths, a swapping and a watering-down of superstitions that should be abandoned. Thus I am not interested in the Pope's meeting with the Archbishop of Canterbury or with the Orthodox Patriarch except as a news item. The doctrinal discussions of these men are well-meaning anachronisms in the global village. These leaders cannot speak for men and women as monarchs and dictators could in the past. If after centuries of living together, after centuries of suffering and war, bitterness and hatred, all they can do is talk and gently qualify their myths, then I am not interested. Who cares about virgin births or valid orders or saints and sins except frightened children? Who cares if Mary was a virgin or if she had ten more children? Who cares if Jesus physically rose from the dead as long as he has conquered death and inspired love and forgiveness. Who cares if Jesus gave his Apostles keys or walking sticks? Who cares if he did or didn't walk on water, or called bread and wine his own body and blood? I don't. I care about wounded and yearning men and women and peace and joy! I care about our helping others not "saving" them. I care about us feeding the hungry and to the extent we can providing the poor with jobs and helping the lonely to find meaning in life. And I care about ending war, not about redeeming souls. I care about becoming the man God had in mind at my "selective" creation. I care about becoming a loving and compassionate and honest man who lives in peace and joy.

I will not waste my time with ecumenical discussions on the nature of religious differences. I will not carry signs for or against abortion, nor try to convince anyone of anything. The Inner Spirit will guide me and everyone else in such matters. Such differences are merely historical relics. By the time the religions of the world agree on their various doctrines, men and women will not care about such things. They will live with reality and uncertainty, to do the best they can and take life as it comes, without the support of the religious myths. They will have found Jesus or Buddha, and the One God Beyond All Myth within themselves.

But realistically the religious institutions will not soon change significantly; they are hesitant to do anything but rearrange their myths. And the power focus of the institutions will not easily change. Most do not have the right structure for change. How do you fire a Pope or file a Referendum after a council, or oust a Bishop? Rome and one of its cardinals will quarrel about the behavior of nuns or Mexican Priests, while in Southeast Asia or Somalia the children search in rubble for their homes. Fundamentalists leaders will quarrel about the virgin birth while the poor of the world are ignored by its members. Churches will build new buildings while Black babies are bitten by rats. The churches will continue to baptize and circumcise and wonder why there are fewer and fewer people in attendance at their services. In some way, this is a tragedy, because religious institutions could be of great service to men if they could abandon their myths and forget their histories and change their sole focus and image.

Instead, they will lose more of their leaders, and more and more of their members. Eventually the traditional faiths will largely cease to be, and millions are committed to assist in their demise. Religious institutions stand in man's way, they are dishonest, they cling to myths that are not true. They are not harmless like a social club. They are dangerous like a propaganda machine. They have weakened man, delayed his

212

growth, severed him from his brother. They have built walls between men and called them "revealed" truths; they have taught distrust and self-righteousness and called it morality, they are responsible for most of a world's wars, if only by docility and silence. They have taught that men are evil, or that they are better than other men, that "salvation" comes from forces outside of man's concern for his fellowmen. Even the splintered New Age groups will continue to splinter and succeed to attract only if they have a "charismatic" leader who could be as dangerous as a Pope in delaying spiritual maturity.

Of God And Promises
Charlie Jordan started a new church,
And promised the believers a Mercedes,
A villa in Spain, and an Hawaiian vacation.
Attendance was up sixty-four percent a month
After twelve weeks of preaching personal fulfullment.
The median income of his flock is $67,000.00

Sid Gilbert's church leans towards Jaguars
If appropriate affirmations
Immediately follow acute visualizations.
After three months Sid had 946 followers
With an increase of four percent a month.
The median income of his flock is $84,000.00.

My church is into bicycles, canoes, and long walks.
The median income in not at all impressive.
We do not visualize, affirm, or know what we believe.
We pray, laugh a lot, and have potlucks once a week.
Membership, besides me, Slats O'Meara, and Johnnycake Jones,
Consists of two blind lepers and twelve fishermen.

From Tears and Laughter Of A Man's Soul

The religions have had their chance to turn the words of Jesus and the prophets into reality. But they have only taught the German to hate the Jew, the Jew to hate the Arab, the American to hate the Communist, the Protestant to distrust the Catholic, the Catholic to stand apart from the rest of men. They have prayed for the world while distrusting its science, criticizing its progress, calling it "immoral," questioning its sincerity, mocking its commitment. They have called its men and women ruthless and faithless, greedy and proud, ambitious and contemptuous and immoral. How history has changed the Church is beyond all reckoning. It is interesting to peruse early writings.

One of the earliest Church documents, written long before John's gospel, the Didache, tells of the election of the bishops by the people. And the primitive Church said the mark of a man elected bishop was one who would give his life for his flock. The bishop was in charge of his Church before papal centralization began under Constantine and Charlemagne, and papal power was glorified at the Vatican Council in 1870 proclaiming infallibility. Now an episcopal appointment is much like one to the Supreme Court (without veto power). John Paul II, for example, has surrounded himself with bishops and cardinals that reflect his own rigid and conservative stance, totally unlike that of Pope John XXIII— though both shared the same office and projected through it what life had taught them about people. American bishops, in particular, have been for the most part, docile administrators, not adventurous and creative pastors.

Under Pope John Paul II, the great majority of appointments to important positions at the Vatican and throughout the world are arch-conservatives who now control the Church. Why? Perhaps because John Paul's whole life perspective was the Polish war against communism that determined his life's focus. There are a few notable exceptions who represent the finest in episcopal stature, but I'll wager they will not stray far from home under John Paul II. This only points out the political activity and a kind of "nepotism" in the Church as in

214

any human institution. I truly accept this without rancor or cynicism. It's the wisdom of the Guiding Spirit that helps wake up individuals to take moral responsibility, and not look for authority figures to grant them rights they already have - like annulments and sexual freedom. The more rigid the leadership, the sooner the people become free. It's called revolution, or better yet, simple maturation, and the modern Catholic has no choice but to grow. Perhaps in the long run, Pope John Paul II can be more effective than the mature Pope John XXIII who was grounded in an historical awareness and much loved. Each projected his own "personal papacy"— equally human for God's own purposes.

With all the cheap and scurrilous scandal surrounding the death of the late Cardinal Cody of Chicago, the wonderful book that he authorized to be assembled by Agnes Cunningham, *The Bishop In The Church*, should be required reading by every bishop in the world. Then they might realize the elected authority they have from the very earliest Church to shepherd their dioceses without Rome's permission. St. Jerome had it right in the 4th century: *"Not all bishops are bishops... Ecclesiastical rank does not make a Christian!"* Or as St. Ambrose, the 4th century Bishop of Milan put it so well: *"There is nothing so fraught with danger before God, so base before men, as for a bishop not to declare freely what he thinks! Who will dare tell you the truth if the bishop does not?"*

The men and women of the global village will pursue the truth themselves. They have no regard for sects or nationalities, no time for boundaries or divisions. They have no faith in the artificial communities that join people together to separate them from other artificial communities. They are not strangers to any man or woman, black or white, American or Russian, Jew or gentile. They are less and less afraid to abandon the religious institution and its mythology for the God within. In fact they have already begun to lay it aside. They cannot respect a synagogue that makes them feel like strangers because they are not Jewish, a Church that has little to say to them because they are not Catholic or Protestant.

They will not wave flags or salute crosses or honor religious stars. They will only strive to know their brother, to be one with him as they are silently guided from within as the primary "authority".

Meanwhile the religious institutions will proved a comfortable home for the men and women who find contentment and solace there and who still want the myths to give substance to their lives, who need its framework to provide them with support. But the man of the global village will reach these people soon, or reach their sons and daughters, and help them to realize that man is strong enough to live with himself and his God. Then men will leave the religions, as they are leaving them now, and find themselves as men with other men and women in whatever spiritual setting they choose.

God is not in the religious institution. He is in the men and women who believe in other men and women. My friend Gene is Jewish. He abandoned the synagogue about two days after his Bar Mitzvah. He has no feelings about sin or an afterlife. He never prays in the synagogue, but enjoys the Jewish memorial and feast days. The world of institutional religion is no more real to him than the struggle of Atlas to uphold the world. But he cares about the poor, the ignorant, the helpless, his own growth and personal peace. Whenever I talk to him he has taken another family under his wing, helped a man to find a job, found a school for a retarded child, or just enjoyed the simple pleasures of the day. He is not Jewish to me, nor am I Catholic or Christian or a "former priest" to him. We are just men, friends, brothers, fellow members of the global village. He would rather give one family hope or spend an evening in chatter and laughter than update a hundred liturgies. So would I. He would rather get one man a job or teach his wife to read, than "save" a thousand souls. So would I.

Now I am gradually living without the stubborn religious myths to which I once gave total allegiance. I can ignore the Church or attend when I choose, and I often flounder and frequently hurt deeply on my own. But my God is forever available wherever I am. And I flounder with a freedom that makes the struggle usually worthwhile. I can see life and death in a dimension that makes me feel a part of the world and a Son of God.

Not long ago a close friend of mine died. He was only fifty-seven. I went to see his body and hear the Rosary recited by his friends. I found it strange to believe that years ago I would have led the Rosary and would have asked God to grant my friend eternal rest. I would have said Mass for him and blessed his body with the traditional holy water and incense, which I grant can have real meaning when stripped of its mythology. I would have prayed that he might not have to spend a long time in purgatory. I would have offered his widow the comfort that he would live in peace with God.

But now I could only think of the last time we talked. I could only be sad and wonder where he was. I could not then say the Rosary, but I assuredly did not mock it because it was not presently of help to me. It was uncomfortable to attend the funeral and hear myths that offended me and my friend. I could not tell the family anything except that I was sad and that I would always love him. I had nothing to lean on except my grief and my personal faith, nothing to save me from the reality that I, too, must die. So I lived with my grief, my uncertainty, my fear, and somehow I knew a little more clearly that life must mean something at the present moment. And in the midst of my sadness I felt a kind of strength that my past idolatry had never provided. I was glad that I did not have a prayer-book full of answers, that I could only be sad, and thank God for a great friend who shared the planet with me—and whom I believed would live joyfully forever.

And as I looked around and saw the sincerity of the loving people saying the rosary for my friend, I knew that the myth would not die easily, nor did it have to. It was their present choice, and to millions it gives comfort, as it daily did my mother till the end. It is not for me righteously to demand that they live or think, grow or wonder or hurt and hope as I do. To me the sound of the beads was the gentle death rattle of the ancient and archaic institution which surely will outlive me even as it changes dramatically. I was only glad that I had escaped from the myth. I was glad that I could only look at the body of my friend and know that I had loved him, glad that I had nothing to give but my friendship and my sadness, and eternal hope, glad that in our growing freedom, union, and demythologizing is the Birth of God beyond all myth forever. And I know that at some point in my life if I choose to say the rosary, I still can.

To transform a world means to live another way. It means to invade cultural institutions that have destroyed or weakened our values, to challenge our own greed, our fear of the future, our need to control every aspect of our lives, our attitudes towards others of any race or creed, to respect child and adult and the elderly as sacred individuals, not measured by their power but by their being. Most of all, it means to trust that all is well, that we are the beloved of God, and that the Father Who knows what we need even before we ask has not conditioned his good gifts on our asking or even on our believing.

It is not to be overwhelmed by Somalia or Sarajevo, to delight in Russia's seeming demise, to be terrified by recession, to be in competition with Japan or Germany, to believe that congress or an ineffective president can in any way interfere with our peace and joy. There is a Power that guides not only the world but each person and particle of it. When I know that, I know all there is to know.

There are times when we cannot believe, when we can just barely hang on, times when the very thought of prayer can make us rebellious and resentful. So many good things have been given me when I never asked for them, I know that prayer and ritual, creed and Church can easily be another way to attempt to control God as our self contained benefactor and universal credit card.

I do not think my moral and spiritual values came from any Church. Somehow they came from within me and from the few people that loved me just the way I am. Just as my love of America has little or nothing to do with its government, my love of God and man has little or nothing to do with any Church or religious assemblage. I can go or not go, even as I can attend a movie, hear a symphony, gaze at a mountain or walk along the ocean's shore.

I liked most of the people in the Church, loved hundreds if not thousands of them, but the institutions themselves, of any variety, have been locked in the past and trapped in the bias and bruises of history. Now I judge a church the same way I do a book or a lecture. Nothing more. God is not contained in a Temple, millions have known this for years. Though Jesus made it most clear, it took me awhile to learn it, but that too was all part of the plan. Had I not been the victim of dogma and harsh legalities, I could not write of the death of destructive mythology and the glorious Birth of God that will rise from the ashes of spiritual museums and lead man deeper within himself where he is united with all of life and the God Who Lives.

Finally

Finally I want so little of life,
Merely to let me run free,
To greet each day with some excitement and
    new found hope.
I ask not fame or fortune, but some quiet tranquility
    that lives within me at all times,
And does not fear loss or storm, life or death, or
    whatever is mine to confront.
I cannot recall the past or remake it, I cannot live with
    regrets of what I have or have not done.
I can only hold on to a Father's hand knowing
    His strength is mine.
Life is this moment, the lady walking the dogs, cars
    parked by the side of the road,
Lovers holding hands briefly in the morning chill.

Fear is a strange and persistent enemy—I find it hard
    to fight him directly lest he overwhelm me.
I let him pass through my being and know that he
    has no more currency
Than strange sounds I heard in the basement as a child.
I've learned too much from fear to hide it under a bushel.
I've traveled too many roads finally to turn back,
    loved too much to be denied.
I no longer want the whole world, just my own gentle
    place of service and love,
And the courage and strength from God to do today
    and tomorrow whatever I was forever meant to do.

From Quiet Water

Chapter 10

The Birth of A Personal God

$\mathcal{T}$here are moments when I find it hard to be concerned about war or the trials of the Blacks, or the effects of drugs on the young. There are moments when I am scarcely concerned about Russia, Africa, or the struggles of India and Eastern Europe, or even the war against poverty. I do not like these moments; I merely acknowledge their existence. When they occur, I seldom read the paper or recognize another man's problem. I must retreat within myself and escape from even my closest friend. I hardly care about the starving children, the horror of life in the inner city, the scars of napalm, or the rising crime rate in our streets. All of my attention and energy is focused on me. I cannot get away from myself.

At times like these I am aware of how fiercely I want to live. I am fighting for my own existence. Sometimes these moments occur when I am struggling with work or a relationship, when I am forced to wonder if life is anything but a complicated game. Or they happen when I am worried about my health, when I feel incapable of writing, when words seem inadequate, or money pressures prominent. At such moments I find it hard to sleep, and when I doze off my imagination is sometimes filled with disconnected pictures that frighten me. I am forced to wonder if I have been honest with others, if I am capable of having a friend, if I am destined to be lonely and distressed.

In moments like this, it would do no good to tell me to help the poor, to urge me to realize how much better off I am than the man who is dying of cancer, than the boy who lies bleeding on a battlefield, starving in a dessert, or dying of AIDS. A weariness comes over me, or a fear, or an impulsive urge to run away and be by myself. At a moment like this no one seems to help; I can find no comfort in my work, and I can find no inner reserve of confidence. I am brought face to face with the feebleness of my own existence. Prayer does not help me, nor entertainment, even alcohol would not let me escape.

I think I would have felt this way if I were a Vietnamese husband and my wife and children were murdered by mortar shells. I would not have cared about the war in Vietnam or the free world's struggle with the Communists. I would only care about my family and I would wonder if life had any further meaning. I think I would feel this way if I were a black in a rat-infested tenement. I would not care about the race problem; I would only want food and shelter and protection for my children. I would feel this way if my wife or lover had left me, or if I could not hold a job. I might feel this way if I were told that I only had a few weeks to live.

I would feel what I sometimes feel even now—and almost without reason—that I am all alone. I recognize that ultimately I am an individual, and I must bear the burden of being one. I cannot lean really on anyone else. This is not to say that I cannot love, that I cannot trust, that I cannot reach out. It is only to say that at times I am thrust back upon my own aloneness, and I cannot appreciate my union with the world or God. It is not that there is no one to reach out to me, it is, rather, that I do not want nor choose to be reached.

Once I dreaded such moments and poured out my heart in prayer. I fell on my knees or face as an adolescent and adult and begged God for hours for deliverance. I joined with Christ in his agony, with the tragic figures of history in a kind of personal anguish. Now I do not pray as often or beg for deliverance. I try as best I can to accept such moments as enriching and strengthening, as a kind of personal surgery in which my own identity is excised from the accumulated artifice of all my illusions about life: success, notoriety, wealth, sex, or perfection. I am certain that I do not suffer as much as many men and women, but when I suffer, it seems to be as much pain as I can bear. I know that I have not been tested ultimately, but it feels like I have, that perhaps some greater trial lies ahead, that even now, someone is suffering an agony that would tear out my heart. But it is at this moment of personal pain, this time of existential anguish, that I am confronted with my own crisis of faith. It is not a crisis that asks me to embrace doctrine or moral teachings. It is far deeper than such facile superficialities. It is the crisis that confronts me with my own aloneness and asks if life has any meaning, if all of existence is not a cruel kind of survival. Maybe you have never experienced it, and if so, I hope you never have to.

I would like to be able to say that it takes a real tragedy to expose this weak and wounded side of myself, that it appears only at rare and important intervals. But this is not true. Usually I can survive my share of real tragedy with comparative ease, but a mere trifle in any objective sense can tear at my being. A difficulty at work, a conflict with a friend, a financial burden I did not anticipate, a gloomy day can sometimes trigger a disproportionate anguish. My whole being is rocked, and I often have little capacity to care for anyone except myself. I am obliged to face myself in my human loneliness.

A psychologist might attribute intelligent interpretations to my moods, but I really doubt I would find his remarks helpful at such times. A religious counselor might offer me reflections on the meaning of life from his well-worn mythology, but he would not hold my interest. An acquaintance might recommend a vacation or a calculated distraction, but I would reject his offer. I consider such painful moments as special times of spiritual growth when gradually I have almost learned to trust God, endure, and know that I am being led to my own place of inner peace. I do not want to dismiss them, to run from them, to interpret them away, to dilute them by some well-meant cliche, and certainly not to create or prolong them. I want to live with them, only when I must, to learn through them, to face the fact of my own individuality and accept it as lovingly as I can.

I refuse to force myself out of this mood as long as it

offers greater self knowledge, although I often feel obliged to hide it and to pretend that it does not exist. I cannot predict its coming or going, its duration or violence. I only know that when it comes and while it stays I am confronted with the meaning of life. It can come when life is seemingly careless and trouble-free. It can come not merely when I am a failure, but even when I feel the flush of success. It only began to come with any degree of intensity when I abandoned the mythology of my Church, when I refused to live with religious placebos and palliatives, when three of my brothers died of cancer and my writings were scarcely valued, when I had no adequate addiction to relieve the pain. I even resisted the God within or any spiritual support for which I was not ready.

Undoubtedly in former years I crowded it out, or I would not let it come to the surface amid the pressure of hard work and pressing responsibilities. More than likely I simply called it a "cross" and refused to look at it. I did not have to face this mood; I only had to be rid of it. So I lost it amid my academic dogmas and my structured rituals, or I dissolved it in the religious fantasies I had learned in childhood. Or I worked 18 hours a day, demanded attention, fought for recognition, and floated on stardom. Now I more often face the painful crisis and ponder seriously the countenance of my life.

And when it comes, I usually sit alone in the woods or mountains, most often in my favorite chair, or stare at the eternal ocean. I do not reflect upon the meaning of my own existence. I do not anticipate a future happiness; I do not predict a life full of emotional enrichment and success. I just permit my own manhood to come to the surface of my consciousness and converse wordlessly with God or Jesus or Mary. I am absorbed with myself. I resist the compulsion to do something or am totally immobilized. I also resist the inclination, nurtured in the religious retreats of my past, to figure something out. I just let my own loneliness happen. And somehow I am more and more in touch with the God within Who is the source of all my strength—far beyond success or psychology.

Fear Stands Like A Dark Forest

Fear stands like a dark forest without a path to freedom,
*   As I wander helplessly amid its foreboding presence.*
Fear emerges like a dark, cold mountain, snow capped
*   and formidable,*
*   As I stare hopelessly at its massive resistance.*
Fear explodes like a roaring river, swollen and ripping at its banks,
*   As I glance timidly at its unmeasured power.*
Fear screams like all the assembled, fiery demons of the earth's core,
*   As I look in terror at its devouring appetite.*

Only courage remains, the least spark of David
*   Versus a giant Goliath,*
But as courage holds its ground
*   —quietly, patiently, relentlessly,*
*   the trees slowly stand aside in the forest,*
*   the mountain silently bows its head,*
*   the river speaks more softly.*
*   the demons pause to listen,*
And the fortitude of a feeble man, frightened, but determined,
Makes his way to peace and serenity and a quiet victory
*   Over the most brutal and overwhelming fear.*

From Loneliness To Love

I do not now speak of the God of religious tradition or the bearded Jew or Michelangelo who may, like me, have considered God for decades, or some living Trinity that religious writers describe. I cannot reduce my God to personal dimensions, nor do I want to. I cannot contain Him in any kind of an image as I can my brother and model, Jesus. Perhaps God is the Life-force of the world, the Unity of all creation, the pervading Spirit of all existence. But, to me, these are just words; finally somehow, He is not the bearded inquisitor. I can only sometimes grasp my God as a kind of meaning in my life, an Inner Guide, a silent voice, a gentle stirring, most of all an abiding presence. He, and I hesitate to call Him "He" or "She," which only compounds my confusion, lives at the root of my own loneliness and somehow makes my life intelligible, my peace grow, and my joy come alive. I am a part of something important; I am of consequence, because God is. I am one with the world, a part of life, capable of knowledge and love and pain because God is. I am here because He wants me here, and I will do a work however minute that no other can do. No greater or less than the work of the most obscure peasant, but the work that I love and was designed to perform even if it takes decades to discover it.

When men or women ask me about Him, I am often at a loss for words. I sometimes hesitate to speak of Him lest I lose Him in syllables and weak symbols. When religious sects try to corner Him or to reduce Him to their human categories, I know they are telling me more about themselves and their needs than about my God. My God understands all, forgives all, loves me with an unconditional love, and asks universal forgiveness of me. He does not have to save me because there is nothing to save me from except my separation from His presence. He does not redeem me because I am not up for redemption. He loves me and somehow I love Him. He is my life shorn of superficiality and phoniness, of synthetic dreams and vain illusions. He is at the center of my being, at the core of my aloneness, at the root of my genuine existence, and if I trust His Inner Voice He leads me to simplicity, generosity, joy, forgiveness, and peace.

He does not really need credit or gratitude, though I give it gratefully. He does not demand a "thank you" or a meditation on His goodness when I am happily myself. I have already found Him at such times. I do not usually think about God when I am playing golf or diving in the ocean, when I am laughing with a friend, enjoying a meal or walking joyously on the beach. I think of life and love, and I treasure the moment that makes me content. At times I briefly turn to

God and thank Him for my happiness, pause and share with Him my joy, but I am already in touch with God because I am in touch with the peace and joy He embodies. It would, at those times be self-conscious to turn aside and to separate myself from God, to sever my implicit contact, to lose my spontaneous absorption in reality with an artificial contact or a guilty obligation to be forever grateful. The essence of gratitude is to be who I really am—God's own Son or Daughter, a unique creation—not chained to my own ego or in competition with the world.

My God does not guiltily demand an expression of sorrow when I have failed a love or unwittingly hurt my friend, nor does He want a litany of repentance when I am faced with my own human weakness. My God wants me to live, to find meaning, to make each day matter, to struggle against the emptiness and boredom, the frustration and self-pity that can suck out all of my life. Most of all He wants me to forgive everyone that I might finally forgive myself. I do not have to worship God; I only have to find purpose in my daily existence, even if that purpose is just to be. My God asks nothing of me beyond my true self because He loves me, and He permits me to know that I count. Nor does His love depend on what I do or don't do, say or don't say! He does not invade my existence to remind me of my responsibilities; my own conscience, experience, and growth can do that. He does not demand that I change before He offers me His love. This would be a selfish and manipulating God formed by men. It is His very love and strength and inner vision that allows me to change. He does not demand my homage, like an ancient Monarch who was projected on our ignorance by history. This would be an egotistical and controlling God created by men who want to rule in His place. He does not demand that I always believe in Him, that I totally trust Him at all times. This would be an insensitive and frightened God fashioned by ancient and New Age "theologians" who have no confidence in themselves, who create new guilts by my failure to control all of my thoughts. Even sickness, in such destructive teaching, is always my own fault. This God is too perfect and inhuman, too fierce and angry for me. My God is, and He lets me be, and in such a relationship there is the essence of love and the fullness of faith that grows at its own pace with His grace and strength.

It is not difficult for me to play a kind of game and to reduce God to the pictures I inherited in my religious tradition, or the more contemporary laws of mind control, seminars, and more guide books. I can rehearse the deep-rooted suggestions of my religious training and call God "omnipotent" or "everlasting" or "omniscient." But when I have such words, I have said nothing. I can speak learnedly and theologically of the relationship between members of the Trinity, the prerogatives of Father, Son, and Holy Spirit; I can speculate about the power and influence of God upon the earth. But when I have finished with my verbalizing, I have achieved nothing of value for my own journey. I can turn my God into freedom from personal responsibility. I can ask Him to do all things that I must do myself; I can make of Him an all-powerful leprechaun or an avenging angel. I can reduce Him to the level of a seducible human friend; I can make of Him an extension of my own self contrived hopes or desires or resentments. I can transform Him into the essence of indulgent fatherhood or motherhood; I can depict Him as a kind of overseeing superman or intransigent judge. But my God is none of these. He is the intangible, elusive, fleeting meaning of my life, the powerful, loving, indefinable presence that is always there for me to become who I already internally and eternally am. And Jesus is always available, as human as I am, to lead me to the Father.

Increasingly, I do not ask my God for anything unless I feel great pain or fear as a helpless child. Usually I just talk to Him as I would to you, and know that He listens, and I try to trust where I am being led. Trust is the foundation of my incipient faith. I also go to the men and women who love me, and know increasingly, in some, tiny deep corner of my being that I now and always will have all I need. If, from habit, I ask Him for peace in the midst of my struggle, I am not really asking at all because He already knows. I am merely connecting with him and admitting that I need something beyond my present, feeble strength that He alone can give. I simply want to feel my permanent union with Him, and that requires practice. I do not expect Him to come rushing to my aid with some "supernatural" power, although many have told me how it happened to them, and assuredly I would not reject immediate relief. I really do not expect Him to come at all because He is already Within. But I want to be aware of His ongoing presence, to know that my life is in His hands. I may even say, as I sometimes do over and over, "God, help me" or "God, give me strength," but I am not really asking for a special kind of infusion of heavenly assistance, merely to reconnect once again. Then I am more ready to hurt, to feel pain, to see more clearly the artificial goals that I unwillingly and helplessly chose. I do not encourage suffering, but it usually tells me I'm relying on my own strength and moving in the wrong direction. Then I am ready to pursue more honestly the genuine meaning of life, to release the massive illusions that I have created to make myself "special", "unique", unlike the "publican".

Similarly, I can accept the stress that is a part of my existence, the medical help I need, the nurturing and friendship. My tension is a revelation to me. It is a protest from my body and it tells me about the struggle of my spirit. It tells me that I am trying to be something that I am not, that I am afraid to be honest. And that's OK and part of being human. I have somehow interrupted the flow of life; I have somehow, mysteriously and unaware, refused to face myself because it was not yet time, I was not ready, or the abundant teachers of my culture were exceedingly effective. I was still seeking that approval that I must first give myself, or I was attempting from past, necessary survival techniques to be other than I am destined to be. The survival techniques may once have kept me alive, but often I cling to them when the need is gone. I am no longer a helpless child, or an abused victim without recourse. My stress is a message from God. It is direct and unmistakable; it demands attention. I can ignore it, as I am often obliged to do, but ultimately I must face it and discover God in the growing serenity of my life. The necessary faith comes when it comes without force or struggle, without self-appointed gurus or gilded god's as part of an unconditional love. God can speak in thousands of ways—if I learn to listen and comprehend.

Some men tell me that without such tension they cannot work. I do not believe them. For me this pressure is an artificial impetus to accomplishment. It kills and compares and is addictively never satisfied. I believe it is an abuse of the marvelous being that man is. It reflects his confusion and artificial goals that will pass away. It is an infallible directive asking man to live his own life, to reflect upon it until he knows who he is and what he truly wants. It comes when he is afraid to tell people the truth, or when he is using them for personal gain. It comes when he is rushing to finish work that he could enjoy at another time. It comes when he permits himself to be in situations that he loathes, relationships that he could have avoided had he the courage to be honest, and in environments in which he is not yet able to be himself. It comes when he feels bound to do too much, to quiet his restlessness and self contempt with activity. My tension tells me that I have not yet arrived, that I am not yet enough. Always I must be more. That is not God's voice but ego and alien pressures. But all that matters is that I am doing the best I can to understand this quiet, unmistakable message that bids me to live in complete honesty to the extent I can, and to love who I am at this moment. Most of all, it asks me to forgive myself.

I Asked The River
I asked the river
Where he was going and how he would know
*   When he got there.*
He only laughed at me

Splashing across the rocks.

I asked the mountain
When he was high enough and how he would know
　　When he reached the heavens.
His echo only laughed
　　Like thunder in the valleys.

I asked the trees
How long they would live and how they would know
　　When they were a forest.
Their leaves only shook with mirth
　　In the joy of a sudden wind storm.

Finally I was silent,
As if there were no one else to please,
　　And I spent my time laughing
With the river, the mountain, and trees.

From Walk Easy On The Earth

　　And in those human struggles to let go, I find my God, even as I find Him in the moods that intensify my loneliness and force me back upon myself. I have learned at such times as these to go apart and to feel again my oneness with the world. I want my being to flow with the rhythm of the sea gull and the heaving ocean. I want my heart to join with the pulse of the wind and the motion of the trees. I want to know the serenity I feel when I swim in the ocean and spy upon the tiny schools of fish, the purple sea urchins, the lobsters under rocks, the lurking eels, and the multicolored starfish. And when I am apart, often I begin to know such serenity and rhythm; I am again in contact with my manhood, or if I am not, I must accept the help that is available and push on!

　　I could not continue to live without these reflective moments when I look at my life and evaluate my place in it with Jesus and the God within. As a child, I used to hit stones

231

with a small baseball bat by the hour. Later I realized I needed this solitude to be in touch with myself. And as a man, I need it still; unstructured time, priceless time, when I do not work or rush or converse, when I am alone with myself, when I realize that I am one being in touch with one world, one man in special contact with his God who has already given me all I need before I ask. Asking just makes me feel better, like the widow in Jesus' story who kept harassing the judge until her request was granted. I am whoever I am at the varied moments of my life when I chat with Jesus, talk to God, or converse with a friend.

And when my reflective times are past, and I am once again in contact with war and poverty, joy and those I love, I usually come away a different man. I find that material comforts do not mean as much, that simplicity of life and needs is a clear goal, that my work is not as important as I thought, that my friendships can become richer and deeper and more real. Such moments and moods are a priceless revelation from my God. Afterward, I can never again be quite the same, not because some divine law demands it, but because I see more clearly the true and honest values of my life and the need for growing simplicity.

I am not sure that I can begin to put these values into words. I can only say that I sense my unity with all of creation, that I am an integral part of life. It is then that I can look at a friend or lover and know how truly beautiful they are. It is then a simple touch can mean as much as the most exciting and passionate moments of love. It is then that I most want to reveal myself to my friends. It is then that I can taste food and enjoy its flavor, then that I want to swim in the ocean and feel the waves on my flesh. It is then that I can see a Black or tormented gay or homeless kid and know that I must help them to endure, then that I can read of war and know that it is futile and mad. It is then that I can see the sun shimmering against the sea and the white water splashing on the rocks and rejoice in the reality of my own life. It is then that I do not have to have any purpose in life, that life is its own purpose, that I am a part of an undying kind of creation. I do not have to turn to my God and say, "thank you!" I am spontaneously grateful and He knows it. I just am and this is quite enough. It is then that I can look at my world and watch the rebirth of God beyond myth, forever available to everyone—asking of us the universal forgiveness that He Himself forever gives.

I know that whenever a man or woman is finding joy and peace, wherever one is helped from darkness and again finds beauty and serenity in life, God is being born. I do not have to call Him "God," for "God" is but a word. I do not have to describe Him or reflect His mind. I can, but do not have to praise Him or to determine His will. I do not have to picture Him as a white-haired patriarch or to put the words of Western civilization in His mouth. I do not have to reduce Him to a system or to place in careful categories the rules that men have offered in His name. It is enough that a man smiles, or enjoys his work, or is freed from slavery, or a mother rejoices in the birth of her child, that an honest businessman or politician cares about his people, that a doctor or lawyer truly serve, that a teacher loves his or her students, that a tradesman refuses to cheat or steal. Then I know that God is being born because man has meaning in his life.

I see the birth of God in the old Italian couple who run a grocery store in my neighborhood. They do not often speak of God or Jesus or salvation, but I know they feel the divine presence. This couple love each other and greet me with a kind word and a smile. They smile when I buy a half-pound of hamburger for some homemade chili. The store is their home, their life, their community. They know almost everyone by name, or at least, by face. They charge more than a supermarket, but they give more. And when I leave the store, I somehow feel more human, more in touch with the realities of life, more a man, closer to God. They work every day from nine till nine. They eat lunch and dinner together while they work. And when I say, "You work too hard," they answer, "This is where we are the happiest." And I believe them. They do not work at all; they spend the day serving their friends. Then they go home, have a glass of wine, and watch TV and say their simple prayers to a friendly God or light a candle to their madonna. Sometimes they play cards or reminisce. Then they go to bed. At times I sing a little when I leave their store, not because I have been "saved," but because in the beauty of this vision of man, I sense in my life the Living God.

It would be humorous to me if someone would tell this couple they must go more frequently to church, to receive more sacraments, to confess their sins more often although they may do all or none of these things. They are already in touch with God because they are in touch with the heart of life. It is enough for them to go to one another, to laugh and cry with their friends, to confess their weariness at the end of a day. And in their simple lives, I see that God Lives.

I see the living God in the stranger with whom I share a drink in a lonely city away from home. He is a salesman, thirtyish, handsome, and alone. He asks about my work and tells me that he sells plywood. He is recently divorced, has two children living with his wife, and believes that any reconciliation is impossible. He has dated a dozen different women in the past few months, but is tired of the chase and wants to settle down. He glances at an attractive blonde who is sitting near us. He sighs, rubs his hand over his right eye, looks at me and says, "What does it all mean?" I answer that I'm not always sure. Guiltily he talks of church and childhood, saying the same things I have heard a thousand times before: "I'm not very religious; the church routine doesn't do much for me." He sips his drink and asks, "Do you believe in God?" "Yes," I answer, "in my own way." "I wish I could," he says, "I've been looking for something all of my life."

I like him; he is honest and real and searching. Maybe for a time he has to wander around to lose the sense of failure that comes from his past, to discover the futility of culture's noisy illusions. But he is absorbed with the question of peace and how to live and these, to me, are the questions of God. He wants to know if life leads anywhere and how he is directed to live it. So for a pair of drinks we reveal a bit of ourselves and then walk anonymously away. I am more at home with him than with the prophets of religion who speak of "sin" and "redemption." I am in touch with a human being who is searching for a God as real as a martini, as fulfilling as the genuine love of a woman, as tangible as the personal exchange of words between friends. And in the reality of his search and gradually emerging peace of soul, I feel that God Lives.

I have a close friend who rejects the very notion of God. Yet he is as "religious" as any man I know. His feelings about God may well reflect the hypocrisy and ignorance he discovered in the Fundamentalist faith of his childhood. Or, it may be the result of his own mature experience. I do not know or really care. But I know that he is trying to make his life mean something. He has no time for God the magician, or the God Who turns men's attention away from life. He only has time for the friends who need him, the students he teaches, the work he loves. He refused several jobs that pay more money but do not mean as much as the job he has. He is sensitive, compassionate, strong, and utterly honest. His children are warm, curious, happy and alive. He takes life as it comes, requires no assurance of an afterlife, can be loyal to his wife without the command of a lawgiver, lives simply without the vows of a monk. He has no time for churches or religions, nor have they time for him. Those who would call him an atheist reveal how little they know of God. For the God in whom I profess faith is not different from the sacred concern my friend has for the meaning of life. It is one and the same God Within beyond historic myth.

I don't think I would live differently if I suddenly recognized that my faith in God were an illusion, for there is finally no other satisfying way to live. Nor would my friend change his way of life if he became aware of a living God. Neither of us is loyal to some way of life that contradicts the inner longing of our own spirit. We do not try to be honest because God has requested it, but because it is the only way we can live comfortably with ourselves. In reality, I do not differ "religiously" from my friend. I do not try to convert him. I listen to him, enjoy him, love him. And in his honesty, I know the God Lives beyond all myth.

My God is alive and mysterious. He does not terrorize me with His laws and punishments, nor does He bore me with dull prayers and empty rituals. He does not harangue me about my weakness when I impulsively choose to indulge it, but teaches me to grow in strength. He does not call me an unworthy son since He has fashioned me through the miracle of millions of years of growth and change. He teaches me to smile at my failures, to try again to do the best I can. He does not reproach me for my sensual weakness, or gathered remnants of past addictions, but teaches me that my weakness and need is the reason that I can be loved and can accept His strength. He does not want me to be instantly perfect, only to be honest and alive and growing. He does not want me to live in fear of Him or to be saturated with guilt; He wants my freedom which is His own. He does not limit His messages to sacred books, nor does He share His powers only with special consecrated persons. He does not communicate in selected sects alone. He speaks to me in the wind and the rain, in a woman's arms, in the curiosity of a child, in the touch of a friend's hand, in the look of one I love.

He is in the water before it is blessed, in the bread and wine before priests pray over it. I speak to Him in intimate and casual conversations, but I do not have to speak to Him at all. I am aware of Him, and that seems enough unless my pain and need grows more desperate. At times I have shouted at Him and eloquently cursed Him. He is most present in me when I am most present to myself, when I am most present and real to other people. He is at the depths of my very own being. I cannot define Him or reduce Him to rules. I cannot fathom His mind or the mystery of His joy. When I am able really to think about Him, I am more apt to smile than frown.

Learned men ask me if He is transcendent or immanent, which means, is He something more than I am, or a mere extension and projection of myself? I do not know how to answer them. I am not sure that I understand their words, or if I do understand, I am not sure that it is really important to me. Somehow the question doesn't seem relevant. I don't know how it can be solved. I can only say that at times He seems to be other than I am, at other times He is so much a part of my own existence that to talk to Him would be like talking to myself. I must leave such speculations to minds that are more differently attuned than mine, since I do not see the possibility or the importance of a solution.

I cannot speak of God as though I am speaking of some exceptional human person. Nor can I picture Him thus. To speak of God's personality or variety of personalities is to create an amalgam of sterile words. The ancient Jews did well not to mention His name. I cannot fathom God; I can only describe my feeble and powerful experience of Him and assert that He gives joy and energy to my life. I can attempt more as I did so eloquently for so many years, but it would not now be real for me. Neither is it real to ask God for particular detailed favors. This reduces God to a comfortable religious myth and permits men to make up rules according to which God is controlled. He gives without my asking, and my specific asking seems only to doubt his unconditional largess. This does not mean I live in mystical peace, or I never beg in fear or pain for release. It is just that it is more a reflection of my struggle than what really is.

Trusting
Trusting the day turning into moonlight,
Trusting snow drifts transformed into meadows,
Trusting the geese will return, and wheat and water will
*   not disappear from the earth.*
Trusting the children will laugh every morning

And hungry babies will cry for their mothers.
Trusting deer will survive the winter and mountains will
*   forever give way to dawn,*

Trusting the love locked in my heart and the light

locked in my eyes
Will shine on every step I take, every voice I hear,
   every face I finally see.
Trusting you, trusting me, trusting life, trusting God!

From Quiet Water

And now, in my search for God, I can appreciate Jesus Christ. I talk to Him as to God—as to my friend and brother. I do not look to him for salvation. He does not mystify me with his words. He does not make love complicated or turn it into a definition. He is not a theologian, but a brother; not a preacher, but a friend. He can get the attention of a man in a bar, a prostitute, a laborer, or a millionaire. He speaks of the hungry, the sick, the prisoners, the sad, and he asks man to give them help without the complexities of law and doctrine.

But most of all, he tells every man that he counts in the sight of God. He tells him this by the attention he gives, by the time he spends, by the patience he had. He has no program, no routine. Even now he goes about doing good, knowing well that he cannot do all of it without you and me, but knowing equally well that he can do some of it and we will do the rest. He announces the living God in his love for men, in his effort to wipe out the distinction between Jew and gentile, slave and free, even man and woman, and to see everyone as good.

This is the Jesus I know. I do not recognize the marble monuments in which frightened men have buried him. Nor do I believe the doting mother-churches that brag that he belongs exclusively to them. Nor do I accept easily the arrogance of men who ask me if Jesus is my Saviour, and who leave me cold when they tell me he is theirs. Such men look at me with hardly human eyes. The Jesus I know is not saved. He is in a rage to love men. He looks at man, not through him. He is a friend. No friend of mine looks at me and asks with self-satisfied pride: "Are you saved?" If he cares one whit, he talks to me, not as a salvation-monger, but as a man. Then

238

somehow he is like Jesus, even if he has never heard his name. Then somehow, like Jesus, he tells me of the living God within.

My God is not dead, the whole world speaks of Him and tells me of His birth. The Blacks' struggle for freedom is the relentless voice of God. Once the Black knew another kind of God and was content to sing mournful hymns and to hang his head. Once he prayed to a white God Who told him to tolerate his slavery and bow to his master in a timid and broken spirit. Now I see the wrath of the true and living God Who marched in Washington and raged in Detroit or Los Angeles. I see that God Lives in the black man's determination to work and eat and send his children to a decent school. I see God in the fire of dark eyes and in the courage of a strong mouth with full lips. I see that God Lives in slums and speeches, in the fight for open housing, in the courage and fire of the gays for their true dignity, and in the strength of brave men and women who are ready to go to jail rather than be denied their human rights. I see the living God because all mankind is demanding a meaningful life and total respect in place of slavery and hostile judgment.

I see God's birth in the struggle to end poverty and in the protests that hope to end war. I see His birth in the hearts of men who wince with every bullet, who shudder at napalm, and who detest every bomb. I see Him born in the screams of the children who do not understand the gunfire that keeps them from playing. I see him in the mothers who will not give their sons to war and violence, in the young women who will not watch their husbands die in vain. I see Him born in the philosophers who insist that the freedom purchased by war is not freedom at all if a child or a spouse is murdered, if a home and family are destroyed.

I see the living God in the comedian who makes me laugh, in the young man who interviews me with trembling lips, in the joy of the World Series, in the excitement of a no-hitter, in a young pitcher's struggle to win twenty games. I see the living God in a heart transplant, in the excitement of the Preakness or the Kentucky Derby, in a child's attempt to walk, in a baby's struggle to say a meaningful word. I see the living God in a work of art that makes me gasp, in a piece of sculpture that tells me something of myself. I see the living God in the whole school of art that reaches beyond the obvious, that insists on more than photographing or rendering, that touches the secrets of existence. I see it in the colors and forms, the shades and contrasts that insist that life is delicate and refined, indescribable and tenuous, bold and exciting. I see that God Lives in an old man's refusal to die, in his determination to endure the operation that may save his life. I see it in a young man's dream, in an adolescent's turmoil. I see the living God wherever man is searching for peace and meaning, wherever life is struggling to express itself, wherever hands are reaching out to grasp other hands, where strong hearts whisper to weak ones; "You can." I can see God especially and most eloquently in forgiveness of those we think have injured us, and to forgive "seventy times seven times."

I see that God Lives in the men who explore the sea to feed the future nations, in the scientists who struggle to regulate a world's population, in the ecologists who purify the air so men can breathe. I see it in the fight for mental health, in the experiments for better education, in the new forms of communication, in the effort to improve impoverished health care. I see that God Lives in the welfare worker who brings help to the poor amid frustration and ingratitude and red tape. I see it in the teachers in the slums, in the men and women of the Peace Corps, in the new housing, in any effort to give men and women hope and to make their lives mean something.

I do not agree with the prophets of doom who maintain that morality is at an end, who deplore the sexual irresponsibility of our age, who assert that modern man wants freedom without discipline. I do not agree with the surplice leaders who plead with men to return to the churches, who refurbish their empty ceremonies and reword their archaic sermons to keep men captive in their religious institutions. God is no longer trapped in the churches, and He is not the legends and myths that frightened and resentful men have fashioned. God is in the struggle of honest men and women to be themselves, in the effort of the brave to care, in the courage of the weak to do the best they can, in the determination of leaders in the global village to provide men and women with the love and equality that is their due.

God is not dead. The religions are. God is not dead. The sects are. God lives and is born in man's effort to be fulfilled and free. Outside my window I can see a little boy at play. He is bouncing a tennis ball against a brick wall, and he may be playing "baseball" like I used to do. I hope he never feels, as I once did, that he has to confess his sins, that he has to appease an angry God, that he has to be rescued or redeemed. I hope that he will make every day mean something, that he will be open and honest enough to have a friend, that his parents will love him and permit him to be free. I hope that he will care about other men, regardless of their race or religion, forgive readily and finally that he will be free enough to search for a joyful, fulfilling life and for God. I hope that he will not have to fight in Vietnam or anywhere else, that he will have time to grow and love and care about his fellow man. I hope that he will be satisfied to do the best he can and to know that no matter what he does or doesn't do, he counts and has his unique contribution of love. I hope he can find meaning amid loneliness, purpose amid discouragement and failure, love in the midst of his search. I hope he knows that in his struggle to be himself, in his effort to find himself in the global village, he is assisting in the rebirth of the God Who lives!

Will You Be My Friend?

Will you be my friend?
There are so many reasons why you never should:
I'm sometimes sullen, often shy, acutely sensitive,
My fear erupts as anger, I find it hard to give,
I talk about myself when I'm afraid
And often spend a day without anything to say.
    But I will make you laugh
    And love you quite a bit
    And hold you when you're sad.
I cry a little almost every day
Because I'm more caring than the strangers ever know,
And, if at times, I show my tender side
(The soft and warmer part I hide)
    I wonder, Will you be my friend?
A friend
    Who far beyond the feebleness of any vow or tie
    Will touch the secret place where I am really I,
    To know the pain of lips that plead and eyes that weep,
    Who will not run away when you find me in the street
    Along and lying mangled by my quota of defeats
But will stop and stay—to tell me of another day
When I was beautiful.

Will you be my friend?
There are so many reasons why you never should:
Often I'm too serious, seldom predictably the same,
Sometimes cold and distant, probably I'll always change.
I bluster and brag, seek attention like a child,
I brood and pout, my anger can be wild,
   But I will make you laugh
   And love you quite a bit
   And be near when you're afraid.
I shake a little almost every day
Because I'm more frightened than the strangers ever know
And, if at times, I show my trembling side
(The anxious, fearful part I hide)
   I wonder, Will you be my friend?
A friend
   Who, when I fear your closeness, feels me push away and
   Stubbornly will stay to share what's left on such a day,
   Who, when no one knows my name or calls me on the phone,
   When there's no other concern for me—what I have or haven't
done—
   And those I've helped and counted on have, oh so deftly, run,
Who, when there's nothing left but me, stripped of charm and subtlety,
Will nonetheless remain.

Will you be my friend?
   For no reason that I know except I want you so.

                              From Will You Be My Friend?

B efore the world was a Global Village, it was possible for each separate culture to give absolute substance to its religious myths. Catholics would consider themselves and their revelations the "one, true faith". Jews could consider themselves the "chosen people". Mormons could maintain that the words of the angel to Joseph Smith were divine and absolute. Buddha, Mohammed, Krishna each had a unique grasp on truth. Protestants divided Catholics a half millennium ago, and soon there were myriad divisions among Protestants, where Calvin improved Luther, Henry VIII and Melancthon modified both, and soon there were dozens of sects East and West each claiming to have the truth. Catholic divided from Orthodox and Protestant, Mohammedan and Shinto divided from Jew, all divided from Hindu and Bhuddist, and North American Indian divided from Inca and Mayan.

That their were similarities in the myths is beyond all question. That there was comfort provided and penetration into the profound truth is beyond doubt. But there was also orthodoxy, dogma, absolutes, and each individual slice of culture was certain of its own truth. Men and women were massacred for myths, bloody wars were but extensions of religious, cultural, and national myths. There were gentle and harmless myths, and fiendish, brutal ones like a Torquemada or a Hitler. Mobs were caught in the myths that made them better, superior, unique, as well as murderous. And the myths continue still as Jew fights Arab, and a Saddam attacks Kuwait, Sikhs, or Shiites. Even as Europe is still divided, and Russian and American were locked in a cold war born of fear and spiritual emptiness that was forever seething.

Now we begin to see our own particular myths as guides and insights and personal paths, no better or worse than other primitives. Thus there are hundreds of ways to the indefinable and limitless God Whose Spirit lives in every man and woman of any color, race, or creed. But until we see the power of this

God in ourselves and in everyone else as a form of Universal Energy and direction, we cannot see the world as one. All science will lead to the same path, as is already happening, physics and chemistry, history and archaeology, astronomy and biology, because there is but One Divine Energy in billions and billions of forms. There cannot be competition between Jesus and Bhuddha, between Yahweh and the Christian, Persian, Mohammedan, or Oriental God. All are but impoverished approximations of what is real.

The measure of a nation is not its economy, its productivity, its power, but its Spirit. There is no longer any system of politics or economy that can save us, and no religion or culture that can in any way completely encapsulate the truth. Political dreamers like Lenin turn to Stalin, and American democracy becomes a manipulated republic, As Nietzche put it, *"The last Christian died on the cross"*. Truth is not saying, defining, or reciting, truth is being! If we find Jesus in a Eucharist, or God in a protective cloud, it is no different than another finding wonder in the wind or joy and flowers in the meadow. It is not consecrated bread that brings me to God, nor consecrated bread that does not. These are but sacred mythologies that helped some along the path and caused others to stumble. When I can see beyond myth, all Gods are mine and none, all Sacraments and none. I know what is true and I have no need to attack another man's truth as falsehood. Nor he to impose his myth on me as absolute and infallible.

What difference a sacrifice of the Mass or a sunset if I am in touch with God and truth? A tabernacle or an ark of the covenant, a giant redwood or a blue beetle on a summer afternoon. This is not to mock another man's myth, or to insist on replacing it with my own. If my myth gives me comfort and attacks no one else, it earns my respect and leads me through life's trials. I do not mock rosaries or oriental prayer beads, Masses or Temple ceremonials, circumcision or baptism. But to move beyond myth as absolute truth and infallible dogma is not to see color, nation, power, empire, possessions. It is to know we are all one, that the earth and all its creatures are sacred and uniquely designed by God. God will forever be only a private projection rather than my present vision until I am willing to move beyond myth or symbol to what truly is, when an inner awareness permits, craves, and demands it.

There is land and food for all, but egotistical myths forbade us share it. It is merely to multiply seven barley loaves that all may have enough. Fear alone has starved and separated us, nuclear power with no real power at all has frightened us into division and bankruptcy while the poor die to a world's shame. Myths have limited and divided the limitless and indefinable, made slaves of one color and kings of another, helped us to forget that the riches of the earth belong to all and all are indeed kings.

I can treasure and find truth in the Bible, the Koran, or Vedic books. I can read and study the myths of dozens of cultures, as I have. They can be interesting, inspiring, and curious, (this is merely a matter of taste) but ultimately I lose my appetite for such studies. Israel is me, so is Jordan, Somalia, Iran and Monaco me. So is the darkness of a Hitler, or the radiance of a prophet. Only beyond all myth does God live. There is nothing to fear, nothing to lose, nothing to harm, only myths, dark and light, beyond which is reality, truth, the eternal Living God—in each of us who lives, whoever has or will!

One Little Man

One little man making his way in a frightening world,
    Frightening only if he walks all by himself,
Or listens to the hollowness of his own wounded heart.
    The only strength is to let go, walking openly with God,
As He gently reveals Himself the way He chooses.
    Even now as the Bhuddist priest says his daily prayers
At some far and undistinguished corner of the earth,
    As a meek charwoman of Mecca looks radiantly to the sun,
And the man of Israel or Ireland seeks his own peace,
    A God beyond Sinai and Pentecost, beyond words and icons
Bends to bless and heal, to make brave and serene.
    The freedom that power and possessions cannot provide,

Is freely given to the little ones in the darkest corners of the earth,
If only they are trusting child enough to ask!

From Quiet Water

Churches are closing and new structures are being built
and many of the new ones will close as well because they are
addicted to the past. Ancient traditions are questioned and new
ones, often as dogmatic and destructive, take their place. But
there is action and change, movement and growth which are
signs of rebirth. It has to be. What we now see as "New Age"
well may become rapidly outmoded because the change is so
profound and personal. The God reborn, the God beyond
churches and myths is the God Within each of us whether we
name Him or not, whether we acknowledge Him or not. His
love is unconditional even for a Judas or a Hitler.

We do not need to hear of our sins, our obvious weaknesses, our faults and mistakes, our failed marriages and abused
families, our fear and despair, shame and guilt. We need to
discover and expand our courage and strength, our innate
goodness and generosity. The mothers who have raised children by themselves, the men who have lost their jobs and
dignity, the myriad individuals who have changed their whole
style of living, who could no longer be seduced by money and
things, who learned to trust with their whole heart and all
their strength the power of God Who selected them from billions of possibilities and loves them eternally and without limit.

This is religion one does not have to sell! Religion one does
not have to terrify people into attendance, one that does not
need to promise some distant and obscure salvation which is
already ours. The Church's mission is pastoral as was Jesus',
not dogmatic and legalist, fearful and condemnatory, rigid and
authoritarian. Certainly not arrogant and absolute, but a
channel of equality where each individual learns to bloom
fully into his or her own destiny. Never to lose hope, never to
give up, never to die in despair! The care that is extended to
sparrows and the love that is lavished on lilies of the field is

even more the right of each one of us.

Religion is comfort and generosity in recession, and hope and courage as well. It is simplifying our needs, extending our love, and heeding the private revelation of God that is given to each of us in inner silence. We are not here by chance. Each is important, each has a mission, each has a destiny that affects everyone else. A life, a love, a part of the world depends on me. It is only, " My God, what would you have me do?" And I will have the courage and power from Within to do it.

Maybe I was not strong enough to be black or poor or Somalian, or maybe such a life can only be saved by me. Maybe I was not brave enough to be a galley slave or a victim of history's atrocities. I did not have the destiny to survive a death camp, to lead an important battle for freedom, to end war, to give my life for my friend. I only have what I have and am what I am. And to become that as best I can is my heritage even as yours is yours. Thus we move beyond myth to reality. We keep the rituals we enjoy or that lead us closer to ourselves and others. We do not impose. It is not for me to decide what myth or even ritual is outmoded or destructive for you. I am not your guru nor are you mine. We are all teachers to one another without teaching at all. Just being who we are.

Religions indeed are dying, just as flowers do so they may reappear, just as clouds do so that the sun may burst forth, just as the moon gives way to morning. It is no disgrace, it is love and health, progress and freedom. Pope Leo XIII a century ago said that *"Man is older than the State"*. He is also older than any religion or any Church. God's primary Temple will always be in the mind and heart of each individual. It is the privilege of religion, community, or Church, or just two together, to be aware of that Temple. Thus even as the religions are dying, even as we are, God is reborn beyond myth—for eternal love and joy is our home within our very own being at this instant. There is God, there is church, there is religion. Above and beyond all, GOD LIVES! Forever!

James Kavanaugh
Chicago, Illinois

It Is Destined

It is destined by some rhythm more powerful than
  religion or even economics
That the earth belongs to us all or none shall possess it.
What Christianity never achieved nor Buddha,
  what Communism never won
    nor Muhammed,
Will finally ensue without prayer or sacred proclamation.
There is no good or bad, malice or virtue, only time
    and circumstance,
And the inexorable hand of a mysterious rhythm dictating
  That art and love and understanding will flower
    Or dust will inherit the earth.
What nobility could never teach, survival's law will demand.
The exploiter will be pitied when exploitation disappears.
  What man refused to share will finally be taken away.
Even as I write in the Manila Hotel where MacArthur governed
And returned to Corregidor to drive out the Japanese,
His grave is silent, but the Kamikazes return
  to go in business with the Filipinos.
Today America salutes Peking and
  Taiwan curses her treachery,
But tomorrow China will host Hong Kong in mutual celebration.
  Not because of virtue or even political compromise,
  But because man is destined to live lovingly on the earth,
    Or he shall not live at all.
Not because of Mao or Marx, Jefferson or Jesus,
But because a rhythm as obvious as water and land
  governs the destiny of man.

Lion will lie with lamb or both be devoured by Leviathan.
Men will not turn swords to plowshares,
   but swords will rust,
    Not because man is noble, but because it is written in reality.
Churches never really changed anyone, nor did a poem.
    Asia is no wiser than the west, man no wiser than woman,
    Black or brown virtue no more enduring than yellow or white.
What socialism could not achieve or Iron Curtains,
   what democracies could not do nor kings and queens,
Will happen of iteslf!
    The Arabs will not be proud because the earth gave them oil,
    Nor America because its soil is lavish of wheat and corn.
All will be as one whether they will or no, and death will
   follow life like winter to spring and summer.
Thus it is written by man's own hand!

From Walk Easy On The Earth

INFORMATION ABOUT BOOKS AND TAPES BY
JAMES KAVANAUGH

In September 1990, all rights to James Kavanaugh books were purchased by Steven J Nash who is now the exclusive publisher of Kavanaugh's books and tapes. For information or to order, write:

Steven J. Nash Publishing
P.O. Box 2115 • Highland Park, IL 60035
or call: 1-800-843-8545

A Modern Priest Looks At His Outdated Church. *25th Anniversary Edition* of the explosive 1967 best-seller reprinted with a new introduction. Psychologist, Dr. Carl Rogers said, "It is one of the most moving human documents I have "ever" read! In an earlier day the author would have been burned at the stake..." **"This is combat religion!"** *Saturday Review*

There Are Men Too Gentle To Live Among Wolves. This James Kavanaugh classic, in its 69th printing; JK writes: *"We searchers are ambitious only for life itself, for everything beautiful it can provide. We want to love and be loved, to live in a relationship that will not prevent our search, nor lock us in prison walls..."*

Will You Be My Friend? *(57th printing)* Kavanaugh writes "Friendship is freedom, is flowing, is rare... It trusts, understands, grows, explores,.. It does not exhaust or cling, expect or demand. It is— and that is enough—and it dreams a lot!"

Laughing Down Lonely Canyons. JK confronts loneliness and fear. "This is a book for the barely brave like me who refuse to abandon their dream... For those who want to make life the joy it was meant to be, who refuse to give up no matter the pain..."

From Loneliness To Love. JK writes: *"To move from loneliness to love means to take a risk, to create the kind of personal environment & support we need. This is a book of hope and reassurance that love is available and loneliness can end."*

Search: A Guide For Those Who Dare Ask Of Life Everything Good And Beautiful. *(Prose)* "**Search** provides 12 proven principles to move from self doubt to self love. It is a celebration of one's creativity and unique beauty, rising from practical psychology to the spiritual power of our Inner Being in a journey to wholeness."

A Lifetime Isn't Long Enough To Love You. These passionate poems confront forces that numb our senses and freeze our souls. Kavanaugh challenges us to be feeling beings,..."*So much of life is spent trying to prove something... Maybe if I loved you more, I wouldn't have to prove anything!*"

Walk Easy On The Earth. It reflects JK's life spent in a remote cabin in the California gold country. *"I do not focus on the world's despair, I am forever renewed by spring splashing over granite rocks, or a cautious deer emerging into twilight. I know then that I will survive all my personal fears to realize my finest dreams."*

A Village Called Harmony-A Fable. A timeless tale in eloquent prose that touches the deepest chords in the human struggle of lust and love, ambition and peace. Dear Abby says: *"A powerful tale of our times. A classic! I loved it!"*

Celebrate The Sun: A Love Story. A moving allegory about the life of Harry Langendorf Pelican, dedicated to *"those who take time to celebrate the sun—and are grateful!"* A stirring tale that, truly, reflects JK's philosophy of life.

The Crooked Angel. James Kavanaugh's only children's story tells of two angels *"with crooked little wings"* who escape from isolation and sadness through friendship and laughter...Says Goldie Hawn:*"My children loved it! So did I."*

Tears And Laughter Of A Man's Soul. "Men are not easy to know, even by other men and it's a rare woman who understands men...We hope another marriage, a secret affair, or more income will revive us, but ingrained habits only assume a new addictive form and depression fills a vacuum of dead dreams. The path to freedom and joy is more exciting than difficult."

Quiet Water. Includes the most memorable of JK's inspirational reflections, his own past favorites as well as new thoughts. He gives hope and courage when life's most difficult passages seem impossible to endure writing with wisdom and compassion born of his own painful discovery of the path to peace and joy. A perfect gift for a struggling friend!...*"There is quiet water in the center of your soul..."*

Mystic Fire: Reflections on Love! All the passion, romance, and tenderness, as well as the humor and pain of love unfold in this beautiful new edition of Kavanaugh's favorites. Men and women of any age, will find herein the perfect gift, to celebrate the expression of love... "Love grew like some mystic fire around my heart..."

America, I Love You But Not Like I Used To: A Powerful ballad that sums up the discontent with the way things are, yet gives us hope as we "reach out and give.. for no reason at all." Walter Cronkite says, *"Another Kavanaugh 10-strike!"*

And On The Sixth Day God Made Man...Honest!: Humorous Reflections on our society, our culture, ourselves. Hilarious and timely — JK is todays Mark Twain.

About The Author...

James Kavanaugh is a poet, author, philosopher, former priest, and clinical psychologist. His best selling book, **A Modern Priest Looks At His Outdated Church**, was a major instrument in the reform of churches in the late 1960's. His poetry books, particularly **There Are Men Too Gentle To Live Among Wolves,** have become modern classics. Often called the modern day Mark Twain, Kavanaugh's words has been lauded by people from all walks of life, from Walter Cronkite to Dear Abby, from Larry Dossey to Dyan Cannon.

Kavanaugh's earthy words touch the hearts and minds of the most common and profound. He radiates a magic aura of hopefulness and laughter that ignites and spreads among those he touches with his words and thoughts and has become the passionate spokesman for the individual. With incisive clarity and perception, in his poetry or prose, JK tells each of us, **"You are your own answer!"**

He reads his poetry at bookstores, gatherings, and other group meetings. He appears on major TV and radio talk shows. He lectures at colleges, universities and at civic functions. He continues to write and travel and expects to have his new book, a novel, completed this year.

TAPES BY JAMES KAVANAUGH

Of Love, Life, And Laughter. This 4-tape set includes selections from JK's books, **Quiet Water, Mystic Fire, Tears And Laughter Of A Man's Soul, and Will You Be My Friend?** Powerfully read by the author, with original music, his poems and honest commentary will touch your soul.

Search: A Guide for Those Who Dare to Ask of Life Everything Good and Beautiful. Two 90-minute tape set by JK exploring the Search principles to compliment the book and learn to "play the long game."

The Creative Process. Creativity reflects one's uniqueness, not imitating what is culturally acceptable. The creator is by definition a rebel otherwise he is a pale imitator who sells out his own soul.

In Search Of One's Self. Identity and self-esteem begin and end with honesty, and the acceptance of who I am "now". "Denial" and "pleasing others" makes real change and consistent growth impossible.

Man and Woman: A Time For Healing. It is time for attack to end, and for awareness, self responsibility, and open communication to begin. There's no one to blame! No one did it to us! Kavanaugh's use of humor softens a tough subject.

There Are Men Too Gentle. The great Elmer Bernstein heard a ranch- hand read Kavanaugh's poetry, called the author, and agreed to write an original score with full orchestra if Kavanaugh would read his own work. Later they performed together to SRO audiences in Los Angeles.

Poetry of James Kavanaugh. William Conrad read James Kavanaugh's poetry and wrote the author asking permission to do this album with an original score by Shelley Mann. The words are classic Kavanaugh, the reading is spectacular Conrad. "I stand in awe of his talent," said Conrad.